Maple 9
Learning Guide

Based in part on the work of B. W. Char

with 10 color figures

Maplesoft, Maple, Maple Application Center, and Maplet are all trademarks of Waterloo Maple Inc.

Windows is a registered trademark of Microsoft Corporation.

Java and all Java based marks are trademarks or registered trademarks of Sun Microsystems, Inc. in the United States and other countries. Maplesoft is independent of Sun Microsystems, Inc.

All other trademarks are the property of their respective owners.

This document was produced using a special version of Maple that reads and updates LaTeX files.

Printed in Canada

ISBN 1-894511-42-5

Contents

Preface

This manual introduces important concepts and builds a framework of knowledge that guides you in your use of the interface and the Maple™ language. This manual provides an overview of the functionality of Maple. It describes both the symbolic and numeric capabilities, introducing the available Maple objects, commands, and methods. Emphasis is placed on finding solutions, plotting or animating results, and exporting worksheets to other formats. More importantly, this manual presents the philosophy and methods of use intended by the designers of the system.

Audience

The information in this manual is intended for first time Maple users. As an adjunct, access to the Maple help system is recommended.

Manual Set

There are three other manuals available for Maple users, the *Maple Getting Started Guide*, the *Maple Introductory Programming Guide*, and the *Maple Advanced Programming Guide.*[1]

- The *Maple Getting Started Guide* contains an introduction to the graphical user interface and a tutorial that outlines using Maple to solve mathematical problems and create technical documents. It also

[1]The Student Edition does not include the *Maple Introductory Programming Guide* and the *Maple Advanced Programming Guide.* These programming guides can be purchased from school and specialty bookstores or directly from Maplesoft.

includes information for new users about the help system, New User's Tour, example worksheets, and the Maplesoft Web site.

- The *Maple Introductory Programming Guide* introduces the basic Maple programming concepts, such as expressions, data structures, looping and decision mechanisms, procedures, input and output, debugging, and the Maplet^{TM} User Interface Customization System.

- The *Maple Advanced Programming Guide* extends the basic Maple programming concepts to more advanced topics, such as modules, input and output, numerical programming, graphics programming, and compiled code.

Whereas this book highlights features of Maple, the help system is a complete reference manual. There are also examples that you can copy, paste, and execute immediately.

Conventions

This manual uses the following typographical conventions.

- `courier` font - Maple command, package name, and option name
- **bold roman** font - dialog, menu, and text field
- *italics* - new or important concept, option name in a list, and manual titles
- **Note** - additional information relevant to the section
- **Important** - information that must be read and followed

Customer Feedback

Maplesoft welcomes your feedback. For suggestions and comments related to this and other manuals, contact doc@maplesoft.com.

1 Introduction to Maple

Maple is a *Symbolic Computation System* or *Computer Algebra System*. Maple manipulates information in a symbolic or algebraic manner. You can obtain exact analytical solutions to many mathematical problems, including integrals, systems of equations, differential equations, and problems in linear algebra. Maple contains a large set of graphics routines for visualizing complicated mathematical information, numerical algorithms for providing estimates and solving problems where exact solutions do not exist, and a complete and comprehensive programming language for developing custom functions and applications.

Worksheet Graphical Interface

Maple mathematical functionality is accessed through its advanced worksheet-based graphical interface. A worksheet is a flexible document for exploring mathematical ideas and for creating sophisticated technical reports. You can access the power of the Maple computation engine through a variety of user interfaces: the standard worksheet, the command-line[1] version, the classic worksheet (not available on Macintosh®), and custom-built Maplet applications. The full Maple system is available through all of these interfaces. In this manual, any references to the graphical Maple interface refer to the standard worksheet interface. For more information on the various interface options, refer to the `?versions` help page.

Modes

You can use Maple in two modes: as an interactive problem-solving environment and as a system for generating technical documents.

[1]The command-line version provides optimum performance. However, the worksheet interface is easier to use and renders typeset, editable math output and higher quality plots.

Interactive Problem-Solving Environment Maple allows you to undertake large problems and eliminates your mechanical errors. The interface provides documentation of the steps involved in finding your result. It allows you to easily modify a step or insert a new one in your solution method. With minimal effort you can compute the new result.

Generating Technical Documents You can create interactive structured documents for presentations or publication that contain mathematics in which you can change an equation and update the solution automatically. You also can display plots. In addition, you can structure your documents by using tools such as outlining, styles, and hyperlinks. Outlining allows you to collapse sections to hide regions that contain distracting detail. Styles identify keywords, headings, and sections. Hyperlinks allow you to create live references that take the reader directly to pages containing related information. The interactive nature of Maple allows you to compute results and answer questions during presentations. You can clearly and effectively demonstrate why a seemingly acceptable solution method is inappropriate, or why a particular modification to a manufacturing process would lead to loss or profit. Since components of worksheets are directly associated with the structure of the document, you can easily translate your work to other formats, for example, HTML, RTF, and LaTeX.

2 Mathematics with Maple: The Basics

This chapter introduces the Maple commands necessary to get you started. Use your computer to try the examples as you read.

In This Chapter

- Exact calculations
- Numerical computations
- Basic symbolic computations and assignment statements
- Basic types of objects
- Manipulation of objects and the commands

Maple Help System

At various points in this guide you are referred to the Maple help system. The help pages provide detailed command and topic information. You may choose to access these pages during a Maple session. To use the help command, at the Maple prompt enter a question mark (?) followed by the name of the command or topic for which you want more information.

```
?command
```

2.1 Introduction

This section introduces the following concepts in Maple.

- Semicolon (;) usage

• Representing exact expressions

The most basic computations in Maple are numeric. Maple can function as a conventional calculator with integers or floating-point numbers. Enter the expression using natural syntax. A *semicolon* (;) marks the end of each calculation. Press ENTER to perform the calculation.

```
> 1 + 2;
```

$$3$$

```
> 1 + 3/2;
```

$$\frac{5}{2}$$

```
> 2*(3+1/3)/(5/3-4/5);
```

$$\frac{100}{13}$$

```
> 2.8754/2;
```

$$1.437700000$$

Exact Expressions

Maple computes exact calculations with rational numbers. Consider a simple example.

```
> 1 + 1/2;
```

$$\frac{3}{2}$$

The result of $1+1/2$ is $3/2$ not 1.5. To Maple, the rational number $3/2$ and the floating-point approximation 1.5 are distinct objects. The ability to *represent exact expressions* allows Maple to preserve more information about their origins and structure. Note that the advantage is greater with more complex expressions. The origin and structure of a number such as

$$0.5235987758$$

are much less clear than for an exact quantity such as

$$\frac{1}{6}\pi$$

Maple can work with rational numbers and arbitrary expressions. It can manipulate integers, floating-point numbers, variables, sets, sequences, polynomials over a ring, and many more mathematical constructs. In addition, Maple is also a complete programming language that contains procedures, tables, and other programming constructs.

2.2 Numerical Computations

This section introduces the following concepts in Maple.

- Integer computations
- Continuation character (\)
- Ditto operator (%)
- Commands for working with integers
- Exact and floating-point representations of values
- Symbolic representation
- Standard mathematical constants
- Case sensitivity
- Floating-point approximations
- Special numbers
- Mathematical functions

Integer Computations

Integer calculations are straightforward. Terminate each command with a semicolon.

```
> 1 + 2;
```

$$3$$

```
> 75 - 3;
```

$$72$$

```
> 5*3;
```

$$15$$

```
> 120/2;
```

$$60$$

Maple can also work with arbitrarily large integers. The practical limit on integers is approximately 2^{28} digits, depending mainly on the speed and resources of your computer. Maple can calculate large integers, count the number of digits in a number, and factor integers. For numbers, or other types of continuous output that span more than one line on the screen, Maple uses the *continuation character* (\) to indicate that the output is continuous. That is, the backslash and following line ending should be ignored.

```
> 100!;
```

933262154439441526816992388562667004907\
159682643816214685929638952175999932299\
156089414639761565182862536979208272237\
582511852109168640000000000000000000000\
00000

```
> length(%);
```

$$158$$

This answer indicates the number of digits in the last example. The *ditto operator*, (%), is a shorthand reference to the result of the previous computation. To recall the second- or third-most previous computation result, use %% and %%%, respectively.

Table 2.1 Commands for Working with Integers

Function	*Description*
`abs`	absolute value of an expression
`factorial`	factorial of an integer
`iquo`	quotient of an integer division
`irem`	remainder of an integer division
`iroot`	approximate integer root of an integer
`isqrt`	approximate integer square root of an integer
`max`, `min`	maximum and minimum of a set of inputs
`mod`	modular arithmetic
`surd`	real root of an integer

Commands for Working With Integers

Maple has many commands for working with integers, some of which allow for calculations of the factorization of an integer, the greatest common divisor (gcd) of two integers, integer quotients and remainders, and primality tests. See the following examples, as well as Table 2.1.

```
> ifactor(60);
```

$$(2)^2\ (3)\ (5)$$

```
> igcd(123, 45);
```

$$3$$

```
> iquo(25,3);
```

$$8$$

```
> isprime(18002676583);
```

$$true$$

Exact Arithmetic—Rationals, Irrationals, and Constants

Maple can perform exact rational arithmetic, that is, work with rational numbers (fractions) without reducing them to floating-point approximations.

```
> 1/2 + 1/3;
```

$$\frac{5}{6}$$

Maple handles the rational numbers and produces an exact result. The distinction between *exact* and *approximate* results is important. The ability to perform exact computations with computers enables you to solve a range of problems. Maple can produce floating-point estimates. Maple can work with floating-point numbers with many thousands of digits, producing accurate estimates of exact expressions.

```
> Pi;
```

$$\pi$$

```
> evalf(Pi, 100);
```

$$\begin{array}{l} 3.1415926535897932384626433832795028841\backslash \\ 9716939937510582097494459230781640628 6\backslash \\ 2089986280348253421170 68 \end{array}$$

Maple distinguishes between *exact and floating-point representations of values*. Here is an example of a rational (exact) number.

```
> 1/3;
```

$$\frac{1}{3}$$

The following is its floating-point approximation (shown to ten digits, by default).

```
> evalf(%);
```

$$0.3333333333$$

These results are not the same mathematically, and they are not the same in Maple.

Important: Whenever you enter a number in decimal form, Maple treats it as a floating-point approximation. The presence of a decimal number in an expression causes Maple to produce an approximate floating-point result, since it cannot produce an exact solution from approximate data. Use floating-point numbers when you want to restrict Maple to working with non-exact expressions.

```
> 3/2*5;
```

$$\frac{15}{2}$$

```
> 1.5*5;
```

$$7.5$$

You can enter exact quantities by using *symbolic representation*, for example, π in contrast to 3.14. Maple interprets irrational numbers as exact quantities. Here is how you represent the square root of two in Maple.

```
> sqrt(2);
```

$$\sqrt{2}$$

Here is another square root example.

```
> sqrt(3)^2;
```

$$3$$

Maple recognizes the *standard mathematical* constants, such as π and the base of the natural logarithms, e. It works with them as exact quantities.

```
> Pi;
```

$$\pi$$

```
> sin(Pi);
```

$$0$$

The exponential function is represented by the Maple function `exp`.

```
> exp(1);
```

$$e$$

```
> ln(exp(5));
```

$$5$$

The example with π may look confusing. When Maple is producing typeset real-math notation, it attempts to represent mathematical expressions as you might write them yourself. Thus, you enter π as `Pi` and Maple displays it as π.

Maple is *case sensitive.* Ensure that you use proper capitalization when stating these constants. The names `Pi`, `pi`, and `PI` are distinct. The names `pi` and `PI` are used to display the lowercase and uppercase Greek letters π and Π, respectively. For more information on Maple constants, enter `?constants` at the Maple prompt.

Floating-Point Approximations

Maple works with exact values, but it can return a floating-point approximation up to about 2^{28} digits, depending upon your computer's resources. Ten or twenty accurate digits in floating-point numbers is adequate for many purposes, but two problems severely limit the usefulness of such a system.

- When subtracting two floating-point numbers of almost equal magnitude, the relative error of the difference may be very large. This is known as *catastrophic cancellation.* For example, if two numbers are identical in their first seventeen (of twenty) digits, their difference is a three-digit number accurate to only three digits. In this case, you would need to use almost forty digits to produce twenty accurate digits in the answer.

- The mathematical form of the result is more concise, compact, and convenient than its numerical value. For instance, an exponential function provides more information about the nature of a phenomenon than a large set of numbers with twenty accurate digits. An exact analytical description can also determine the behavior of a function when extrapolating to regions for which no data exists.

The **evalf** command converts an exact numerical expression to a floating-point number.

```
> evalf(Pi);
```

$$3.141592654$$

By default, Maple calculates the result using ten digits of accuracy, but you can specify any number of digits. Indicate the number after the numerical expression, using the following notation.

```
> evalf(Pi, 200);
```

$$3.1415926535897932384626433832795028841\backslash$$
$$97169399375105820974944592307816406286\backslash$$
$$20899862803482534211706798214808651328\backslash$$
$$23066470938446095505822317253594081284\backslash$$
$$81117450284102701938521105559644622948\backslash$$
$$9549303820$$

You can also force Maple to do all its computations with floating-point approximations by including at least one floating-point number in each expression. Floats are *contagious*: if an expression contains one floating-point number, Maple evaluates the entire expression using floating-point arithmetic.

```
> 1/3 + 1/4 + 1/5.3;
```

$$0.7720125786$$

```
> sin(0.2);
```

$$0.1986693308$$

The optional second argument to **evalf** controls the number of floating-point digits for that particular calculation, and the special variable **Digits** sets the number of floating-point digits for all subsequent calculations.

```
> Digits := 20;
```

$$Digits := 20$$

```
> sin(0.2);
```

$$0.1986693307950612154\,6$$

Digits is now set to twenty, which Maple then uses at each step in a calculation. Maple works like a calculator or an ordinary computer application in this respect. When you evaluate a complicated numerical expression, errors can accumulate to reduce the accuracy of the result to less than twenty digits. In general, setting Digits to produce a given accuracy is not easy, as the final result depends on your particular question. Using larger values, however, usually gives you some indication. If required, Maple can provide extreme floating-point accuracy.

Arithmetic with Special Numbers

Maple can work with complex numbers. I is the Maple default symbol for the square root of minus one, that is, $I = \sqrt{-1}$.

```
> (2 + 5*I) + (1 - I);
```

$$3 + 4\,I$$

```
> (1 + I)/(3 - 2*I);
```

$$\frac{1}{13} + \frac{5}{13}\,I$$

You can also work with other *bases and number systems.*

```
> convert(247, binary);
```

$$11110111$$

```
> convert(1023, hex);
```

$$3FF$$

```
> convert(17, base, 3);
```

$$[2, 2, 1]$$

Maple returns an integer base conversion as a list of digits; otherwise, a line of numbers, like 221, may be ambiguous, especially when dealing with large bases. Note that Maple lists the digits in order from least significant to most significant.

Maple also supports arithmetic in *finite rings and fields.*

```
> 27 mod 4;
```

$$3$$

Symmetric and *positive representations* are both available.

```
> mods(27,4);
```

$$-1$$

```
> modp(27,4);
```

$$3$$

The default for the `mod` command is positive representation, but you can change this option. For details, refer to `?mod`.

Maple can work with *Gaussian Integers*. The `GaussInt` package has about thirty commands for working with these special numbers. For information about these commands, refer to `?GaussInt` help page.

Mathematical Functions

Maple contains all the standard mathematical functions (see Table 2.2 for a partial list).

```
> sin(Pi/4);
```

$$\frac{1}{2}\sqrt{2}$$

```
> ln(1);
```

$$0$$

Table 2.2 Select Mathematical Functions in Maple

Function	*Description*
`sin`, `cos`, `tan`, etc.	trigonometric functions
`sinh`, `cosh`, `tanh`, etc.	hyperbolic trigonometric functions
`arcsin`, `arccos`, `arctan`, etc.	inverse trigonometric functions
`exp`	exponential function
`ln`	natural logarithmic function
`log[10]`	logarithmic function base 10
`sqrt`	algebraic square root function
`round`	round to the nearest integer
`trunc`	truncate to the integer part
`frac`	fractional part
`BesselI`, `BesselJ`, `BesselK`, `BesselY`	Bessel functions
`binomial`	binomial function
`erf`, `erfc`	error & complementary error functions
`Heaviside`	Heaviside step function
`Dirac`	Dirac delta function
`MeijerG`	Meijer G function
`Zeta`	Riemann Zeta function
`LegendreKc`, `LegendreKc1`, `LegendreEc`, `LegendreEc1`, `LegendrePic`, `LegendrePic1`	Legendre's elliptic integrals
`hypergeom`	hypergeometric function

Note: When Maple cannot find a simpler form, it leaves the expression as it is rather than convert it to an inexact form.

```
> ln(Pi);
```

$$\ln(\pi)$$

2.3 Basic Symbolic Computations

Maple can work with mathematical unknowns, and expressions which contain them.

```
> (1 + x)^2;
```

$$(1+x)^2$$

```
> (1 + x) + (3 - 2*x);
```

$$4-x$$

Note that Maple automatically simplifies the second expression.

Maple has hundreds of commands for working with symbolic expressions. For a partial list, see Table 2.2.

```
> expand((1 + x)^2);
```

$$1+2\,x+x^2$$

```
> factor(%);
```

$$(1+x)^2$$

As mentioned in **2.2 Numerical Computations**, the ditto operator, %, is a shorthand notation for the previous result.

```
> Diff(sin(x), x);
```

$$\frac{d}{dx}\sin(x)$$

```
> value(%);
```

$$\cos(x)$$

```
> Sum(n^2, n);
```

$$\sum_{n} n^2$$

```
> value(%);
```

$$\frac{1}{3}n^3-\frac{1}{2}n^2+\frac{1}{6}n$$

Divide one polynomial in x by another.

```
> rem(x^3+x+1, x^2+x+1, x);
```

$$2+x$$

Create a series.

```
> series(sin(x), x=0, 10);
```

$$x-\frac{1}{6}x^3+\frac{1}{120}x^5-\frac{1}{5040}x^7+\frac{1}{362880}x^9+\mathrm{O}(x^{10})$$

All the mathematical functions mentioned in the previous section also accept unknowns as arguments.

2.4 Assigning Expressions to Names

This section introduces the following concepts in Maple.

- Naming an object
- Guidelines for Maple names
- Maple arrow notation (->)
- Assignment operator (:=)
- Predefined and reserved names

Syntax for Naming an Object

Using the ditto operator, or retyping a Maple expression every time you want to use it, is not always convenient, so Maple enables you to name an object. Use the following syntax for naming.

```
name := expression;
```

You can assign *any* Maple expression to a name.

```
> var := x;
```

$$var := x$$

```
> term := x*y;
```

$$term := x\,y$$

You can assign equations to names.

```
> eqn := x = y + 2;
```

$$eqn := x = y + 2$$

Guidelines for Maple Names

Maple names can include any alphanumeric characters and underscores, but they *cannot start with a number.* Do not start names with an underscore because Maple uses these names for internal classification.

- Examples of valid Maple names are `polynomial`, `test_data`, `RoOt_lOcUs_pLoT`, and `value2`.
- Examples of *invalid* Maple names are `2ndphase` (because it begins with a number) and `x&y` (because `&` is not an alphanumeric character).

Maple Arrow Notation in Defining Functions

Define functions by using the Maple *arrow notation* (`->`). This notation allows you to evaluate a function when it appears in Maple expressions. You can do simple graphing of the function by using the `plot` command.

```
> f := x -> 2*x^2 -3*x +4;
```

$$f := x \rightarrow 2\,x^2 - 3\,x + 4$$

```
> plot (f(x), x= -5..5);
```

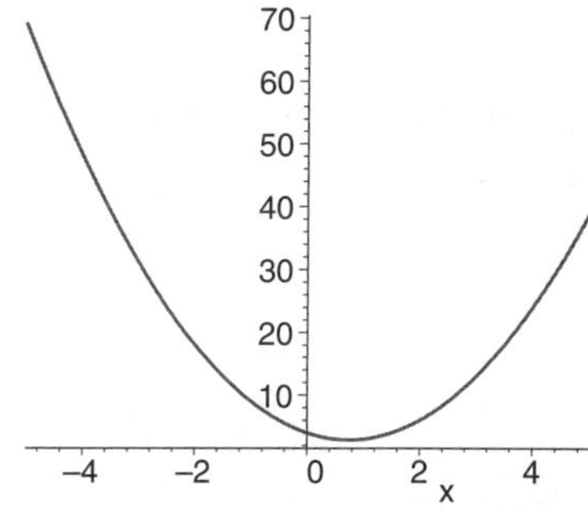

For more information on the `plot` command, see chapter 5 or enter `?plot` at the Maple prompt.

The Assignment Operator

The assignment (`:=`) operator associates a function name with a function definition. The name of the function is on the left-hand side of the `:=`. The function definition (using the arrow notation) is on the right-hand side. The following statement defines `f` as the *squaring function.*

```
> f := x -> x^2;
```

$$f := x \to x^2$$

Evaluating `f` at an argument produces the square of the argument of `f`.

```
> f(5);
```

$$25$$

```
> f(y+1);
```

$$(y+1)^2$$

Predefined and Reserved Names

Maple has some predefined and reserved names. If you try to assign to a name that is predefined or reserved, Maple displays a message, informing you that the name you have chosen is protected.

```
> Pi := 3.14;
```

```
Error, attempting to assign to `Pi` which is protected
```

```
> set := {1, 2, 3};
```

```
Error, attempting to assign to `set` which is protected
```

2.5 Basic Types of Maple Objects

This section examines basic types of Maple objects, including *expression sequences*, *lists*, *sets*, *arrays*, *tables*, and *strings*. These ideas are essential to the discussion in the rest of this book. Also, the following concepts in Maple are introduced.

- Concatenation operator
- Square bracket usage
- Curly braces usage
- Mapping
- Colon (:) for suppressing output
- Double quotation mark usage

Types Expressions belong to a class or group that share common properities. The classes and groups are known as *types*. For a complete list of types in Maple, refer to the `?type` help page.

Expression Sequences

The basic Maple data structure is the *expression sequence*. This is a group of Maple expressions separated by commas.

```
> 1, 2, 3, 4;
```

$$1, 2, 3, 4$$

```
> x, y, z, w;
```

$$x, y, z, w$$

Expression sequences are neither lists nor sets. They are a distinct data structure within Maple and have their own properties.

- Expression sequences preserve the order and repetition of their elements. Items stay in the order in which you enter them. If you enter an element twice, both copies remain.
- Sequences are often used to build more sophisticated objects through such operations as concatenation.

Other properties of sequences will become apparent as you progress through this manual. Sequences extend the capabilities of many basic Maple operations. For example, concatenation is a basic name-forming operation. The *concatenation operator* in Maple is "||". You can use the operator in the following manner.

```
> a||b;
```

$$ab$$

When applying concatenation to a sequence, the operation affects each element. For example, if S is a sequence, then you can prepend the name a to each element in S by concatenating a and S.

```
> S := 1, 2, 3, 4;
```

$$S := 1, 2, 3, 4$$

```
> a||S;
```

$$a1, a2, a3, a4$$

You can also perform multiple assignments using expression sequences. For example

```
> f,g,h := 3, 6, 1;
```

$$f, g, h := 3, 6, 1$$

```
> f;
```

$$3$$

```
> h;
```

$$1$$

Lists

You create a *list* by enclosing any number of Maple objects (separated by commas) in *square brackets.*

```
> data_list := [1, 2, 3, 4, 5];
```

$$data\_list := [1, 2, 3, 4, 5]$$

```
> polynomials := [x^2+3, x^2+3*x-1, 2*x];
```

$$polynomials := [x^2 + 3,\ x^2 + 3\,x - 1,\ 2\,x]$$

```
> participants := [Kathy, Frank, Rene, Niklaus, Liz];
```

$$participants := [Kathy,\ Frank,\ Rene,\ Niklaus,\ Liz]$$

Thus, a list is an expression sequence enclosed in square brackets.

Order Maple preserves the order and repetition of elements in a list. Thus, `[a,b,c]`, `[b,c,a]`, and `[a,a,b,c,a]` are all different.

```
> [a,b,c], [b,c,a], [a,a,b,c,a];
```

$$[a, b, c], [b, c, a], [a, a, b, c, a]$$

Because order is preserved, you can extract a particular element from a list without searching for it.

```
> letters := [a,b,c];
```

$$letters := [a, b, c]$$

```
> letters[2];
```

$$b$$

Use the `nops` command to determine the number of elements in a list.

```
> nops(letters);
```

$$3$$

Section **2.6 Expression Manipulation** discusses this command, including its other uses, in more detail.

Sets

Maple supports *sets* in the mathematical sense. Commas separate the objects, as they do in a sequence or list, but the enclosing *curly braces* identify the object as a set.

```
> data_set := {1, -1, 0, 10, 2};
```

$$data\_set := \{-1, 0, 1, 2, 10\}$$

```
> unknowns := {x, y, z};
```

$$unknowns := \{x, y, z\}$$

Thus, a set is an expression sequence enclosed in curly braces.

Order Maple does *not* preserve order or repetition in a set. That is, Maple sets have the same properties as sets do in mathematics. Thus, the following three sets are identical.

```
> {a,b,c}, {c,b,a}, {a,a,b,c,a};
```

$$\{a, b, c\}, \{a, b, c\}, \{a, b, c\}$$

For Maple, the integer 2 is distinct from the floating-point approximation 2.0. Thus, the following set has three elements, not two.

```
> {1, 2, 2.0};
```

$$\{1, 2, 2.0\}$$

The properties of sets make them a particularly useful concept in Maple, just as they are in mathematics. Maple provides many operations on sets, including the basic operations of *intersection* and *union* using the notation `intersect` and `union`.

```
> {a,b,c} union {c,d,e};
```

$$\{a, b, c, d, e\}$$

```
> {1,2,3,a,b,c} intersect {0,1,y,a};
```

$$\{1, a\}$$

The nops command counts the number of elements in a set or list.

```
> nops(%);
```

$$2$$

For more details on the nops command, see **2.6 Expression Manipulation**.

Mapping A common and useful command, often used on sets, is map. Mapping applies a function simultaneously to all the elements of any structure.

```
> numbers := {0, Pi/3, Pi/2, Pi};
```

$$numbers := \{0, \pi, \frac{1}{3}\pi, \frac{1}{2}\pi\}$$

```
> map(g, numbers);
```

$$\{g(0), g(\pi), g(\frac{1}{3}\pi), g(\frac{1}{2}\pi)\}$$

```
> map(sin, numbers);
```

$$\{0, 1, \frac{1}{2}\sqrt{3}\}$$

Further examples demonstrating the use of map appear in **2.6 Expression Manipulation** and **6.3 Structural Manipulations**.

Operations on Sets and Lists

The member command verifies membership in sets and lists.

```
> participants := [Kate, Tom, Steve];
```

$$participants := [Kate, Tom, Steve]$$

```
> member(Tom, participants);
```

$$true$$

```
> data_set := {5, 6, 3, 7};
```

$$data\_set := \{3, 5, 6, 7\}$$

```
> member(2, data_set);
```

$$false$$

To select items from lists, use the subscript notation, `[n]`, where n identifies the position of the desired element in the list.

```
> participants[2];
```

$$Tom$$

Maple recognizes *empty* sets and lists, that is, lists or sets that have no elements.

```
> empty_set := {};
```

$$empty\_set := \{\}$$

```
> empty_list := [];
```

$$empty\_list := []$$

You can create a new set from other sets by using, for example, the `union` command. Delete items from sets by using the `minus` command.

```
> old_set := {2, 3, 4} union {};
```

$$old\_set := \{2, 3, 4\}$$

```
> new_set := old_set union {2, 5};
```

$$new\_set := \{2, 3, 4, 5\}$$

```
> third_set := old_set minus {2, 5};
```

$$third\_set := \{3, 4\}$$

Arrays

Arrays are an extension of the concept of the list data structure. Think of a list as a group of items in which you associate each item with a positive integer, its index, that represents its position in the list. The Maple `array` data structure is a generalization of this idea. Each element is still associated with an index, but an array is not restricted to one dimension. In addition, indices can also be zero or negative. Furthermore, you can define or change the array's individual elements without redefining it entirely.

Declare the array to indicate dimensions.

```
> squares := array(1..3);
```

$$squares := \mathrm{array}(1..3, [])$$

Assign the array elements. Multiple commands can be entered at one command prompt provided each ends with a colon or semicolon.

```
> squares[1] := 1;  squares[2] := 2^2;  squares[3] := 3^2;
```

$$squares_1 := 1$$

$$squares_2 := 4$$

$$squares_3 := 9$$

Or do both simultaneously.

```
> cubes := array( 1..3, [1,8,27] );
```

$$cubes := [1, 8, 27]$$

You can select a single element using the same notation applied to lists.

```
> squares[2];
```

$$4$$

You must declare arrays in advance. To see the array's contents, you must use a command such as `print`.

```
> squares;
```

$$squares$$

```
> print(squares);
```

$$[1, 4, 9]$$

The preceding array has only one dimension, but arrays can have more than one dimension. Define a 3×3 array.

```
> pwrs := array(1..3,1..3);
```

$$pwrs := \mathrm{array}(1..3, 1..3, [])$$

This array has dimension two (two sets of indices). To begin, assign the array elements of the first row.

```
> pwrs[1,1] := 1;  pwrs[1,2] := 1;  pwrs[1,3] := 1;
```

$$pwrs_{1,1} := 1$$

$$pwrs_{1,2} := 1$$

$$pwrs_{1,3} := 1$$

Continue for the rest of the array. If you prefer, you can end each command with a colon (:), instead of the usual semicolon (;), to *suppress the output.* Both the colon and semicolon are statement separators.

```
> pwrs[2,1] := 2:  pwrs[2,2] := 4:  pwrs[2,3] := 8:
> pwrs[3,1] := 3:  pwrs[3,2] := 9:  pwrs[3,3] := 27:
> print(pwrs);
```

$$\begin{bmatrix} 1 & 1 & 1 \\ 2 & 4 & 8 \\ 3 & 9 & 27 \end{bmatrix}$$

You can select an element by specifying both the row and column.

```
> pwrs[2,3];
```

$$8$$

You can define a two-dimensional array and its elements simultaneously by using a similar method employed for the one-dimensional example shown earlier. To do so, use lists within lists. That is, make a list where each element is a list that contains the elements of one row of the array. Thus, you could define the pwrs array as follows.

```
> pwrs2 := array( 1..3, 1..3, [[1,1,1], [2,4,8], [3,9,27]] );
```

$$pwrs2 := \begin{bmatrix} 1 & 1 & 1 \\ 2 & 4 & 8 \\ 3 & 9 & 27 \end{bmatrix}$$

Arrays are not limited to two dimensions, but those of higher order are more difficult to display. You can declare all the elements of the array as you define its dimension.

```
> array3 := array( 1..2, 1..2, 1..2,
> [[[1,2],[3,4]], [[5,6],[7,8]]] );
```

$$\begin{aligned}
&array3 := \mathrm{array}(1..2,\ 1..2,\ 1..2,\ [\\
&(1,\ 1,\ 1) = 1\\
&(1,\ 1,\ 2) = 2\\
&(1,\ 2,\ 1) = 3\\
&(1,\ 2,\ 2) = 4\\
&(2,\ 1,\ 1) = 5\\
&(2,\ 1,\ 2) = 6\\
&(2,\ 2,\ 1) = 7\\
&(2,\ 2,\ 2) = 8\\
&])
\end{aligned}$$

Maple does not automatically expand the name of an array to the representation of all elements. In some commands, you must specify explicitly that you want to perform an operation on the elements.

Suppose that you want to define a new array identical to `pwr`, but with each occurrence of the number 2 in `pwrs` replaced by the number 9. To perform this substitution, use the `subs` command. The basic syntax is

```
subs( x=expr1, y=expr2, ... , main_expr )
```

Note: The subs command does not modify the value of main_expr. It returns an object of the same type with the specified substitutions. For example, to substitute $x + y$ for z in an expression, do the following.

```
> expr := z^2 + 3;
```

$$expr := z^2 + 3$$

```
> subs( {z=x+y}, expr);
```

$$(x + y)^2 + 3$$

Note that the following call to subs does not work.

```
> subs( {2=9}, pwrs );
```

$$pwrs$$

You must instead force Maple to fully evaluate the name of the array to the component level and not just to its name, using the command evalm.

```
> pwrs3:=subs( {2=9}, evalm(pwrs) );
```

$$pwrs3 := \begin{bmatrix} 1 & 1 & 1 \\ 9 & 4 & 8 \\ 3 & 9 & 27 \end{bmatrix}$$

This causes the substitution to occur in the components and full evaluation displays the array's elements, similar to using the print command.

```
> evalm(pwrs3);
```

$$\begin{bmatrix} 1 & 1 & 1 \\ 9 & 4 & 8 \\ 3 & 9 & 27 \end{bmatrix}$$

Tables

A *table* is an extension of the concept of the array data structure. The difference between an array and a table is that a table can have *anything* for indices, not just integers.

```
> translate := table([one=un,two=deux,three=trois]);
```

$$translate := \mathrm{table}([two = deux,\ three = trois,\ one = un])$$

```
> translate[two];
```

$$deux$$

Although at first they may seem to have little advantage over arrays, table structures are very powerful. Tables enable you to work with natural notation for data structures. For example, you can display the physical properties of materials using a Maple table.

```
> earth_data := table( [ mass=[5.976*10^24,kg],
>                        radius=[6.378164*10^6,m],
>                        circumference=[4.00752*10^7,m] ] );
```

$$\begin{aligned}&earth\_data := \mathrm{table}([mass = [0.5976000000\,10^{25},\ kg],\\&radius = [0.6378164000\,10^{7},\ m],\\&circumference = [0.4007520000\,10^{8},\ m]\\&])\end{aligned}$$

```
> earth_data[mass];
```

$$[0.5976000000\,10^{25},\ kg]$$

In this example, each index is a name and each entry is a list. Often, much more general indices are useful. For example, you could construct a table which has algebraic formulæ for indices and the derivatives of these formulæ as values.

Strings

A *string* is also an object in Maple and is created by enclosing any number of characters in *double quotes*.

```
> "This is a string.";
```

"This is a string."

They are nearly indivisible constructs that stand only for themselves; they cannot be assigned a value.

```
> "my age" := 32;
Error, invalid left hand side of assignment
```

Like elements of lists or arrays, the individual characters of a string can be indexed with square bracket notation.

```
> mystr := "I ate the whole thing.";
```

$$mystr := \text{"I ate the whole thing."}$$

```
> mystr[3..5];
```

"ate"

```
> mystr[11..-2];
```

"whole thing"

A negative index represents a character position counted from the right end of the string. In the example above, -2 represents the second last character.

The concatenation operator, "`||`", or the `cat` command is used to join two strings together, and the `length` command is used to determine the number of characters in a string.

```
> newstr := cat("I can't believe ", mystr);
```

$$newstr := \text{"I can't believe I ate the whole thing."}$$

```
> length(newstr);
```

38

For examples of commands that operate on strings and take strings as input, refer to the `?StringTools` help page.

2.6 Expression Manipulation

Many Maple commands concentrate on manipulating expressions. This includes manipulating results of Maple commands into a familiar or useful form. This section introduces the most commonly used commands in this area.

The `simplify` Command

You can use this command to apply simplification rules to an expression. Maple has simplification rules for various types of expressions and forms, including trigonometric functions, radicals, logarithmic functions, exponential functions, powers, and various special functions.

```
> expr := cos(x)^5 + sin(x)^4 + 2*cos(x)^2
> - 2*sin(x)^2 - cos(2*x);
```

$$expr := \cos(x)^5 + \sin(x)^4 + 2\cos(x)^2 - 2\sin(x)^2 - \cos(2\,x)$$

```
> simplify(expr);
```

$$\cos(x)^4\,(\cos(x) + 1)$$

To perform only a certain type of simplification, specify the type you want.

```
> simplify(sin(x)^2 + ln(2*y) + cos(x)^2);
```

$$1 + \ln(2) + \ln(y)$$

```
> simplify(sin(x)^2 + ln(2*y) + cos(x)^2, 'trig');
```

$$1 + \ln(2\,y)$$

```
> simplify(sin(x)^2 + ln(2*y) + cos(x)^2, 'ln');
```

$$\sin(x)^2 + \ln(2) + \ln(y) + \cos(x)^2$$

With the *side relations* feature, you can apply your own simplification rules.

```
> siderel := {sin(x)^2 + cos(x)^2 = 1};
```

$$siderel := \{\sin(x)^2 + \cos(x)^2 = 1\}$$

```
> trig_expr := sin(x)^3 - sin(x)*cos(x)^2 + 3*cos(x)^3;
```

$$trig\_expr := \sin(x)^3 - \sin(x)\cos(x)^2 + 3\cos(x)^3$$

```
> simplify(trig_expr, siderel);
```

$$2\sin(x)^3 - 3\cos(x)\sin(x)^2 + 3\cos(x) - \sin(x)$$

The factor Command

This command factors polynomial expressions.

```
> big_poly := x^5 - x^4 - 7*x^3 + x^2 + 6*x;
```

$$big\_poly := x^5 - x^4 - 7\,x^3 + x^2 + 6\,x$$

```
> factor(big_poly);
```

$$x\,(x-1)\,(x-3)\,(x+2)\,(x+1)$$

```
> rat_expr := (x^3 - y^3)/(x^4 - y^4);
```

$$rat\_expr := \frac{x^3 - y^3}{x^4 - y^4}$$

Both the numerator and denominator contain the common factor $x-y$. Thus, factoring cancels these terms.

```
> factor(rat_expr);
```

$$\frac{x^2 + x\,y + y^2}{(y+x)\,(x^2+y^2)}$$

Maple can factor both univariate and multivariate polynomials over the domain the coefficients specify. You can also factor polynomials over algebraic extensions. For details, refer to the ?factor help page.

The expand Command

The expand command is essentially the reverse of factor. It causes the expansion of multiplied terms as well as a number of other expansions. This is among the most useful of the manipulation commands. Although you might imagine that with a name like expand the result would be larger and more complex than the original expression; this is not always the case. In fact, expanding some expressions results in substantial simplification.

```
> expand((x+1)*(x+2));
```

$$x^2 + 3\,x + 2$$

```
> expand(sin(x+y));
```

$$\sin(y)\cos(x) + \cos(y)\sin(x)$$

```
> expand(exp(a+ln(b)));
```

$$e^a\, b$$

The expand command is quite flexible. You can you specify that certain subexpressions be unchanged by the expansion and program custom expansion rules.

Although the simplify command may seem to be the most useful command, this is misleading. Unfortunately, the word *simplify* is rather vague. When you request to simplify an expression, Maple examines your expression, tests many techniques, and then tries applying the appropriate simplification rules. However, this might take a little time. As well, Maple may not be able to determine what you want to accomplish since universal mathematical rules do not define what is simpler.

When you do know which manipulations will make your expression simpler for you, specify them directly. In particular, the expand command is among the most useful. It frequently results in substantial simplification, and also leaves expressions in a convenient form for many other commands.

The convert Command

This command converts expressions between different forms. For a list of common conversions, see Table 2.3.

```
> convert(cos(x),exp);
```

Table 2.3 Common Conversions

Argument	*Description*
polynom	series to polynomials
exp, expln, expsincos	trigonometric expressions to exponential form
parfrac	rational expressions to partial fraction form
rational	floating-point numbers to rational form
radians, degrees	between degrees and radians
set, list, listlist	between data structures
temperature	between temperature scales
units	between units

$$\frac{1}{2}e^{(x\,I)} + \frac{1}{2}\frac{1}{e^{(x\,I)}}$$

```
> convert(1/2*exp(x) + 1/2*exp(-x),trig);
```

$$\cosh(x)$$

```
> A := Matrix([[a,b],[c,d]]);
```

$$A := \begin{bmatrix} a & b \\ c & d \end{bmatrix}$$

```
> convert(A, 'listlist');
```

$$[[a,\, b],\, [c,\, d]]$$

```
> convert(A, 'set');
```

$$\{a,\, b,\, d,\, c\}$$

```
> convert(%, 'list');
```

$$[a,\, b,\, d,\, c]$$

The normal Command

This command transforms rational expressions into *factored normal form*,

$$\frac{numerator}{denominator},$$

where the *numerator* and *denominator* are relatively prime polynomials with integer coefficients.

```
> rat_expr_2 := (x^2 - y^2)/(x - y)^3 ;
```

$$rat\_expr\_2 := \frac{x^2 - y^2}{(-y + x)^3}$$

```
> normal(rat_expr_2);
```

$$\frac{y + x}{(-y + x)^2}$$

```
> normal(rat_expr_2, 'expanded');
```

$$\frac{y + x}{y^2 - 2\,x\,y + x^2}$$

The **expanded** option transforms rational expressions into *expanded normal form*.

The combine Command

This command combines terms in sums, products, and powers into a single term. These transformations are, in some cases, the reverse of the transformations that **expand** applies.

```
> combine(exp(x)^2*exp(y),exp);
```

$$e^{(2\,x+y)}$$

```
> combine((x^a)^2, power);
```

$$x^{(2\,a)}$$

The map Command

This command is useful when working with lists, sets, or arrays. It provides a means for working with multiple solutions or for applying an operation to each element of an array.

The map command applies a command to each element of a data structure or expression. While it is possible to write program structures such as loops to accomplish these tasks, you should not underestimate the convenience and power of the map command. The map command is one of the most useful commands in Maple.

```
> map( f, [a,b,c] );
```

$$[\mathrm{f}(a),\ \mathrm{f}(b),\ \mathrm{f}(c)]$$

```
> data_list := [0, Pi/2, 3*Pi/2, 2*Pi];
```

$$\mathit{data\_list} := [0,\ \frac{1}{2}\,\pi,\ \frac{3}{2}\,\pi,\ 2\,\pi]$$

```
> map(sin, data_list);
```

$$[0,\ 1,\ -1,\ 0]$$

If you give the map command more than two arguments, Maple passes the last argument(s) to the initial command.

```
> map( f, [a,b,c], x, y );
```

$$[\mathrm{f}(a,\ x,\ y),\ \mathrm{f}(b,\ x,\ y),\ \mathrm{f}(c,\ x,\ y)]$$

For example, to differentiate each item in a list with respect to x, you can use the following commands.

```
> fcn_list := [sin(x),ln(x),x^2];
```

$$\mathit{fcn\_list} := [\sin(x),\ \ln(x),\ x^2]$$

```
> map(Diff, fcn_list, x);
```

$$[\frac{d}{dx}\sin(x),\ \frac{d}{dx}\ln(x),\ \frac{d}{dx}(x^2)]$$

```
> map(value, %);
```

$$[\cos(x), \frac{1}{x}, 2\,x]$$

You can also create an operation to map onto a list. For example, suppose that you want to square each element of a list. Replace each element (represented by x) with its square (x^2).

```
> map(x->x^2, [-1,0,1,2,3]);
```

$$[1, 0, 1, 4, 9]$$

The lhs and rhs Commands

These two commands take the left-hand side and right-hand side of an expression, respectively.

```
> eqn1 := x+y=z+3;
```

$$eqn1 := y + x = z + 3$$

```
> lhs(eqn1);
```

$$y + x$$

```
> rhs(eqn1);
```

$$z + 3$$

The numer and denom Commands

These two commands take the numerator and denominator of a rational expression, respectively.

```
> numer(3/4);
```

$$3$$

```
> denom(1/(1 + x));
```

$$x + 1$$

The nops and op Commands

These two commands are useful for breaking expressions into parts and extracting subexpressions.

The nops command returns the number of parts in an expression.

```
> nops(x^2);
```

$$2$$

```
> nops(x + y + z);
```

$$3$$

The op command allows you to access the parts of an expression. It returns the parts as a sequence.

```
> op(x^2);
```

$$x, 2$$

You can also specify items by number or range.

```
> op(1, x^2);
```

$$x$$

```
> op(2, x^2);
```

$$2$$

```
> op(2..-2, x+y+z+w);
```

$$y, z$$

Common Questions about Expression Manipulation

1. How do I substitute for a product of two unknowns? Use side relations to specify an identity. Substituting directly does not usually work because Maple searches for an exact match before substituting.

```
> expr := a^3*b^2;
```

$$expr := a^3\, b^2$$

```
> subs(a*b=5, expr);
```

$$a^3\, b^2$$

The **subs** command was unsuccessful in its attempt to substitute. Use the **simplify** command.

```
> simplify(expr, {a*b=5});
```

$$25\, a$$

You can also use the **algsubs** command, which performs an algebraic substitution.

```
> algsubs(a*b=5, expr);
```

$$25\, a$$

2. How do I factor out the constant from $2x + 2y$? Currently, this operation is not possible in Maple because its simplifier automatically distributes the number over the product, believing that a sum is simpler than a product. In most cases, this is true.

If you enter the following expression, Maple automatically multiplies the constant into the expression.

```
> 2*(x + y);
```

$$2\, x + 2\, y$$

How can you then deal with such expressions, when you need to factor out constants, or negative signs? To factor such expressions, try this substitution.

```
> expr3 := 2*(x + y);
```

$$expr3 := 2\, x + 2\, y$$

```
> subs( 2=two, expr3 );
```

$$x\,two + y\,two$$

```
> factor(%);
```

$$two\,(x + y)$$

2.7 Conclusion

In this chapter you have seen many of the types of objects which Maple is capable of manipulating, including sequences, sets, and lists. You have seen a number of commands, including **`expand`**, **`factor`**, and **`simplify`**, that are useful for manipulating and simplifying algebraic expressions. Others, such as **`map`**, are useful for sets, lists, and arrays. Meanwhile, **`subs`** is useful almost any time.

In the next chapter, you will learn to apply these concepts to solve systems of equations, one of the most fundamental problems in mathematics. As you learn about new commands, observe how the concepts of this chapter are used in setting up problems and manipulating solutions.

3 Finding Solutions

This chapter introduces the key concepts needed for quick, concise problem solving in Maple. Several commands are presented along with information on how they interoperate.

In This Chapter

- Solving equations symbolically using the `solve` command
- Manipulations, plotting, and evaluating solutions
- Solving equations numerically using the `fsolve` command
- Specialized solvers in Maple
- Functions that act on polynomials
- Tools for solving problems in calculus

3.1 The Maple `solve` Command

The Maple `solve` command is a general-purpose equation solver. It takes a set of one or more equations and attempts to solve them exactly for the specified set of unknowns. (Recall from **2.5 Basic Types of Maple Objects** that you use braces to denote a set.)

Examples Using the `solve` Command

In the following examples, you are solving one equation for one unknown. Each set contains only one element.

```
> solve({x^2=4}, {x});
```

$$\{x = 2\}, \{x = -2\}$$

```
> solve({a*x^2+b*x+c=0}, {x});
```

$$\{x = \frac{1}{2}\frac{-b + \sqrt{b^2 - 4\,a\,c}}{a}\}, \{x = \frac{1}{2}\frac{-b - \sqrt{b^2 - 4\,a\,c}}{a}\}$$

Maple returns each possible solution as a set. Since both of these equations have two solutions, Maple returns a sequence of solution sets.

Solving for All Unknowns If you do not specify any unknowns in the equation, Maple solves for all of them.

```
> solve({x+y=0});
```

$$\{x = -y, y = y\}$$

Here, the result is one solution set containing two equations. This means that y can take any value, while x is the negative of y. This solution is parameterized with respect to y.

Expression versus Equation If you give an expression rather than an equation, Maple automatically assumes that the expression is equal to zero.

```
> solve({x^3-13*x+12}, {x});
```

$$\{x = 1\}, \{x = 3\}, \{x = -4\}$$

Systems of Equations The `solve` command can also handle systems of equations.

```
> solve({x+2*y=3, y+1/x=1}, {x,y});
```

$$\{x = -1, y = 2\}, \{x = 2, y = \frac{1}{2}\}$$

Returning the Solution as a Set Although you do not always need the braces (denoting a set) around either the equation or variable, using them forces Maple to return the solution as a set, which is usually the most convenient form. For example, it is a common practice to check your solutions by substituting them into the original equations. The following example demonstrates this procedure.

As a set of equations, the solution is in an ideal form for the `subs` command. You might first give the set of equations a name, like `eqns`, for instance.

```
> eqns := {x+2*y=3, y+1/x=1};
```

$$eqns := \{x + 2\,y = 3,\ y + \frac{1}{x} = 1\}$$

Then solve.

```
> soln := solve( eqns, {x,y} );
```

$$soln := \{x = -1,\ y = 2\},\ \{x = 2,\ y = \frac{1}{2}\}$$

This produces two solutions:

```
> soln[1];
```

$$\{x = -1,\ y = 2\}$$

and

```
> soln[2];
```

$$\{x = 2,\ y = \frac{1}{2}\}$$

Verifying Solutions

To check the solutions, substitute them into the original set of equations by using the two-parameter `eval` command.

```
> eval( eqns, soln[1] );
```

$$\{1 = 1,\ 3 = 3\}$$

```
> eval( eqns, soln[2] );
```

$$\{1 = 1,\ 3 = 3\}$$

For verifying solutions, you will find that this method is generally the most convenient.

Observe that this application of the `eval` command has other uses. To extract the value of x from the first solution, use the `eval` command.

```
> x1 := eval( x, soln[1] );
```

$$x1 := -1$$

Alternatively, you could extract the first solution for y.

```
> y1 := eval(y, soln[1]);
```

$$y1 := 2$$

Converting Solution Sets to Other Forms You can use this evaluation to convert solution sets to other forms. For example, you can construct a `list` from the first solution where x is the first element and y is the second. First construct a `list` with the *variables* in the same order as you want the corresponding *solutions*.

```
> [x,y];
```

$$[x, y]$$

Evaluate this list at the first solution.

```
> eval([x,y], soln[1]);
```

$$[-1, 2]$$

The first solution is now a list.

Instead, if you prefer that the solution for y comes first, evaluate `[y,x]` at the solution.

```
> eval([y,x], soln[1]);
```

$$[2, -1]$$

Since Maple typically returns solutions in the form of sets (in which the order of objects is uncertain), remembering this method for extracting solutions is useful.

Applying One Operation to All Solutions The map command is another useful command that allows you to apply one operation to all solutions. For example, try substituting *both* solutions.

The map command applies the operation specified as its first argument to its second argument.

```
> map(f, [a,b,c], y, z);
```

$$[\mathrm{f}(a,\, y,\, z),\, \mathrm{f}(b,\, y,\, z),\, \mathrm{f}(c,\, y,\, z)]$$

Due to the syntactical design of map, it cannot perform multiple function applications to sequences. Consider the previous solution sequence, for example,

```
> soln;
```

$$\{x = -1,\, y = 2\},\, \{x = 2,\, y = \frac{1}{2}\}$$

Enclose soln in square brackets to convert it to a list.

```
> [soln];
```

$$[\{x = -1,\, y = 2\},\, \{x = 2,\, y = \frac{1}{2}\}]$$

Use the following command to substitute *each* of the solutions simultaneously into the original equations, eqns.

```
> map(subs, [soln], eqns);
```

$$[\{1 = 1,\, 3 = 3\},\, \{1 = 1,\, 3 = 3\}]$$

This method can be valuable if your equation has many solutions, or if you are unsure of the number of solutions that a certain command produces.

Restricting Solutions

You can limit solutions by specifying inequalities with the solve command.

```
> solve({x^2=y^2},{x,y});
```

$$\{x = -y,\ y = y\},\ \{y = y,\ x = y\}$$

```
> solve({x^2=y^2, x<>y},{x,y});
```

$$\{x = -y,\ y = y\}$$

Consider this system of five equations in five unknowns.

```
> eqn1 := x+2*y+3*z+4*t+5*u=41:
> eqn2 := 5*x+5*y+4*z+3*t+2*u=20:
> eqn3 := 3*y+4*z-8*t+2*u=125:
> eqn4 := x+y+z+t+u=9:
> eqn5 := 8*x+4*z+3*t+2*u=11:
```

Solve the system for all variables.

```
> s1 := solve({eqn1,eqn2,eqn3,eqn4,eqn5}, {x,y,z,t,u});
```

$$s1 := \{x = 2,\ t = -11,\ z = -1,\ y = 3,\ u = 16\}$$

Solving for a Subset of Unknowns You can also solve for a subset of the unknowns. Maple returns the solutions in terms of the other unknowns.

```
> s2 := solve({eqn1,eqn2,eqn3}, { x, y, z});
```

$$s2 := \{x = -\frac{527}{13} - 7\,t - \frac{28}{13}\,u,\ z = -\frac{70}{13} - 7\,t - \frac{59}{13}\,u,$$
$$y = \frac{635}{13} + 12\,t + \frac{70}{13}\,u\}$$

Exploring Solutions

You can explore the parametric solutions found at the end of the previous section. For example, evaluate the solution at $u = 1$ and $t = 1$.

```
> eval( s2, {u=1,t=1} );
```

$$\{x = \frac{-646}{13},\ y = \frac{861}{13},\ z = \frac{-220}{13}\}$$

Suppose that you require the solutions from `solve` in a particular order. Since you cannot fix the order of elements in a set, `solve` does not necessarily return your solutions in the order x, y, z. However, lists do preserve order. Try the following.

```
> eval( [x,y,z], s2 );
```

$$[-\frac{527}{13} - 7t - \frac{28}{13}u, \frac{635}{13} + 12t + \frac{70}{13}u, -\frac{70}{13} - 7t - \frac{59}{13}u]$$

This command fixed the order and extracted the right-hand side of the equations. Because the order is fixed, you know the solution for each variable. This capability is particularly useful if you want to plot the solution surface.

```
> plot3d(%, u=0..2, t=0..2, axes=BOXED);
```

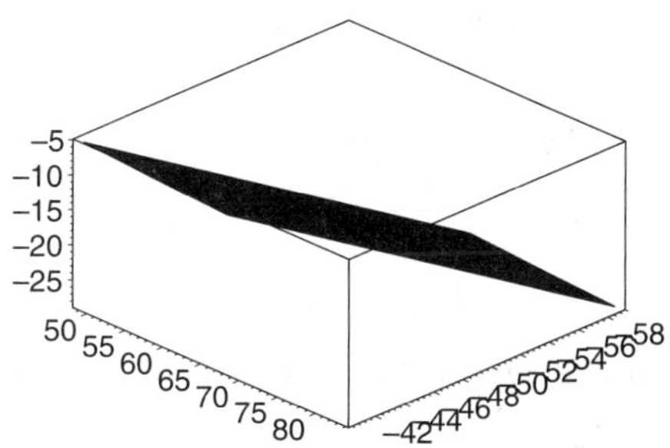

The unapply Command

For convenience, define $x = x(u,t)$, $y = y(u,t)$, and $z = z(u,t)$, that is, convert the solutions to functions. Recall that you can easily select a solution *expression* for a particular variable using eval.

```
> eval( x, s2 );
```

$$-\frac{527}{13} - 7t - \frac{28}{13}u$$

However, this is an *expression* for x and not a function.

```
> x(1,1);
```

$$\mathrm{x}(1,\ 1)$$

To convert the expression to a function, use the unapply command. Provide unapply with the expression *and* the independent variables. For example,

```
> f := unapply(x^2 + y^2 + 4, x, y);
```

$$f := (x,\, y) \to x^2 + y^2 + 4$$

produces the function, f, of x and y that maps (x, y) to $x^2 + y^2 + 4$. This new function is easy to use.

```
> f(a,b);
```

$$a^2 + b^2 + 4$$

Thus, to make your solution for x a function of both u and t, obtain the *expression* for x, as above.

```
> eval(x, s2);
```

$$-\frac{527}{13} - 7\,t - \frac{28}{13}\,u$$

Use `unapply` to turn it into a function of u and t.

```
> x := unapply(%, u, t);
```

$$x := (u,\, t) \to -\frac{527}{13} - 7\,t - \frac{28}{13}\,u$$

```
> x(1,1);
```

$$\frac{-646}{13}$$

You can create the functions y and z in the same manner.

```
> eval(y,s2);
```

$$\frac{635}{13} + 12\,t + \frac{70}{13}\,u$$

```
> y := unapply(%,u,t);
```

$$y := (u,\, t) \to \frac{635}{13} + 12\,t + \frac{70}{13}\,u$$

```
> eval(z,s2);
```

$$-\frac{70}{13} - 7\,t - \frac{59}{13}\,u$$

```
> z := unapply(%, u, t);
```

$$z := (u,\, t) \to -\frac{70}{13} - 7\,t - \frac{59}{13}\,u$$

```
> y(1,1), z(1,1);
```

$$\frac{861}{13},\, \frac{-220}{13}$$

The assign Command

The **assign** command allocates values to unknowns. For example, instead of defining x, y, and z as functions, assign each to the expression on the right-hand side of the corresponding equation.

```
> assign( s2 );
> x, y, z;
```

$$-\frac{527}{13} - 7\,t - \frac{28}{13}\,u,\, \frac{635}{13} + 12\,t + \frac{70}{13}\,u,\, -\frac{70}{13} - 7\,t - \frac{59}{13}\,u$$

Think of the **assign** command as turning the "=" signs in the solution set into ":=" signs.

The **assign** command is convenient if you want to assign expressions to names. *While this command is useful for quickly assigning solutions, it cannot create functions.*

This next example incorporates solving differential equations, which section **3.6 Solving Differential Equations Using the dsolve Command** discusses in further detail. To begin, assign the solution.

```
> s3 := dsolve( {diff(f(x),x)=6*x^2+1, f(0)=0}, {f(x)} );
```

$$s3 := \mathrm{f}(x) = 2\,x^3 + x$$

```
> assign( s3 );
```

However, you have yet to create a function.

```
> f(x);
```

$$2\,x^3 + x$$

produces the expected answer, but despite appearances, f(x) is simply a name for the *expression* $2x^3 + x$ and *not* a *function.* Call the function f using an argument other than x.

```
> f(1);
```

$$\mathrm{f}(1)$$

The reason for this behavior is that the **assign** command performs the following assignment

```
> f(x) := 2*x^3 + x;
```

$$\mathrm{f}(x) := 2\,x^3 + x$$

which is *not* the same as the assignment

```
> f := x -> 2*x^3 + x;
```

$$f := x \to 2\,x^3 + x$$

- The former defines the value of the function f for only the special argument x.
- The latter defines the function $f\colon x \mapsto 2x^3 + x$ so that it works whether you say $f(x)$, $f(y)$, or $f(1)$.

To define the solution f as a function of x, use **unapply**.

```
> eval(f(x),s3);
```

$$2\,x^3 + x$$

```
> f := unapply(%, x);
```

$$f := x \to 2\,x^3 + x$$

```
> f(1);
```

$$3$$

The RootOf Command

Maple occasionally returns solutions in terms of the **RootOf** command. The following example demonstrates this point.

```
> solve({x^5 - 2*x + 3 = 0},{x});
```

$$\{x = \mathrm{RootOf}(\_Z^5 - 2\,\_Z + 3,\ index = 1)\},$$
$$\{x = \mathrm{RootOf}(\_Z^5 - 2\,\_Z + 3,\ index = 2)\},$$
$$\{x = \mathrm{RootOf}(\_Z^5 - 2\,\_Z + 3,\ index = 3)\},$$
$$\{x = \mathrm{RootOf}(\_Z^5 - 2\,\_Z + 3,\ index = 4)\},$$
$$\{x = \mathrm{RootOf}(\_Z^5 - 2\,\_Z + 3,\ index = 5)\}$$

`RootOf(`*`expr`*`)` is a placeholder for all the roots of *expr*. This indicates that x is a root of the polynomial $z^5 - 2z + 3$, while the index parameter numbers and orders the solutions. This can be useful if your algebra is over a field different from the complex numbers. By using the **evalf** command, you obtain an explicit form of the complex roots.

```
> evalf(%);
```

$$\{x = 0.9585321812 + 0.4984277790\,I\},$$
$$\{x = -0.2467292569 + 1.320816347\,I\},$$
$$\{x = -1.423605849\},$$
$$\{x = -0.2467292569 - 1.320816347\,I\},$$
$$\{x = 0.9585321812 - 0.4984277790\,I\}$$

A general expression for the roots of degree five polynomials in terms of radicals does not exist.

3.2 Solving Numerically Using the fsolve Command

The `fsolve` command is the numeric equivalent of `solve`. The `fsolve` command finds the roots of the equation(s) by using a variation of Newton's method, producing approximate (floating-point) solutions.

```
> fsolve({cos(x)-x = 0}, {x});
```

$$\{x = 0.7390851332\}$$

For a general equation, `fsolve` searches for a single real root. For a polynomial, however, it searches for all *real* roots.

```
> poly :=3*x^4 - 16*x^3 - 3*x^2 + 13*x + 16;
```

$$poly := 3\,x^4 - 16\,x^3 - 3\,x^2 + 13\,x + 16$$

```
> fsolve({poly},{x});
```

$$\{x = 1.324717957\},\ \{x = 5.333333333\}$$

To search for more than one root of a general equation, use the `avoid` option.

```
> fsolve({sin(x)=0}, {x});
```

$$\{x = 0.\}$$

```
> fsolve({sin(x)=0}, {x}, avoid={x=0});
```

$$\{x = -3.141592654\}$$

To find a specified number of roots in a polynomial, use the `maxsols` option.

```
> fsolve({poly}, {x}, maxsols=1);
```

$$\{x = 1.324717957\}$$

By using the `complex` option, Maple searches for complex roots in addition to real roots.

```
> fsolve({poly}, {x}, complex);
```

$$\{x = -0.6623589786 - 0.5622795121\, I\},\\ \{x = -0.6623589786 + 0.5622795121\, I\},\\ \{x = 1.324717957\}, \{x = 5.333333333\}$$

You can also specify a range in which to look for a root.

```
> fsolve({cos(x)=0}, {x}, Pi..2*Pi);
```

$$\{x = 4.712388980\}$$

In some cases, `fsolve` may fail to find a root even if one exists. In these cases, specify a range. To increase the accuracy of the solutions, increase the value of the special variable, `Digits`. Note that in the following example the solution is not guaranteed to be accurate to thirty digits, but rather, Maple performs all steps in the solution to at least thirty significant digits rather than the default of ten.

```
> Digits := 30;
```

$$\mathit{Digits} := 30$$

```
> fsolve({cos(x)=0}, {x});
```

$$\{x = 1.57079632679489661923132169164\}$$

Limitations on `solve`

The `solve` command cannot solve all problems. Maple has an algorithmic approach, and it cannot necessarily use the shortcuts that you might use when solving the problem by hand.

- Mathematically, polynomials of degree five or higher do not have a solution in terms of radicals. Maple attempts to solve them, but you may need to use a numerical solution.
- Solving trigonometric equations can also be difficult. In fact, working with any transcendental equation is quite difficult.

```
> solve({sin(x)=0}, {x});
```

$$\{x = 0\}$$

Note: Maple returns only one of an infinite number of solutions. However, if you set the environment variable `_EnvAllSolutions` to true, Maple returns the entire set of solutions.

```
> _EnvAllSolutions := true;
```

$$\_EnvAllSolutions := true$$

```
> solve({sin(x)=0}, {x});
```

$$\{x = \pi \_Z1\tilde{}\}$$

The prefix _Z on the variable indicates that it has integer values. The *tilde* (~) indicates that there is an assumption on the variable, namely that it is an integer. In addition, with the `fsolve` command you can specify the range in which to look for a solution. Thereby you may gain more control over the solution.

```
> fsolve({sin(x)=0}, {x}, 3..4);
```

$$\{x = 3.14159265358979323846264338328\}$$

These types of problems are common to all symbolic computation systems, and are symptoms of the natural limitations of an algorithmic approach to equation solving. When using `solve`, check your results.

Removable Singularities The following example highlights an issue that can arise with removable singularities.

```
> expr := (x-1)^2/(x^2-1);
```

$$expr := \frac{(x-1)^2}{x^2-1}$$

Maple finds a solution

```
> soln := solve({expr=0},{x});
```

$$soln := \{x = 1\}$$

but when you evaluate the expression at 1, you get 0/0.

```
> eval(expr, soln);
```

```
Error, numeric exception: division by zero
```

The limit shows that $x = 1$ is nearly a solution.

```
> Limit(expr, x=1);
```

$$\lim_{x \to 1} \frac{(x-1)^2}{x^2 - 1}$$

```
> value (%);
```

$$0$$

Maple displays a vertical line at the asymptote, unless you specify discont=true.

```
> plot(expr, x=-5..5, y=-10..10);
```

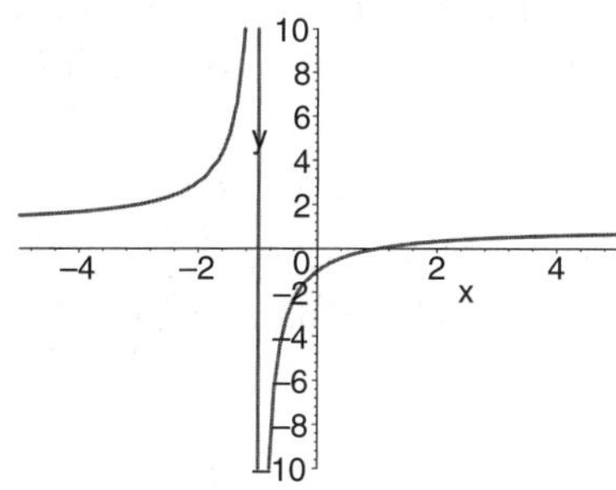

Maple removes the singularity $x = 1$ from the expression before solving it. Independent of the method or tools you use to solve equations, always check your results using the eval command.

3.3 Other Solvers

Maple contains many specialized solve commands. This section briefly mentions some of them. If you require more details on any of these commands, use the help system by entering ? and the command name at the Maple prompt.

Finding Integer Solutions

The `isolve` command finds integer solutions to equations, solving for all unknowns in the expression(s).

```
> isolve({3*x-4*y=7});
```

$$\{x = 5 + 4\_Z1, y = 2 + 3\_Z1\}$$

Maple uses the global names `_Z1`, ..., `_Zn` to denote the integer parameters of the solution.

Finding Solutions Modulo m

The `msolve` command solves equations in the integers modulo m (the positive representation for integers), solving for all unknowns in the expression(s).

```
> msolve({3*x-4*y=1,7*x+y=2},17);
```

$$\{y = 6, x = 14\}$$

```
> msolve({2^n=3},19);
```

$$\{n = 13 + 18\_Z1\tilde{}\}$$

The *tilde* (~) on `_Z1` indicates that `msolve` has placed an assumption on `_Z1`, in this case that `_Z1` is an integer.

```
> about( _Z1 );

Originally _Z1, renamed _Z1~:
  is assumed to be: integer
```

Section **6.2 Assumptions** describes how you can place assumptions on unknowns.

Solving Recurrence Relations

The `rsolve` command solves recurrence equations, returning an expression for the general term of the function.

```
> rsolve({f(n)=f(n-1)+f(n-2),f(0)=1,f(1)=1},{f(n)});
```

$$\{f(n) = (\frac{1}{2} + \frac{1}{10}\sqrt{5})(\frac{1}{2}\sqrt{5} + \frac{1}{2})^n + (\frac{1}{2} - \frac{1}{10}\sqrt{5})(-\frac{1}{2}\sqrt{5} + \frac{1}{2})^n\}$$

For more information, refer to `?LREtools`.

3.4 Polynomials

A *polynomial* in Maple is an expression containing unknowns. Each term in the polynomial contains a product of the unknowns. For example, if the polynomial contains only one unknown, x, then the terms might contain x^3, $x^1 = x$, and $x^0 = 1$ as in the case of the polynomial $x^3 - 2x + 1$. If more than one unknown exists, then a term may also contain a product of the unknowns, as in the polynomial $x^3 + 3x^2y + y^2$. Coefficients can be integers (as in the previous examples), rational numbers, irrational numbers, floating-point numbers, complex numbers, or other variables.

```
> x^2 - 1;
```

$$x^2 - 1$$

```
> x + y + z;
```

$$x + y + z$$

```
> 1/2*x^2 - sqrt(3)*x - 1/3;
```

$$\frac{1}{2}x^2 - \sqrt{3}\,x - \frac{1}{3}$$

```
> (1 - I)*x + 3 + 4*I;
```

$$(1 - I)\,x + 3 + 4\,I$$

```
> a*x^4 + b*x^3 + c*x^2 + d*x + f;
```

$$a\,x^4 + b\,x^3 + c\,x^2 + d\,x + f$$

Maple possesses commands for many kinds of manipulations and mathematical calculations with polynomials. The following sections investigate some of them.

Sorting and Collecting

The `sort` command arranges a polynomial into descending order of powers of the unknowns. Rather than making another copy of the polynomial with the terms in order, `sort` modifies the way Maple stores the original polynomial in memory. In other words, if you display your polynomial after sorting it, it retains the new order.

```
> sort_poly := x + x^2 - x^3 + 1 - x^4;
```

$$sort\_poly := x + x^2 - x^3 + 1 - x^4$$

```
> sort(sort_poly);
```

$$-x^4 - x^3 + x^2 + x + 1$$

```
> sort_poly;
```

$$-x^4 - x^3 + x^2 + x + 1$$

Maple sorts multivariate polynomials in two ways.

- The default method sorts them by total degree of the terms. Thus, x^2y^2 will come before both x^3 and y^3.
- The other option sorts by pure lexicographic order (`plex`), first by the powers of the first variable in the variable list (second argument) and then by the powers of the second variable in the variable list.

The difference between these sorts is best shown by an example.

```
> mul_var_poly := y^3 + x^2*y^2 + x^3;
```

$$mul\_var\_poly := y^3 + x^2\,y^2 + x^3$$

```
> sort(mul_var_poly, [x,y]);
```

$$x^2\,y^2 + x^3 + y^3$$

```
> sort(mul_var_poly, [x,y], 'plex');
```

$$x^3 + x^2\,y^2 + y^3$$

The `collect` command groups coefficients of like powers in a polynomial. For example, if the terms ax and bx are in a polynomial, Maple collects them as $(a + b)x$.

```
> big_poly:=x*y + z*x*y + y*x^2 - z*y*x^2 + x + z*x;
```

$$big\_poly := x\,y + z\,x\,y + y\,x^2 - z\,y\,x^2 + x + z\,x$$

```
> collect(big_poly, x);
```

$$(y - z\,y)\,x^2 + (y + z\,y + 1 + z)\,x$$

```
> collect(big_poly, z);
```

$$(x\,y - y\,x^2 + x)\,z + x\,y + y\,x^2 + x$$

Mathematical Operations

You can perform many mathematical operations on polynomials. Among the most fundamental is division, that is, to divide one polynomial into another and determine the quotient and remainder. Maple provides the commands `rem` and `quo` to find the remainder and quotient of a polynomial division.

```
> r := rem(x^3+x+1, x^2+x+1, x);
```

$$r := 2 + x$$

```
> q := quo(x^3+x+1, x^2+x+1, x);
```

$$q := x - 1$$

```
> collect( (x^2+x+1) * q + r, x );
```

$$x^3 + x + 1$$

Sometimes it is sufficient to know whether one polynomial divides into another polynomial exactly. The `divide` command tests for exact polynomial division.

```
> divide(x^3 - y^3, x - y);
```

$$true$$

```
> rem(x^3 - y^3, x - y, x);
```

$$0$$

You evaluate polynomials at values as you would with any expression, by using `eval`.

```
> poly := x^2 + 3*x - 4;
```

$$poly := x^2 + 3\,x - 4$$

```
> eval(poly, x=2);
```

$$6$$

```
> mul_var_poly := y^2*x - 2*y + x^2*y + 1;
```

$$mul\_var\_poly := y^2\,x - 2\,y + y\,x^2 + 1$$

```
> eval(mul_var_poly, {y=1,x=-1});
```

$$-1$$

Coefficients and Degrees

The commands `degree` and `coeff` determine the degree of a polynomial and provide a mechanism for extracting coefficients.

```
> poly := 3*z^3 - z^2 + 2*z - 3*z + 1;
```

Table 3.1 Commands for Finding Polynomial Coefficients

Command	*Description*
`coeff`	extract coefficient
`lcoeff`	find the leading coefficient
`tcoeff`	find the trailing coefficient
`coeffs`	return a sequence of all the coefficients
`degree`	determine the (highest) degree of the polynomial
`ldegree`	determine the lowest degree of the polynomial

$$poly := 3\,z^3 - z^2 - z + 1$$

```
> coeff(poly, z^2);
```

$$-1$$

```
> degree(poly,z);
```

$$3$$

Root Finding and Factorization

The `solve` command determines the roots of a polynomial whereas the `factor` command expresses the polynomial in fully factored form.

```
> poly1 := x^6 - x^5 - 9*x^4 + x^3 + 20*x^2 + 12*x;
```

$$poly1 := x^6 - x^5 - 9\,x^4 + x^3 + 20\,x^2 + 12\,x$$

```
> factor(poly1);
```

$$x\,(x-2)\,(x-3)\,(x+2)\,(x+1)^2$$

```
> poly2 := (x + 3);
```

$$poly2 := x + 3$$

```
> poly3 := expand(poly2^6);
```

Table 3.2 Functions that Act on Polynomials

Function	*Description*
`content`	content of a multivariate polynomial
`compoly`	polynomial decomposition
`discrim`	discriminant of a polynomial
`gcd`	greatest common divisor
`gcdex`	extended Euclidean algorithm
`interp`	polynomial interpolation
`lcm`	least common multiple
`norm`	norm of a polynomial
`prem`	pseudo-remainder
`primpart`	primitive part of a multivariate polynomial
`randpoly`	random polynomial
`recipoly`	reciprocal polynomial
`resultant`	resultant of two polynomials
`roots`	roots over an algebraic number field
`sqrfree`	square-free factorization

$$poly3 := x^6 + 18\,x^5 + 135\,x^4 + 540\,x^3 + 1215\,x^2 + 1458\,x + 729$$

```
> factor(poly3);
```

$$(x + 3)^6$$

```
> solve({poly3=0}, {x});
```

$$\{x = -3\}, \{x = -3\}, \{x = -3\}, \{x = -3\}, \{x = -3\}, \{x = -3\}$$

```
> factor(x^3 + y^3);
```

$$(x + y)\,(x^2 - x\,y + y^2)$$

Maple factors the polynomial over the ring implied by the coefficients, for example, the integers or rational numbers. The `factor` command also allows you to specify an algebraic number field over which to factor the polynomial. For more information, refer to the `?factor` help page. For a list of functions that act on polynomials, see Table 3.2.

3.5 Calculus

Maple provides many powerful tools for solving problems in calculus. This section presents the following concepts.

- Computing the limits of functions by using the `Limit` command
- Creating series approximations of a function by using the `series` command
- Symbolically computing derivatives, indefinite integrals, and definite integrals

About Calculus Examples in This Manual This and the following section provide an introduction to the Maple commands for calculus problems. A more extensive look at the `Student[Calculus]` package and the calculus commands in the main library is provided in chapter 4 and chapter 7. Also, detailed information is available in the Maple help system.

Using the `Limit` Command Compute the limit of a rational function as x approaches 1.

```
> f := x -> (x^2-2*x+1)/(x^4 + 3*x^3 - 7*x^2 + x+2);
```

$$f := x \to \frac{x^2 - 2\,x + 1}{x^4 + 3\,x^3 - 7\,x^2 + x + 2}$$

```
> Limit(f(x), x=1);
```

$$\lim_{x \to 1} \frac{x^2 - 2\,x + 1}{x^4 + 3\,x^3 - 7\,x^2 + x + 2}$$

```
> value(%);
```

$$\frac{1}{8}$$

Taking the limit of an expression from either the positive or the negative direction is also possible. For example, consider the limit of $\tan(x)$ as x approaches $\pi/2$.

Calculate the left-hand limit by using the option `left`.

```
> Limit(tan(x), x=Pi/2, left);
```

$$\lim_{x \to (1/2\,\pi)-} \tan(x)$$

```
> value(%);
```

$$\infty$$

Calculate the right-hand limit.

```
> Limit(tan(x), x=Pi/2, right);
```

$$\lim_{x \to (1/2\,\pi)+} \tan(x)$$

```
> value(%);
```

$$-\infty$$

Using the series Command To create a series approximation of a function, note the following example.

```
> f := x -> sin(4*x)*cos(x);
```

$$f := x \to \sin(4\,x)\cos(x)$$

```
> fs1 := series(f(x), x=0);
```

$$fs1 := 4\,x - \frac{38}{3}\,x^3 + \frac{421}{30}\,x^5 + \mathrm{O}(x^6)$$

By default, the `series` command generates an order 6 polynomial. By changing the value of the special variable, `Order`, you can increase or decrease the order of a polynomial series.

Using `convert(fs1, polynom)` removes the order term from the series so that Maple can plot it.

```
> p := convert(fs1,polynom);
```

$$p := 4\,x - \frac{38}{3}\,x^3 + \frac{421}{30}\,x^5$$

```
> plot({f(x), p},x=-1..1, -2..2);
```

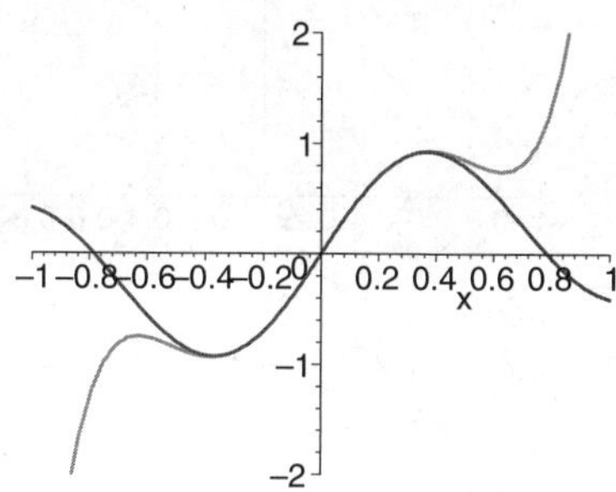

If you increase the order of truncation of the series to 12 and try again, you see the expected improvement in the accuracy of the approximation.

```
> Order := 12;
```

$$Order := 12$$

```
> fs1 := series(f(x), x=0);
```

$$fs1 := 4\,x - \frac{38}{3}\,x^3 + \frac{421}{30}\,x^5 - \frac{10039}{1260}\,x^7 + \frac{246601}{90720}\,x^9 - \frac{6125659}{9979200}\,x^{11} + \mathrm{O}(x^{12})$$

```
> p := convert(fs1,polynom);
```

$$p := 4\,x - \frac{38}{3}\,x^3 + \frac{421}{30}\,x^5 - \frac{10039}{1260}\,x^7 + \frac{246601}{90720}\,x^9 - \frac{6125659}{9979200}\,x^{11}$$

```
> plot({f(x), p}, x=-1..1, -2..2);
```

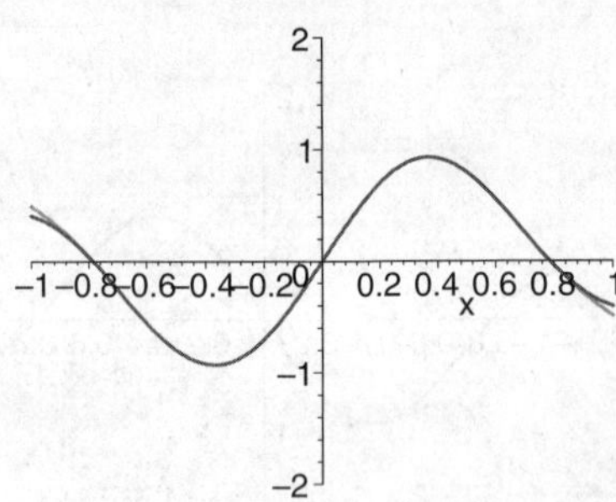

Computing Derivatives and Integrals Maple can symbolically compute derivatives and integrals. For example, differentiate an expression, calculate the *indefinite integral* of its result, and compare it with the original expression. For more information on definite integration in Maple, see the next example.

```
> f := x -> x*sin(a*x) + b*x^2;
```

$$f := x \to x\sin(a\,x) + b\,x^2$$

```
> Diff(f(x),x);
```

$$\frac{\partial}{\partial x}\left(x\sin(a\,x) + b\,x^2\right)$$

```
> df := value(%);
```

$$df := \sin(a\,x) + x\cos(a\,x)\,a + 2\,b\,x$$

```
> Int(df, x);
```

$$\int \sin(a\,x) + x\cos(a\,x)\,a + 2\,b\,x\,dx$$

```
> value(%);
```

$$-\frac{\cos(a\,x)}{a} + \frac{\cos(a\,x) + a\,x\sin(a\,x)}{a} + b\,x^2$$

```
> simplify(%);
```

$$x\,(\sin(a\,x) + b\,x)$$

`Diff` and `Int` are the inert forms of the `diff` and `int` commands. The inert form of a command returns a typeset form of the operation instead of performing the operation. In the previous examples, the inert forms of the commands have been used in conjunction with the `value` command. Note that it is unnecessary to use the inert forms; derivatives and integrals can be calculated in single commands by using `diff` and `int`, respectively. For more information on these commands, refer to the `?diff` and `?int` help pages.

You can also perform *definite integrations.* For example, recompute the previous integral on the interval $x = 1$ to $x = 2$.

```
> Int(df,x=1..2);
```

$$\int_1^2 \sin(a\,x) + x\cos(a\,x)\,a + 2\,b\,x\,dx$$

```
> value(%);
```

$$-\sin(a) + 3\,b + 2\sin(2\,a)$$

Consider a more complicated integral.

```
> Int(exp(-x^2), x);
```

$$\int e^{(-x^2)}\,dx$$

```
> value(%);
```

$$\frac{1}{2}\sqrt{\pi}\,\mathrm{erf}(x)$$

If Maple cannot clearly determine whether a variable is real or complex, it may return an unexpected result.

```
> g := t -> exp(-a*t)*ln(t);
```

$$g := t \to e^{(-a\,t)}\ln(t)$$

```
> Int (g(t), t=0..infinity);
```

$$\int_0^\infty e^{(-a\,t)}\ln(t)\,dt$$

```
> value(%);
```

$$\lim_{t\to\infty} -\frac{e^{(-a\,t)}\ln(t)+\mathrm{Ei}(1,\,a\,t)+\gamma+\ln(a)}{a}$$

Maple assumes that the parameter a is a complex number. Hence, it returns a more general answer.

For situations where you know that a is a positive, real number, indicate this by using the assume command.

```
> assume(a > 0):
> ans := Int(g(t), t=0..infinity);
```

$$ans := \int_0^\infty e^{(-a\tilde{}\,t)}\ln(t)\,dt$$

```
> value(%);
```

$$-\frac{\ln(a\tilde{})}{a\tilde{}}-\frac{\gamma}{a\tilde{}}$$

The result is much simpler. The only non-elementary term is the constant gamma. The tilde (˜) indicates that a carries an assumption. Remove the assumption to proceed to more examples. You must do this in two steps. The answer, ans, contains a with assumptions. To reset and continue using ans, replace all occurrences of $a\tilde{}$ with a.

```
> ans := subs(a ='a', ans );
```

$$ans := \int_0^\infty e^{(-a\,t)}\ln(t)\,dt$$

The first argument, a = 'a', deserves special attention. If you type a after making an assumption about a, Maple automatically assumes you mean a~. In Maple, single quotes *delay evaluation*. In this case, they ensure that Maple interprets the second a as a and not as a~.

Now that you have removed the assumption on a inside ans, you can remove the assumption on a itself by assigning it to its own name.

```
> a := 'a':
```

Use single quotes here to remove the assumption on a. For more information on assumptions, see **6.2 Assumptions**.

3.6 Solving Differential Equations Using the dsolve Command

Maple can symbolically solve many ordinary differential equations (ODEs), including initial value and boundary value problems.

Define an ODE. Note that the diff command and not the inert form Diff is used in this example.

```
> ode1 := {diff(y(t),t,t) + 5*diff(y(t),t) + 6*y(t)  = 0};
```

$$ode1 := \{(\frac{d^2}{dt^2}\,\mathrm{y}(t)) + 5\,(\frac{d}{dt}\,\mathrm{y}(t)) + 6\,\mathrm{y}(t) = 0\}$$

Define initial conditions.

```
> ic := {y(0)=0, D(y)(0)=1};
```

$$ic := \{\mathrm{D}(y)(0) = 1,\ \mathrm{y}(0) = 0\}$$

Solve with dsolve by using the union operator to form the union of the two sets.

```
> soln := dsolve(ode1 union ic, {y(t)});
```

$$soln := \mathrm{y}(t) = -e^{(-3\,t)} + e^{(-2\,t)}$$

To evaluate the solution at points or plot it, first use the unapply command to define a proper Maple function. For more information, see **3.1 The Maple solve Command**.

To extract a value from a solution set, use the eval command.

```
> eval( y(t), soln );
```

$$-e^{(-3\,t)}+e^{(-2\,t)}$$

Define y as a function of t by using the **unapply** command.

```
> y1:= unapply(%, t );
```

$$y1:=t\to -e^{(-3\,t)}+e^{(-2\,t)}$$

```
> y1(a);
```

$$-e^{(-3\,a)}+e^{(-2\,a)}$$

Verify that `y1` is a solution to the ODE:

```
> eval(ode1, y=y1);
```

$$\{0=0\}$$

and that `y1` satisfies the initial conditions.

```
> eval(ic, y=y1);
```

$$\{0=0,\,1=1\}$$

Another method for solution checking is also available. Assign the new solution to `y` instead of `y1`.

```
> y := unapply( eval(y(t), soln), t );
```

$$y:=t\to -e^{(-3\,t)}+e^{(-2\,t)}$$

When you enter an equation containing `y`, Maple uses this function and evaluates the result, in one step.

```
> ode1;
```

$$\{0=0\}$$

```
> ic;
```

$$\{0 = 0, \ 1 = 1\}$$

To change the differential equation, or the definition of $y(t)$, remove the definition with the following command.

```
> y := 'y';
```

$$y := y$$

With Maple, you can use special functions, such as the Dirac delta function, also called the impulse function, used in physics.

```
> ode2 := 10^6*diff(y(x),x,x,x,x) = Dirac(x-2) -
>   Dirac(x-4);
```

$$ode2 := 1000000\,(\frac{d^4}{dx^4}\,\mathrm{y}(x)) = \mathrm{Dirac}(x-2) - \mathrm{Dirac}(x-4)$$

Specify boundary conditions

```
> bc := {y(0)=0, D(D(y))(0)=0, y(5)=0};
```

$$bc := \{\mathrm{y}(0) = 0, \ \mathrm{y}(5) = 0, \ (\mathrm{D}^{(2)})(y)(0) = 0\}$$

and an initial value.

```
> iv := {D(D(y))(5)=0};
```

$$iv := \{(\mathrm{D}^{(2)})(y)(5) = 0\}$$

```
> soln := dsolve({ode2} union bc union iv, {y(x)});
```

$$soln := \mathrm{y}(x) = \frac{1}{6000000}\,\mathrm{Heaviside}(x-2)\,x^3$$
$$-\frac{1}{750000}\,\mathrm{Heaviside}(x-2) + \frac{1}{500000}\,\mathrm{Heaviside}(x-2)\,x$$
$$-\frac{1}{1000000}\,\mathrm{Heaviside}(x-2)\,x^2$$
$$-\frac{1}{6000000}\,\mathrm{Heaviside}(x-4)\,x^3 + \frac{1}{93750}\,\mathrm{Heaviside}(x-4)$$
$$-\frac{1}{125000}\,\mathrm{Heaviside}(x-4)\,x + \frac{1}{500000}\,\mathrm{Heaviside}(x-4)\,x^2$$
$$-\frac{1}{15000000}\,x^3 + \frac{1}{1250000}\,x$$

```
> eval(y(x), soln);
```

$$\frac{1}{6000000}\,\mathrm{Heaviside}(x-2)\,x^3 - \frac{1}{750000}\,\mathrm{Heaviside}(x-2)$$
$$+\frac{1}{500000}\,\mathrm{Heaviside}(x-2)\,x$$
$$-\frac{1}{1000000}\,\mathrm{Heaviside}(x-2)\,x^2$$
$$-\frac{1}{6000000}\,\mathrm{Heaviside}(x-4)\,x^3 + \frac{1}{93750}\,\mathrm{Heaviside}(x-4)$$
$$-\frac{1}{125000}\,\mathrm{Heaviside}(x-4)\,x + \frac{1}{500000}\,\mathrm{Heaviside}(x-4)\,x^2$$
$$-\frac{1}{15000000}\,x^3 + \frac{1}{1250000}\,x$$

```
> y := unapply(%, x);
```

$$y := x \rightarrow \frac{1}{6000000}\,\mathrm{Heaviside}(x-2)\,x^3$$
$$-\frac{1}{750000}\,\mathrm{Heaviside}(x-2) + \frac{1}{500000}\,\mathrm{Heaviside}(x-2)\,x$$
$$-\frac{1}{1000000}\,\mathrm{Heaviside}(x-2)\,x^2$$
$$-\frac{1}{6000000}\,\mathrm{Heaviside}(x-4)\,x^3 + \frac{1}{93750}\,\mathrm{Heaviside}(x-4)$$
$$-\frac{1}{125000}\,\mathrm{Heaviside}(x-4)\,x + \frac{1}{500000}\,\mathrm{Heaviside}(x-4)\,x^2$$
$$-\frac{1}{15000000}\,x^3 + \frac{1}{1250000}\,x$$

This value of y satisfies the differential equation, the boundary conditions, and the initial value.

```
> ode2;
```

$$-12\,\mathrm{Dirac}(1,\,x-2)-\frac{1}{6}\,\mathrm{Dirac}(3,\,x-4)\,x^3+8\,\mathrm{Dirac}(2,\,x-2)$$
$$+\,24\,\mathrm{Dirac}(1,\,x-4)+4\,\mathrm{Dirac}(x-2)-4\,\mathrm{Dirac}(x-4)$$
$$-\,6\,\mathrm{Dirac}(1,\,x-4)\,x+16\,\mathrm{Dirac}(2,\,x-4)\,x$$
$$-\,2\,\mathrm{Dirac}(2,\,x-4)\,x^2-8\,\mathrm{Dirac}(2,\,x-2)\,x$$
$$+\,2\,\mathrm{Dirac}(2,\,x-2)\,x^2+\frac{1}{6}\,\mathrm{Dirac}(3,\,x-2)\,x^3$$
$$+\,\frac{32}{3}\,\mathrm{Dirac}(3,\,x-4)-\frac{4}{3}\,\mathrm{Dirac}(3,\,x-2)-8\,\mathrm{Dirac}(3,\,x-4)\,x$$
$$+\,2\,\mathrm{Dirac}(3,\,x-4)\,x^2+2\,\mathrm{Dirac}(3,\,x-2)\,x$$
$$-\,\mathrm{Dirac}(3,\,x-2)\,x^2+6\,\mathrm{Dirac}(1,\,x-2)\,x$$
$$-\,32\,\mathrm{Dirac}(2,\,x-4)=\mathrm{Dirac}(x-2)-\mathrm{Dirac}(x-4)$$

```
> simplify(%);
```

$$\mathrm{Dirac}(x-2)-\mathrm{Dirac}(x-4)=\mathrm{Dirac}(x-2)-\mathrm{Dirac}(x-4)$$

```
> bc;
```

$$\{0=0\}$$

```
> iv;
```

$$\{0=0\}$$

```
> plot(y(x), x=0..5, axes=BOXED);
```

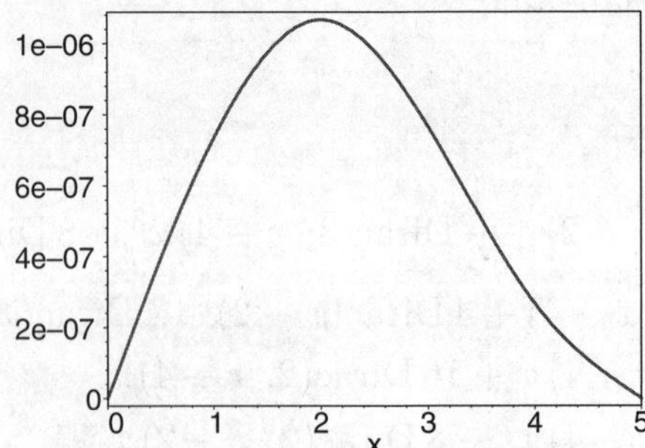

Unassign y now since you are done with it.

```
> y := 'y';
```

$$y := y$$

Maple can also solve systems of differential equations. For example, solve the following system of two simultaneous, second order equations.

```
> de_sys := { diff(y(x),x,x)=z(x), diff(z(x),x,x)=y(x) };
```

$$de\_sys := \{\frac{d^2}{dx^2}\,\mathrm{z}(x) = \mathrm{y}(x),\ \frac{d^2}{dx^2}\,\mathrm{y}(x) = \mathrm{z}(x)\}$$

```
> soln := dsolve(de_sys, {z(x),y(x)});
```

$$soln := \{\mathrm{z}(x) = \_C1\ e^x + \_C2\ e^{(-x)} + \_C3\sin(x) + \_C4\cos(x),$$
$$\mathrm{y}(x) = \_C1\ e^x + \_C2\ e^{(-x)} - \_C3\sin(x) - \_C4\cos(x)\}$$

If you solve the system without providing additional conditions, Maple automatically generates the appropriate constants `_C1`, ..., `_C4`.

You can extract and define the solutions by using the `eval` and `unapply` commands.

```
> y := unapply(eval(y(x), soln), x );
```

$$y := x \rightarrow \_C1\ e^x + \_C2\ e^{(-x)} - \_C3\sin(x) - \_C4\cos(x)$$

```
> y(1);
```

$$\_C1\, e + \_C2\, e^{(-1)} - \_C3 \sin(1) - \_C4 \cos(1)$$

You can unassign it again when you are finished.

```
> y := 'y';
```

$$y := y$$

3.7 Conclusion

This chapter encompasses fundamental Maple features that will assist you greatly as you learn more complicated problem-solving methods. Sections 3.1 and 3.2 introduced the `solve` and `fsolve` commands, and how to evaluate and plot solutions. The final section of this chapter introduced specialized solvers, and commands for solving calculus problems.

4 Maple Organization

This chapter introduces the organization of Maple, including the library and built-in packages of specialized commands.

In This Chapter

- The Maple Library
- List of Maple Packages
- The `Student` Package
- The `LinearAlgebra` Package
- The `Matlab` Package
- The `Statistics` Package
- The `simplex` Linear Optimization Package

4.1 The Organization of Maple

The kernel is the base of the Maple system. It contains fundamental and primitive commands.

- Maple language interpreter (which converts the commands you enter into machine instructions your computer processor can understand)
- Algorithms for basic numerical calculation
- Routines to display results and perform other input and output operations

The kernel consists of highly optimized *C* code—approximately 10% of the system's total size. The kernel has been kept small for speed and efficiency. The Maple kernel implements the most frequently used routines for integer and rational arithmetic and simple polynomial calculations.

The remaining 90% of the Maple mathematical algorithms is written in the Maple language and resides in the Maple library.

The Maple Library

The Maple library divides into two groups: the *main* library and the packages. These groups of functions sit above the kernel.

The *main* library contains the most frequently used Maple commands (other than those in the kernel). The last commands in the library are in the packages. Each package contains a group of commands for related calculations. For example, the `LinearAlgebra` package contains commands for the manipulation of Matrices.

You can use a command from a package in three ways.

1. Use the complete name of the package and the command name.

   ```
   package[cmd]( ... )
   ```

   If the package has a subpackage, use the complete name of the package, the complete name of the subpackage, and the command name.

   ```
   package[subpackage][cmd]( ... )
   ```

2. Activate the short form of the names for all the commands in a package by using the `with` command.

   ```
   with(package)
   ```

   If the package has a subpackage, use the following `with` command.

   ```
   with(package[subpackage])
   ```

   Then use the short name for the command.

```
cmd(...)
```

3. Activate the short name for a single command from a package.

```
with(package, cmd)
```

If the package has a subpackage, use the following command.

```
with(package[subpackage], cmd)
```

Then use the short form of the command name.

```
cmd(...)
```

The following example uses the `Tangent` command in the `Student[Calculus1]` package to calculate the slope of the tangent of the expression $sin(x)$ at the point $x = 0$.

```
> with(Student[Calculus1]);
```

$$[AntiderivativePlot, AntiderivativeTutor, ApproximateInt, ApproximateIntTutor, ArcLength, ArcLengthTutor, Asymptotes, Clear, CriticalPoints, CurveAnalysisTutor, DerivativePlot, DerivativeTutor, DiffTutor, ExtremePoints, FunctionAverage, FunctionAverageTutor, FunctionChart, FunctionPlot, GetMessage, GetNumProblems, GetProblem, Hint, InflectionPoints, IntTutor, Integrand, InversePlot, InverseTutor, LimitTutor, MeanValueTheorem, MeanValueTheoremTutor, NewtonQuotient, NewtonsMethod, NewtonsMethodTutor, PointInterpolation, RiemannSum, RollesTheorem, Roots, Rule, Show, ShowIncomplete, ShowSteps, Summand, SurfaceOfRevolution, SurfaceOfRevolutionTutor, Tangent, TangentSecantTutor, TangentTutor, TaylorApproximation, TaylorApproximationTutor, Understand, Undo, VolumeOfRevolution, VolumeOfRevolutionTutor, WhatProblem]$$

```
> Tangent(sin(x), x = 0);
```

$$x$$

When you enter the `with(package);` command, a list of the short forms of all command names in the package is displayed. A warning message is displayed if it has redefined any pre-existing names. To suppress the display of the shorts forms of all command names, end the command with a colon, for example, `with(package):`.

4.2 The Maple Packages

Maple has packages of specialized commands perform tasks from an extensive variety of disciplines, from Student Calculus to General Relativity Theory. The examples in this section are not intended to be comprehensive. They are simply examples of a few commands in selected packages, to give you a glimpse of Maple functionality.

List of Packages

Many Maple packages are listed below. For a complete list of packages, refer to the `?packages` help page. For a full list of commands in a particular package, refer to the `?`*`packagename`* help page.

`algcurves` tools for studying the one-dimensional algebraic varieties (curves) defined by multi-variate polynomials.

`CodeGeneration` functions that translate Maple code to other programming languages such as C, Fortran, Java™, MATLAB®, and Visual Basic®.

`combinat` combinatorial functions, including commands for calculating permutations and combinations of lists, and partitions of integers. (Use the `combstruct` package instead, where possible.)

`combstruct` commands for generating and counting combinatorial structures, as well as determining generating function equations for such counting.

`context` tools for building and modifying context-sensitive menus in the Maple graphical user interface (for example, when right-clicking on an output expression).

`CurveFitting` commands that support curve-fitting.

`DEtools` tools for manipulating, solving, and plotting systems of differential equations, phase portraits, and field plots.

`diffalg` commands for manipulating systems of differential polynomial equations (ODEs or PDEs).

`difforms` commands for handling differential forms; for problems in differential geometry.

`Domains` commands to create *domains of computation*; supports computing with polynomials, matrices, and series over number rings, finite fields, polynomial rings, and matrix rings.

`ExternalCalling` commands that link to external functions.

`finance` commands for financial computations.

`FileTools` commands for file manipulation. Contains two subpackages: `Text` for manipulating text files and `Binary` for working with files of binary data.

`GaussInt` commands for working with Gaussian Integers; that is, numbers of the form $a + bI$ where a and b are integers. Commands for finding GCDs, factoring, and primality testing.

`genfunc` commands for manipulating rational generating functions.

`geom3d` commands for three-dimensional Euclidean geometry; to define and manipulate points, lines, planes, triangles, spheres, polyhedra, etcetera, in three dimensions.

`geometry` commands for two-dimensional Euclidean geometry; to define and manipulate points, lines, triangles, and circles in two dimensions.

`Groebner` commands for Gröbner basis computations; in particular tools for Ore algebras and D-modules.

`group` commands for working with permutation groups and finitely-presented groups.

`inttrans` commands for working with integral transforms and their inverses.

`LibraryTools` commands for library manipulation and processing.

`liesymm` commands for characterizing the contact symmetries of systems of partial differential equations.

`LinearAlgebra` enhanced linear algebra commands for creating special types of Matrices, calculating with large numeric Matrices, and performing Matrix algebra.

`LinearFunctionalSystems` commands that solve linear functional systems with polynomial coefficients, find the universal denominator of a rational solution, and transform a matrix recurrence system into an equivalent system with a nonsingular leading or trailing matrix.

`ListTools` commands that manipulate lists.

`LREtools` commands for manipulating, plotting, and solving linear recurrence equations.

`Maplets` package commands for creating windows, dialogs, and other visual interfaces that interact with a user to provide the power of Maple.

`MathML` commands that import and export Maple expressions to and from MathML text.

`Matlab` commands to use several MATLAB numerical matrix functions, including eigenvalues and eigenvectors, determinants, and LU-decomposition. (Only accessible if MATLAB is installed on your system.)

`MatrixPolynomialAlgebra` set of tools for the algebraic manipulation of matrix polynomials.

`networks` tools for constructing, drawing, and analyzing combinatorial networks. Facilities for handling directed graphs, and arbitrary expressions for edge and vertex weights.

`numapprox` commands for calculating polynomial approximations to functions on a given interval.

`numtheory` commands for classic number theory, primality testing, finding the nth prime, factoring integers, generating cyclotomic polynomials. This package also contains commands for handling convergents.

`Ore_algebra` routines for basic computations in algebras of linear operators.

`OrthogonalSeries` commands for manipulating series of classical orthogonal polynomials or, more generally, hypergeometric polynomials.

`orthopoly` commands for generating various types of orthogonal polynomials; useful in differential equation solving.

`padic` commands for computing p-adic approximations to real numbers.

`PDEtools` tools for manipulating, solving and plotting partial differential equations.

`plots` commands for different types of specialized plots, including contour plots, two- and three-dimensional implicit plotting, plotting text, and plots in different coordinate systems.

`plottools` commands for generating and manipulating graphical objects.

`PolynomialTools` commands for manipulating polynomial objects.

`powseries` commands to create and manipulate formal power series represented in general form.

`process` the commands in this package allow you to write multi-process Maple programs under UNIX®.

`RandomTools` commands for working with random objects.

`RationalNormalForms` commands that construct the polynomial normal form or rational canonical forms of a rational function, or minimal representation of a hypergeometric term.

`RealDomain` provides an environment in which the assumed underlying number system is the real number system not the complex number system.

`ScientificConstants` commands that provide access to the values of various constant physical quantities that occur in fields such as chemistry and physics.

`ScientificErrorAnalysis` commands that provide representation and construction of numerical quantitites that have a central value and associated uncertainty or error. This allows users to determine the uncertainty in, for example, the product of quantities-with-error.

`simplex` commands for linear optimization using the simplex algorithm.

`Slode` commands for finding formal power series solutions of linear ODEs.

`Sockets` commands for network communication in Maple. The routines in this package enable you to connect to processes on remote hosts on a network (such as an Intranet or the Internet) and exchange data with these processes.

`SolveTools` commands that solve systems of algebraic equations. This package gives expert users access to the routines used by the `solve` command for greater control over the solution process.

`Spread` tools for working with spreadsheets in Maple.

`stats` simple statistical manipulation of data; includes averaging, standard deviation, correlation coefficients, variance, and regression analysis.

`StringTools` optimized commands for string manipulation.

`Student` contains subpackages that are course specific. In general, the subpackages contain computation, interactive, and visualization components. The following is a description of three subpackages.

`Precalculus` interactive tutors, which help with some of the fundamental concepts that lead to calculus.

`Calculus1` commands for stepping through differentiation, integration, and limit problems, visualization of Newton's method, Riemann sums, arc length, volume of rotation and others, as well as routines for finding points of interest of an expression.

`LinearAlgebra` commands to help instructors present and students learn the basic material of a standard first course in linear algebra. Visualization routines use Maple plotting facilities to represent various concepts and computations, for example, displaying two 3-D Vectors and their cross products. Interactive routines allow students to work interactively through a particular type of linear algebra problem, such as finding the eigenvalues of a square matrix. The subpackage also includes routines for Matrix computations, such as constructing a Matrix of Jordon blocks.

`SumTools` tools for finding closed forms of definite and indefinite sums.

`tensor` commands for calculating with tensors and their applications in General Relativity Theory.

`TypeTools` commands for extending the set of recognized types in the type command.

`Units` commands for converting values between units, and environments for performing calculations with units.

`VariationalCalculus` commands for Calculus of Variations computations.

`VectorCalculus` procedures to perform multivariate and Vector calculus operations on objects based on the rtable datatype.

`Worksheet` commands that provide an infrastructure for generating and manipulating Maple worksheets by using the Maple language.

`XMLTools` commands that manipulate Maple's internal representation of XML documents.

Example Packages

The following section provides examples from five Maple packages.

- `Student[Calculus1]`
- `LinearAlgebra`
- `Matlab`
- Statistics
- `simplex` Linear Optimization

The Student Package

The `Student` package contains subpackages designed to assist with the teaching and learning of undergraduate mathematics. There are many routines for displaying functions, computations, and theorems. In general, the `Student` package contains computation, interactive, and visualization components. For a complete list of subpackages, refer to the `?Student` help page. The following provides examples from the `Student[Calculus1]` subpackage.

The Student Calculus1 Subpackage (Single Variable) This subpackage helps you step through differentiation, integration, and limit computations. The package contains visualization and interactive routines, and single-step computation. For details about the `Student[Calculus1]` package, refer to the `?Student[Calculus1]` help page.

Finding the Derivative of a Function You can find the derivative of a function by using the DiffTutor Maplet application, an interactive routine in the Student[Calculus1] package. For example, the following code invokes the interactive DiffTutor.

```
> with(Student[Calculus1]);
> DiffTutor();
> DiffTutor(x*cos(x));
> DiffTutor(x*cos(x),x);
```

See the ?Student[Calculus1][DiffTutor] help page and copy the example into you worksheet.

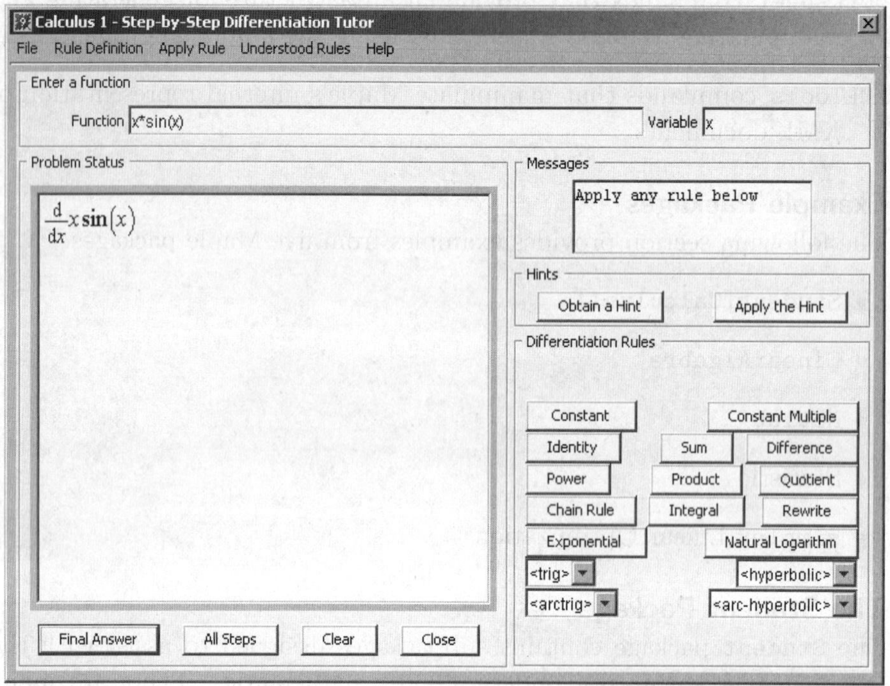

Worksheet Examples

The following examples are generated using the Student[Calculus1] subpackage.

Derivative Given the function 4*x^2, find its derivative. First, activate the short forms of all the command names in the package by using the with command.

```
> with(Student[Calculus1]):
> infolevel[Student[Calculus1]] := 1:
```

To view a list of all the commands that Maple is loading, replace the colon at the end of the command with a semicolon.

```
> Diff(4*x^2, x);
```

$$\frac{d}{dx}\,(4\,x^2)$$

Use the `constantmultiple` rule.

```
> Rule[constantmultiple](%);
```

```
Creating problem #1
```

$$\frac{d}{dx}\,(4\,x^2) = 4\,(\frac{d}{dx}\,(x^2))$$

Use the `power` rule.

```
> Rule[power](%);
```

$$\frac{d}{dx}\,(4\,x^2) = 8\,x$$

Integration Consider the following integration example. Integrate $x * cos(x) + x$ from $x = 0$ to $x = \pi$.

```
> Int(x*cos(x) + x, x=0..Pi);
```

$$\int_0^{\pi} x\cos(x) + x\,dx$$

Use the `sum` rule.

```
> Rule[sum](%);
```

```
Creating problem #2
```

$$\int_0^\pi x\cos(x) + x\,dx = \int_0^\pi x\cos(x)\,dx + \int_0^\pi x\,dx$$

Use the `power` rule.

```
> Rule[power](%);
```

$$\int_0^\pi x\cos(x) + x\,dx = \int_0^\pi x\cos(x)\,dx + \frac{1}{2}\pi^2$$

Use the `Hint` command to determine a possible next step for the problem.

```
> Hint(%);
```

$$[parts,\ x,\ \sin(x)]$$

Use the hint with the `Rule` command.

```
> Rule[%](%%);
```

$$\int_0^\pi x\cos(x) + x\,dx = -\int_0^\pi \sin(x)\,dx + \frac{1}{2}\pi^2$$

Use the `sin` rule to complete this computation.

```
> Rule[sin](%);
```

$$\int_0^\pi x\cos(x) + x\,dx = -2 + \frac{1}{2}\pi^2$$

Calculating Limits Calculate the limit of $(1+1/x)^x$. Use the `Understand` command to use rules for calculating the `Limit` without explicitly applying them. To add the constant, constant multiple, power, and sum `Limit` rules to the list of understood rules for the following example, use the `Understand` command.

```
> Understand(Limit, constant, `c*`, power, sum);
```

$$Limit = [constant,\ constantmultiple,\ power,\ sum]$$

```
> Limit((1 + 1/x)^x, x=infinity);
```

$$\lim_{x \to \infty} (1 + \frac{1}{x})^x$$

Request a hint for the next step of the computation.

```
> Hint(%);
```

```
Creating problem #3
```

```
Rewrite the expression as an exponential to prepare for using l'Hopital's r
```

$$[rewrite, (1 + \frac{1}{x})^x = e^{(x \ln(1+\frac{1}{x}))}]$$

Use the rule that is returned by `Hint`.

```
> Rule[%](%%);
```

$$\lim_{x \to \infty} (1 + \frac{1}{x})^x = \lim_{x \to \infty} e^{(x \ln(1+\frac{1}{x}))}$$

```
> Hint(%);
```

$$[\exp]$$

```
> Rule[%](%%);
```

$$\lim_{x \to \infty} (1 + \frac{1}{x})^x = e^{(\lim_{x \to \infty} x \ln(1+\frac{1}{x}))}$$

```
> Hint(%);
```

$$[lhopital, \ln(1 + \frac{1}{x})]$$

```
> Rule[%](%%);
```

$$\lim_{x \to \infty} (1 + \frac{1}{x})^x = e^{(\lim_{x \to \infty} \frac{x}{x+1})}$$

```
> Hint(%);
```

$$\left[rewrite, \frac{x}{x+1} = \frac{1}{1+\frac{1}{x}} \right]$$

```
> Rule[%](%%);
```

$$\lim_{x \to \infty} (1 + \frac{1}{x})^x = e$$

Plotting a Function and A Tangent Line Consider the function $-2/3 * x^2 + x$. Plot the function and its tangent line at $x = 0$.

```
> Tangent(-2/3*x^2+x, x=0, -2..2, output=plot,
>        showtangent=true);
```

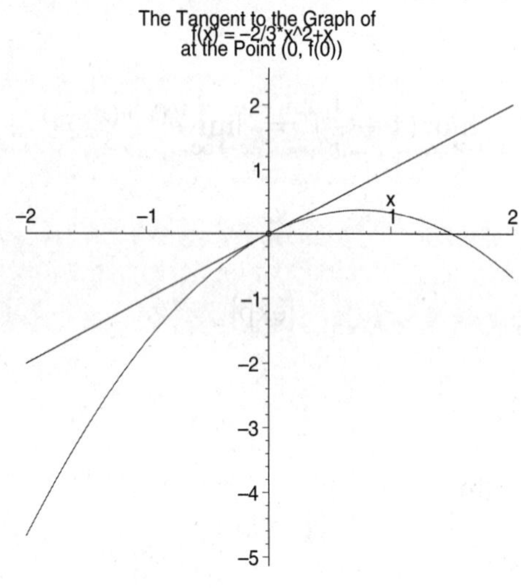

Where does this curve cross the x-axis?

```
> Roots(-2/3*x^2+x);
```

$$[0, \frac{3}{2}]$$

You can find the area under the curve between these two points by using Riemann sums.

```
> ApproximateInt(-2/3*x^2+x, x=0..3/2, method=midpoint,
>             output=plot, view=[0..1.6, -0.15..0.4]);
```

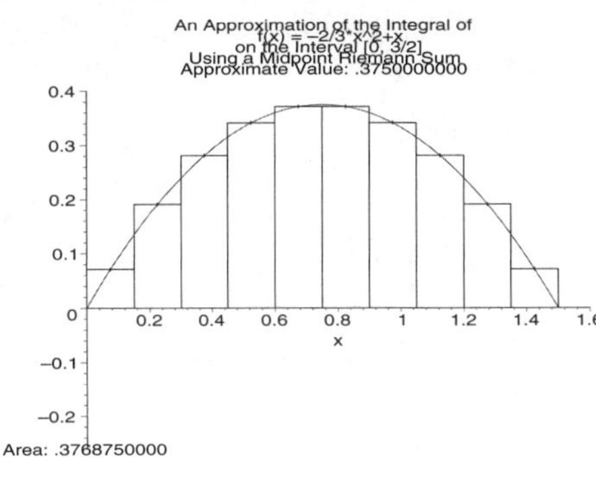

Since the result is not a good approximation, increase the number of boxes used to forty.

```
> ApproximateInt(-2/3*x^2+x, x=0..3/2, method=midpoint,
>             output=plot, view=[0..1.6, -0.15..0.4],
>             partition=40);
```

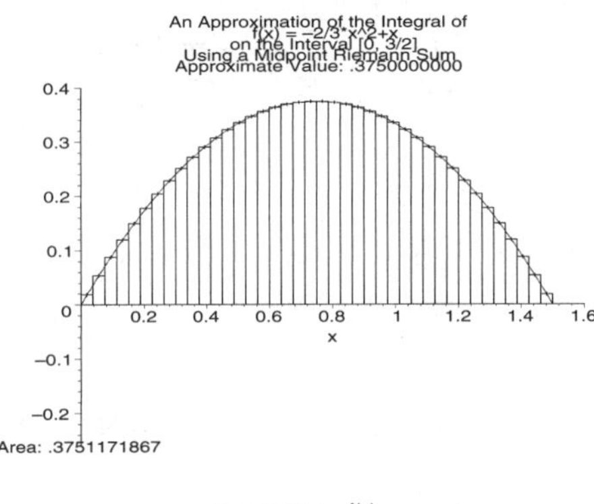

To determine the actual value, take the limit as n goes to ∞. Use n boxes and change the output to sum .

```
> ApproximateInt(-2/3*x^2+x, x=0..3/2, method=midpoint,
>             output=sum, partition=n);
```

$$\frac{3}{2}\,\frac{\displaystyle\sum_{i=0}^{n-1}\left(-\frac{3}{2}\,\frac{(i+\frac{1}{2})^2}{n^2}+\frac{3}{2}\,\frac{i+\frac{1}{2}}{n}\right)}{n}$$

Take the limit as n goes to ∞.

```
> Limit( %, n=infinity );
```

$$\lim_{n\to\infty}\frac{3}{2}\,\frac{\displaystyle\sum_{i=0}^{n-1}\left(-\frac{3}{2}\,\frac{(i+\frac{1}{2})^2}{n^2}+\frac{3}{2}\,\frac{i+\frac{1}{2}}{n}\right)}{n}$$

```
> value(%);
```

$$\frac{3}{8}$$

Observe that you can obtain the same result by using an integral.

```
> Int(-2/3*x^2+x, x=0..3/2 );
```

$$\int_0^{3/2} -\frac{2}{3}\,x^2+x\,dx$$

```
> value(%);
```

$$\frac{3}{8}$$

For more information on calculus with Maple, see chapter 7.

The LinearAlgebra Package

The `LinearAlgebra` package contains routines for computational linear algebra.

- For a complete list of commands, refer to the `?LinearAlgebra` help page.
- For the student version, refer to the `?Student[LinearAlgebra]` help page.

The following examples are generated using the **LinearAlgebra** package. In linear algebra, a set of linearly independent vectors that generates a vector space is a basis. That is, you can uniquely express any element in the vector space as a linear combination of the elements of the basis.

A set of vectors $\{v_1, v_2, v_3, \ldots, v_n\}$ is linearly independent if and only if

$$c_1v_1 + c_2v_2 + c_3v_3 + \cdots + c_nv_n = 0$$

implies

$$c_1 = c_2 = c_3 = \cdots = c_n = 0.$$

Determining a Basis Determine a basis for the vector space generated by the vectors $[1, -1, 0, 1]$, $[5, -2, 3, -1]$, and $[6, -3, 3, 0]$. Express the vector $[1, 2, 3, -5]$ with respect to this basis.

Enter the vectors.

```
> with(LinearAlgebra):
> v1:=<1|-1|0|1>:
> v2:=<5|-2|3|-1>:
> v3:=<6|-3|3|0>:
> vector_space:=<v1,v2,v3>;
```

$$vector\_space := \begin{bmatrix} 1 & -1 & 0 & 1 \\ 5 & -2 & 3 & -1 \\ 6 & -3 & 3 & 0 \end{bmatrix}$$

If the vectors are linearly independent, then they form a basis. To test linear independence, set up the equation $c_1v_1 + c_2v_2 + c_3v_3 = 0$

$$c_1[1, -1, 0, 1] + c_2[5, -2, 3, -1] + c_3[6, -3, 3, 0] = [0, 0, 0, 0]$$

which is equivalent to

$$\begin{aligned} c_1 + 5c_2 + 6c_3 &= 0 \\ -c_1 - 2c_2 - 3c_3 &= 0 \\ 3c_2 + 3c_3 &= 0 \\ c_1 - c_2 &= 0 \end{aligned}$$

```
> LinearSolve( Transpose(vector_space), <0,0,0,0> );
```

$$\begin{bmatrix} -\_t0_3 \\ -\_t0_3 \\ \_t0_3 \end{bmatrix}$$

The vectors are linearly dependent since each is a linear product of a variable. Thus, they cannot form a basis. The `RowSpace` command returns a basis for the vector space.

```
> b:=RowSpace(vector_space);
```

$$b := [[1, 0, 1, -1], [0, 1, 1, -2]]$$

```
> b1:=b[1]; b2:=b[2];
```

$$b1 := [1, 0, 1, -1]$$

$$b2 := [0, 1, 1, -2]$$

```
> basis:=<b1,b2>;
```

$$basis := \begin{bmatrix} 1 & 0 & 1 & -1 \\ 0 & 1 & 1 & -2 \end{bmatrix}$$

Express $[1, 2, 3, -5]$ in coordinates with respect to this basis.

```
> LinearSolve( Transpose(basis), <1|2|3|-5> );
```

$$\begin{bmatrix} 1 \\ 2 \end{bmatrix}$$

The Matlab Package

The Matlab package enables you to call selected MATLAB functions from a Maple session, provided you have MATLAB installed on your system.[1] MATLAB is an abbreviation of **mat**rix **lab**oratory and is a popular numerical computation package, used extensively by engineers and other computing professionals.

[1] There is also a *Symbolic Computation Toolbox* available for MATLAB that allows you to call Maple commands from MATLAB.

To establish the connection between the two products, enter the command

```
> with(Matlab):
```

The call to the `Matlab` library automatically executes the `openlink` command.

To determine the eigenvalues and eigenvectors of a matrix of integers, first define the matrix in Maple syntax.

```
> A := Matrix([[1,2,3],[1,2,3],[2,5,6]]):
```

Then the following call to `eig` is made.

```
> P,W := eig(A, eigenvectors=true):
```

Notice what is to the left of the assignment operator. The `(P,W)` specifies that *two* outputs are to be generated and assigned to variables — the eigenvalues to `W` and the eigenvectors to `P`. This multiple assignment is available to standard Maple commands is rarely used because existing Maple commands are designed to create a single result.

Consider the individual results.

```
> W;
```

$$\begin{bmatrix} 9.321825 & 0. & 0. \\ 0. & -.5612673\ 10^{-15} & 0. \\ 0. & 0. & -.3218253 \end{bmatrix}$$

```
> P;
```

$$\begin{bmatrix} -.3940365889964673 & -.9486832980505138 & -.5567547110202646 \\ -.3940365889964672 & -2.758331802155925\ 10^{-16} & -.5567547110202655 \\ -.8303435030540421 & .3162277660168383 & .6164806432593667 \end{bmatrix}$$

The commands in this package can also take input in MATLAB format. For more information on acceptable input, refer to the `?Matlab` help page.

The Statistics Package

The `stats` package has many commands for data analysis and manipulation, and various types of statistical plotting. It also contains a wide range of statistical distributions.

The `stats` package contains subpackages. Within each subpackage, the commands are grouped by functionality.

```
> with(stats);
```

$$[anova, describe, fit, importdata, random, statevalf, statplots, transform]$$

The `stats` package works with data in *statistical lists*, which can be standard Maple lists. A statistical list can also contain ranges and weighted values. The difference is best shown using an example. The name `marks` is assigned a standard list,

```
> marks :=
> [64,93,75,81,45,68,72,82,76,73];
```

$$marks := [64, 93, 75, 81, 45, 68, 72, 82, 76, 73]$$

as is `readings`

```
> readings := [ 0.75, 0.75, .003, 1.01, .9125,
>               .04, .83, 1.01, .874, .002 ];
```

$$readings := [0.75, 0.75, 0.003, 1.01, 0.9125, 0.04, 0.83, 1.01, 0.874, 0.002]$$

which is equivalent to the following statistical list.

```
> readings := [ Weight(.75, 2), .003, Weight(1.01, 2),
>               .9125, .04, .83, .874, .002 ];
```

$$readings := [\mathrm{Weight}(0.75, 2), 0.003, \mathrm{Weight}(1.01, 2), 0.9125, 0.04, 0.83, 0.874, 0.002]$$

The expression `Weight(x,n)` indicates that the value x appears n times in the list.

If differences less than 0.01 are so small that they are not meaningful, you can group them together, and give a range (using ". .").

```
> readings := [ Weight(.75, 2), Weight(1.01, 2), .9125,
>              .04, .83, .874, Weight(0.002..0.003, 2) ];
```

$$readings := [\text{Weight}(0.75, 2), \text{Weight}(1.01, 2), 0.9125, 0.04, 0.83, 0.874, \text{Weight}(0.002..0.003, 2)]$$

The `describe` subpackage contains commands for data analysis.

```
> describe[mean](marks);
```

$$\frac{729}{10}$$

```
> describe[range](marks);
```

$$45..93$$

```
> describe[range](readings);
```

$$0.002..1.01$$

```
> describe[standarddeviation](readings);
```

$$0.4038750457$$

This package contains many statistical distributions. Generate some random data using the normal distribution, group it into ranges, and then plot a histogram of the ranges.

```
> random_data:=[random[normald](50)];
```

$$random\_data := [-0.4386378394, -1.140005385, 0.1529160443, 0.7487697029, -0.4908898750, -0.6385850228, 0.7648245898, -0.04721150696, -1.463572278, 0.4470293004, 1.342701867, 2.162605068, -0.2620109124, 0.1093403084, -0.9886372087, -0.7765483851, -0.1231141571, 0.3876183720, 1.625165927, 1.095665255, -0.2068680316, -1.283733823, 1.583279600, 0.3045008349, -0.7304597374, 0.4996033128, 0.8670709448, -0.1729739933, -0.6819890237, 0.005183053789, 0.8876933468, -0.3758638317, 1.452138520, 2.858250470, 0.6917100232, 0.6341448687, 0.6707087107, 0.5872984199, 0.03801888006, -0.1238893314, -0.01231563388, -0.7709242575, -1.599692668, 0.8181350112, 0.08547526754, 0.09467224460, -1.407989130, 0.4128440679, -0.9586605355, -0.08180943597]$$

```
> ranges:=[-5..-2,-2..-1,-1..0,0..1,1..2,2..5];
```

$$ranges := [-5.. -2, -2.. -1, -1..0, 0..1, 1..2, 2..5]$$

```
> data_list:=transform[tallyinto](random_data,ranges);
```

$$data\_list := [\mathrm{Weight}(2..5, 2), \mathrm{Weight}(0..1, 20), \mathrm{Weight}(-5.. -2, 0), \mathrm{Weight}(-2.. -1, 5), \mathrm{Weight}(1..2, 5), \mathrm{Weight}(-1..0, 18)]$$

```
> statplots[histogram](data_list);
```

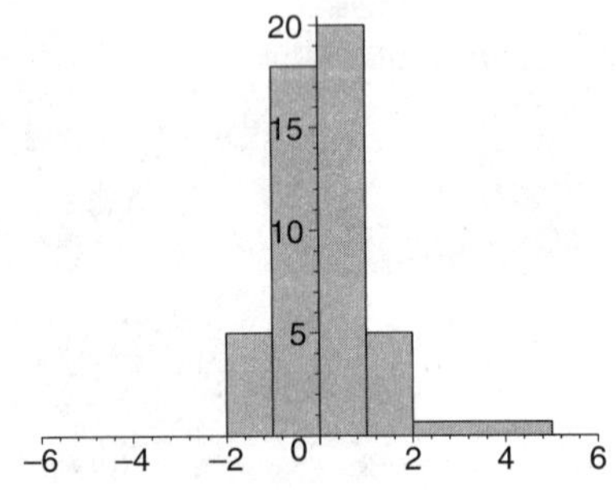

The `simplex` Linear Optimization Package

The **simplex** package contains commands for linear optimization, using the simplex algorithm. Linear optimization involves finding optimal solutions to equations under constraints.

An example of a classic optimization problem is the pizza delivery problem. You have four pizzas to deliver, to four different places, spread throughout the city. You want to deliver all four using as little gas as possible. You also must get to all four locations in under twenty minutes, so that the pizzas stay hot. If you can create mathematical equations representing the routes to the four places and the distances, you can find the optimal solution. That is, you can determine what route you should take to get to all four places in as little time and using as little gas as possible. The constraints on this particular system are that you have to deliver all four pizzas within twenty minutes of leaving the restaurant.

Here is a very small system as an example.

```
> with(simplex);

Warning, the name basis has been redefined
Warning, the protected names maximize and minimize have
been redefined and unprotected
```

$$[basis, convexhull, cterm, define\_zero, display, dual, feasible, maximize, minimize, pivot, pivoteqn, pivotvar, ratio, setup, standardize]$$

To maximize the expression `w`, enter

```
> w  := -x+y+2*z;
```

$$w := -x + y + 2\,z$$

subject to the constraints `c1`, `c2`, and `c3`.

```
> c1 := 3*x+4*y-3*z   <= 23;
```

$$c1 := 3\,x + 4\,y - 3\,z \le 23$$

```
> c2 := 5*x-4*y-3*z   <= 10;
```

$$c2 := 5\,x - 4\,y - 3\,z \le 10$$

```
> c3 := 7*x +4*y+11*z <= 30;
```

$$c3 := 7\,x + 4\,y + 11\,z \leq 30$$

```
> maximize(w, {c1,c2,c3});
```

In this case, no answer means that Maple cannot find a solution. You can use the `feasible` command to determine if the set of constraints is valid.

```
> feasible({c1,c2,c3});
```

$$true$$

Try again and place an additional restriction on the solution.

```
> maximize(w, {c1,c2,c3}, NONNEGATIVE);
```

$$\{z = \frac{1}{2},\, y = \frac{49}{8},\, x = 0\}$$

4.3 Conclusion

This chapter introduced the organization of Maple and the Maple library. Additionally, examples from five packages were provided. This information serves as context for references and concepts in the following chapters.

5 Plotting

Maple can produce several forms of graphs. Maple accepts explicit, implicit, and parametric forms, and recognizes many coordinate systems.

In This Chapter

- Graphing in two dimensions
- Graphing in three dimensions
- Animation
- Annotating plots
- Composite plots
- Special plots
- Manipulating graphical objects
- Code for color plates
- Interactive plot builder

Plotting Commands in Main Maple Library

The command-line plotting feature of Maple contains plotting functions in the main library and in packages. The `plot` and `plot3d` commands reside in the main Maple library. These functions can be called any time during a Maple session. For details about these commands, refer to the `?plot` and `?plot3d` help pages.

Plotting Commands in Packages

Many functions reside in the `plots` and `plottools` packages. These packages must be accessed by using the long or short form in the command calling sequence. For details about these packages, refer to the `?plots` and `?plottools` help pages. For command calling sequence information, refer to the `?UsingPackages` help page.

Publishing Material with Plots

Plots created with the default thickness of 0 are sometimes too faint for professionally published documents. It is recommended that you increase plot line thickness to 3 before submitting documents for professional printing. For information about this feature, see the ?plot[options] help page.

5.1 Graphing in Two Dimensions

When plotting an explicit function, $y = f(x)$, Maple requires the function and the domain.

```
> plot( sin(x), x=-2*Pi..2*Pi );
```

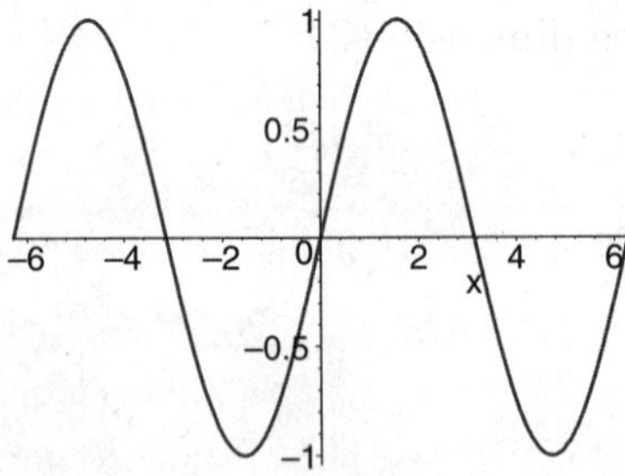

Click a point in the plot window to display particular coordinates. The menus (found on the menu bar or by right-clicking the plot) allow you to modify various characteristics of the plots or use many of the plotting command options listed in the ?plot,options help page.

Maple can also graph user-defined functions.

```
> f := x -> 7*sin(x) + sin(7*x);
```

$$f := x \to 7\sin(x) + \sin(7\,x)$$

```
> plot(f(x), x=0..10);
```

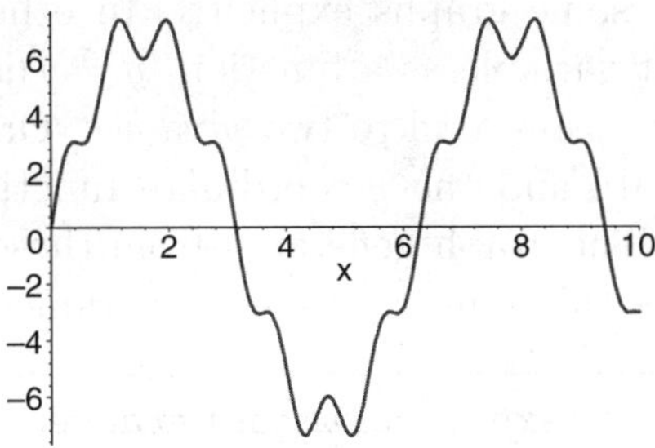

Maple allows you to focus on a specified section in the x- and y-dimensions.

```
> plot(f(x), x=0..10, y=4..8);
```

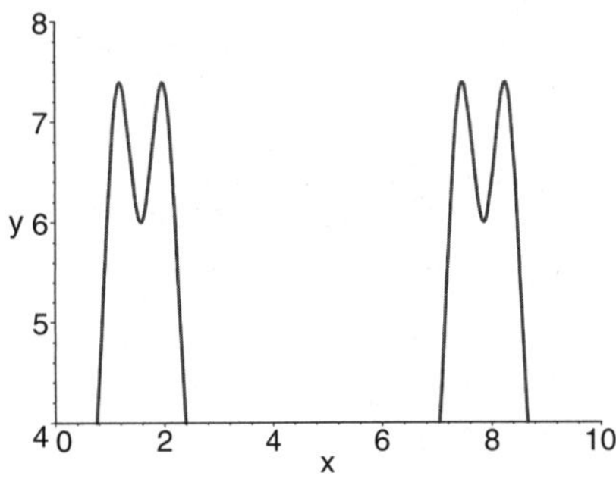

Maple can plot *infinite domains.*

```
> plot( sin(x)/x, x=0..infinity);
```

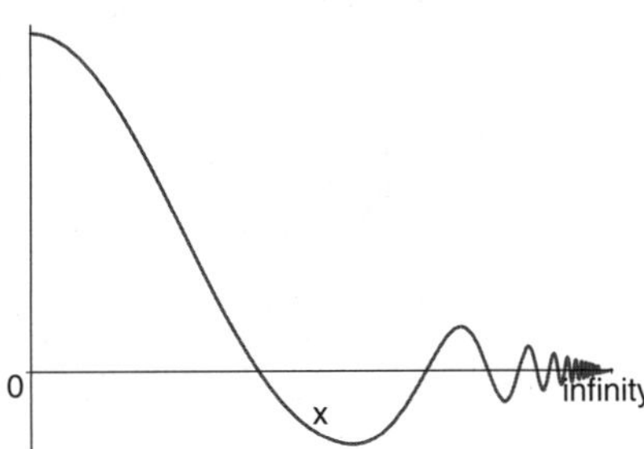

Parametric Plots

You cannot specify some graphs explicitly. In other words, you cannot write the dependent variable as a function, $y = f(x)$. For example, on a circle most x values correspond to two y values. One solution is to make both the x-coordinate and the y-coordinate functions of some parameter, for example, t. The graph generated from these functions is called a *parametric* plot. Use this syntax to specify parametric plots.

```
plot( [ x-expr, y-expr, parameter=range ] )
```

Plot a list containing the *x-expr*, the *y-expr*, and the name and range of the parameter. For example

```
> plot( [ t^2, t^3, t=-1..1 ] );
```

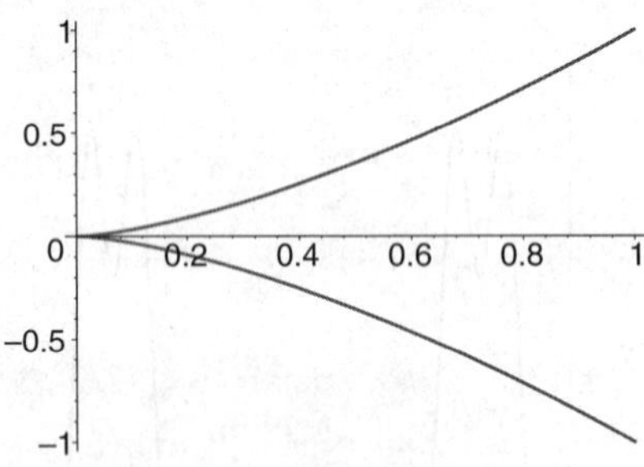

The points $(\cos t, \sin t)$ lie on a circle.

```
> plot( [ cos(t), sin(t), t=0..2*Pi ] );
```

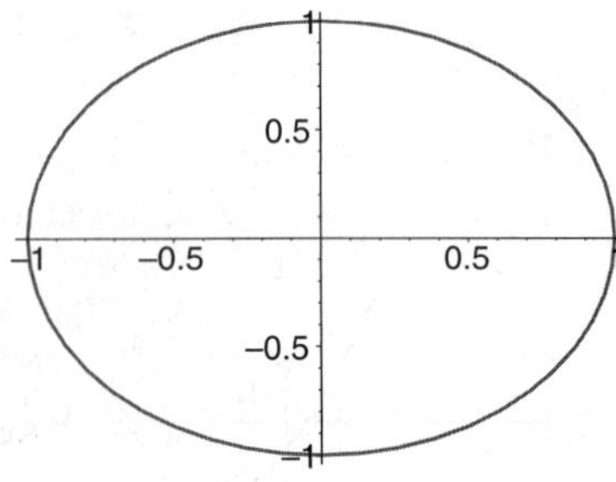

The above plot resembles an ellipse because Maple, by default, scales the plot to fit the window. Here is the same plot again but with

scaling=constrained. To change the scaling, use the context-sensitive menu or the **scaling** option.

```
> plot( [ cos(t), sin(t), t=0..2*Pi ], scaling=constrained );
```

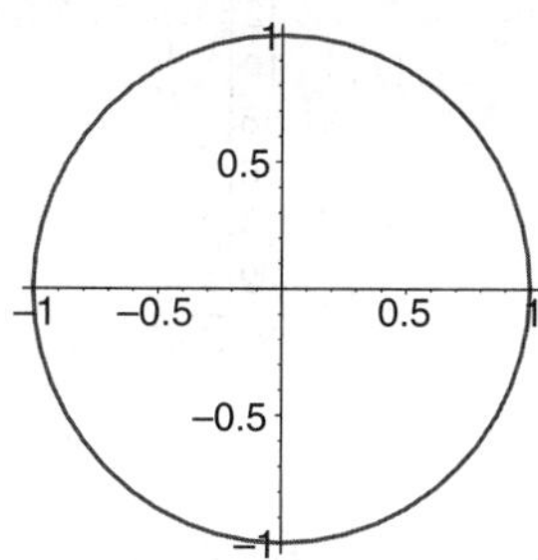

The drawback of **constrained scaling** is that it may obscure important details when the features in one dimension occur on a much smaller or larger scale than the others. The following plot is **unconstrained**.

```
> plot( exp(x), x=0..3 );
```

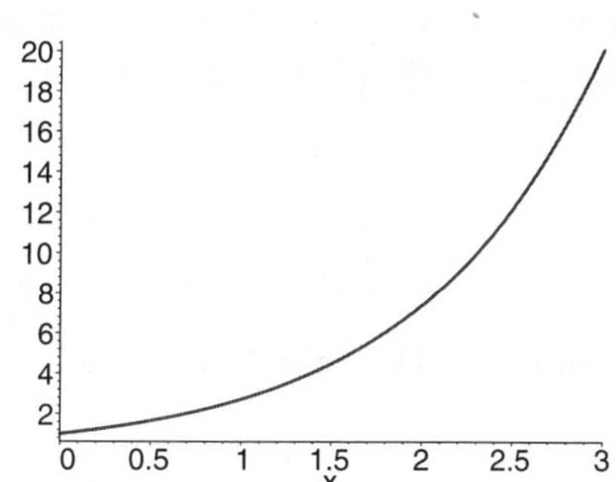

The following is the **constrained** version of the same plot.

```
> plot( exp(x), x=0..3, scaling=constrained);
```

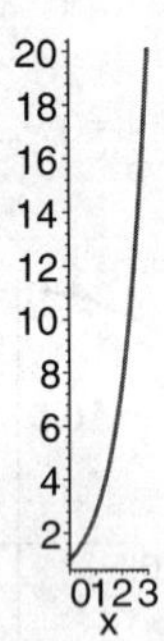

Polar Coordinates

Cartesian (ordinary) coordinates is the Maple default and is one among many ways of specifying a point in the plane. Polar coordinates, (r, θ), can also be used.

In polar coordinates, r is the distance from the origin to the point, while θ is the angle, measured in the counterclockwise direction, between the x-axis and the line through the origin and the point.

You can plot a function in polar coordinates by using the `polarplot` command in the `plots` package. To access the short form of this command, you must first employ the `with(plots)` command.

```
> with(plots):
```

Figure 4.1 The Polar Coordinate System

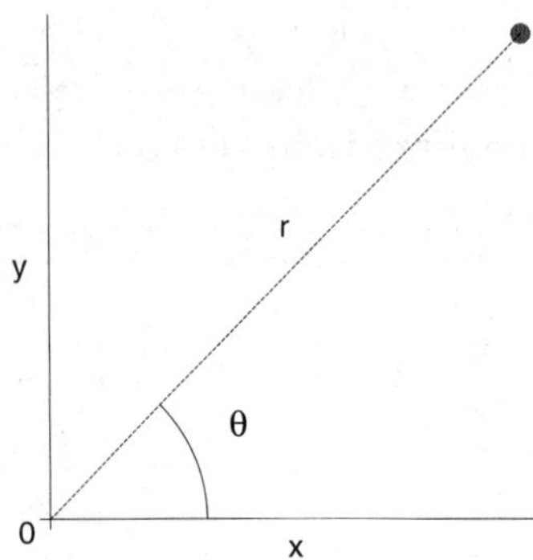

Use the following syntax to plot graphs in polar coordinates.

```
polarplot( r-expr, angle=range )
```

In polar coordinates, you can specify the circle explicitly, namely as $r = 1$.

```
> polarplot( 1, theta=0..2*Pi, scaling=constrained );
```

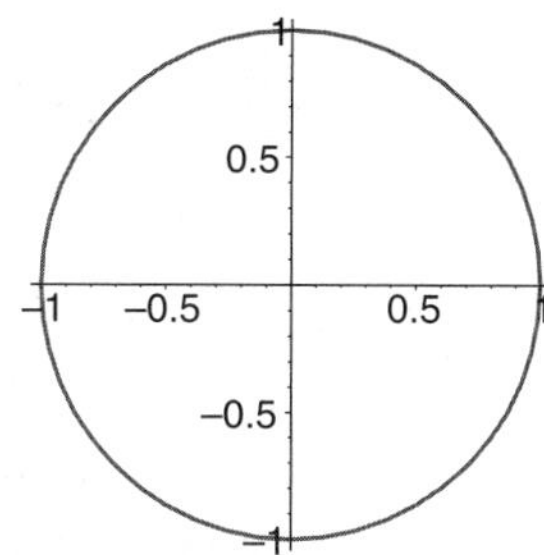

Use the `scaling=constrained` option to make the circle appear round. Here is the graph of $r = \sin(3\theta)$.

```
> polarplot( sin(3*theta), theta=0..2*Pi );
```

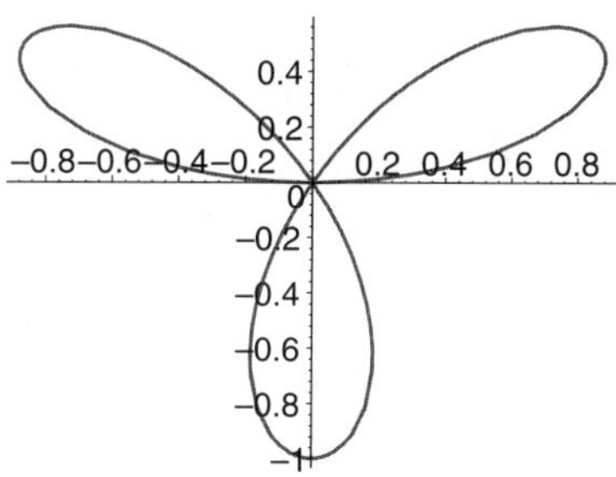

The graph of $r = \theta$ is a spiral.

```
> polarplot(theta, theta=0..4*Pi);
```

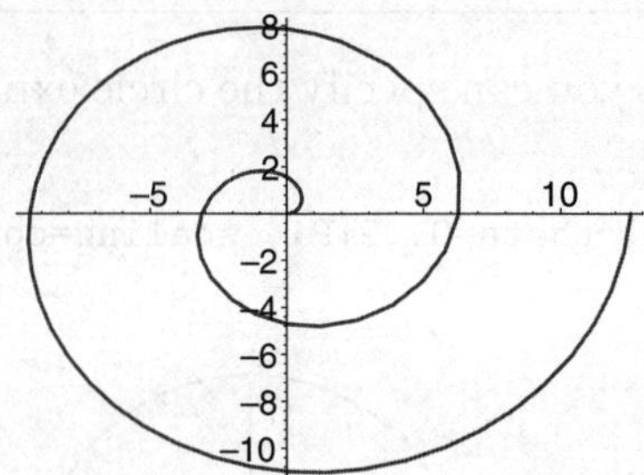

The `polarplot` command also accepts parametrized plots. That is, you can express the radius and angle coordinates in terms of a parameter, for example, t. The syntax is similar to a parametrized plot in Cartesian (ordinary) coordinates. See this section, page 106.

```
polarplot( [ r-expr, angle-expr, parameter=range ] )
```

The equations $r = \sin(t)$ and $\theta = \cos(t)$ define the following graph.

```
> polarplot( [ sin(t), cos(t), t=0..2*Pi ] );
```

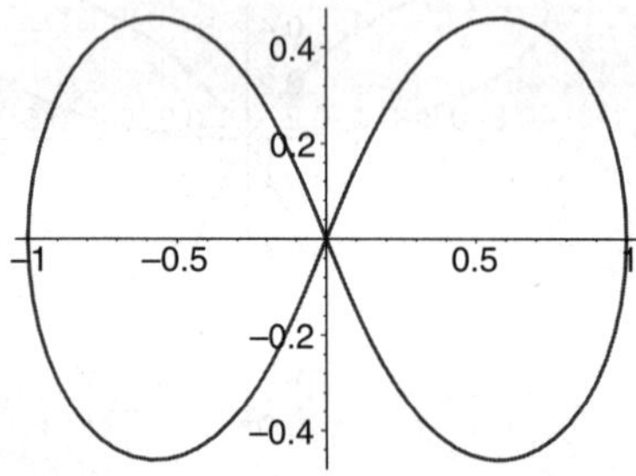

Here is the graph of $\theta = \sin(3r)$.

```
> polarplot( [ r, sin(3*r), r=0..7 ] );
```

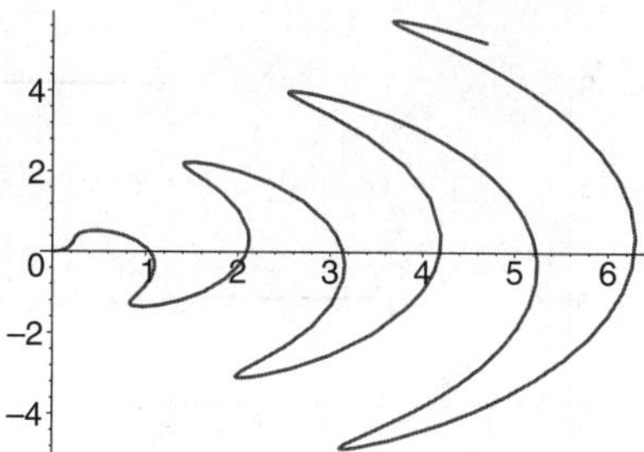

Functions with Discontinuities

Functions with discontinuities require extra attention. This function has two discontinuities, at $x = 1$ and at $x = 2$.

$$f(x) = \begin{cases} -1 & \text{if } x < 1, \\ 1 & \text{if } 1 \le x < 2, \\ 3 & \text{otherwise.} \end{cases}$$

Define $f(x)$ in Maple.

```
> f := x -> piecewise( x<1, -1, x<2, 1, 3 );
```

$$f := x \to \text{piecewise}(x < 1, -1, x < 2, 1, 3)$$

```
> plot(f(x), x=0..3);
```

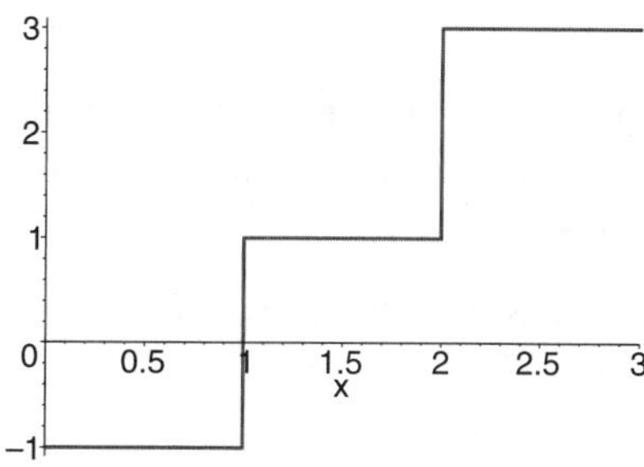

Maple draws almost vertical lines near the point of a discontinuity. The option `discont=true` indicates that there may be discontinuities.

```
> plot(f(x), x=0..3, discont=true);
```

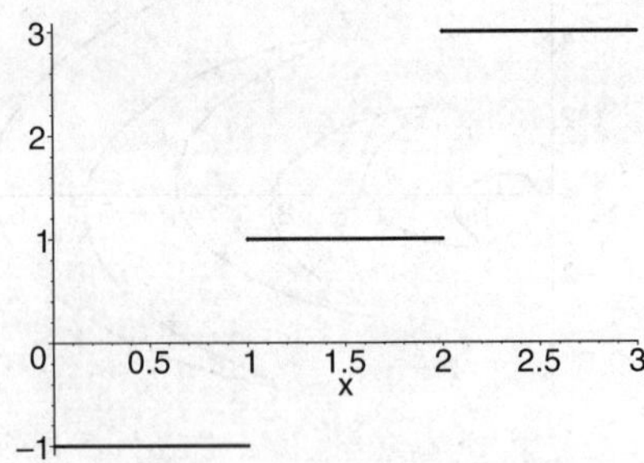

Functions with Singularities

Functions with singularities, that is, those functions which become arbitrarily large at some point, constitute another special case. The function $x \mapsto 1/(x-1)^2$ has a singularity at $x = 1$.

```
> plot( 1/(x-1)^2, x=-5..6 );
```

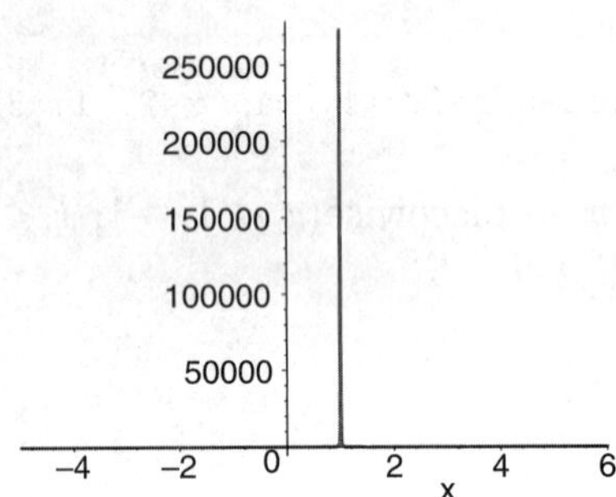

In the previous plot, all the interesting details of the graph are lost because there is a spike at $x = 1$. The solution is to view a narrower range, perhaps from $y = -1$ to 7.

```
> plot( 1/(x-1)^2, x=-5..6, y=-1..7 );
```

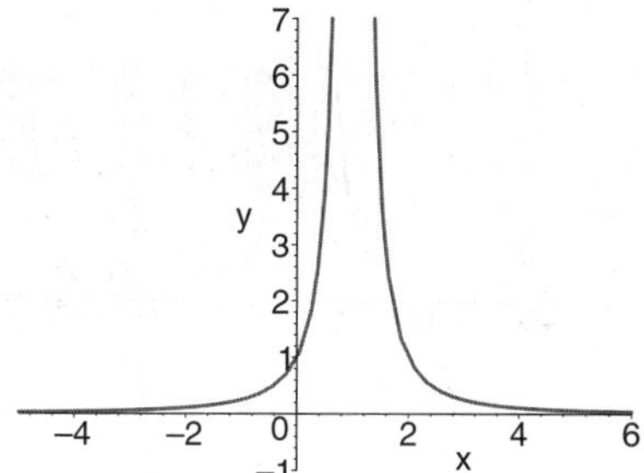

The tangent function has singularities at $x = \frac{\pi}{2} + \pi n$, where n is any integer.

```
> plot( tan(x), x=-2*Pi..2*Pi );
```

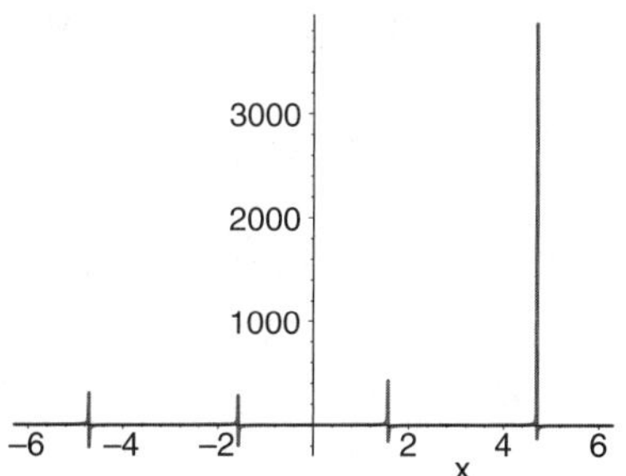

To see the details, reduce the range to $y = -4$ to 4.

```
> plot( tan(x), x=-2*Pi..2*Pi, y=-4..4 );
```

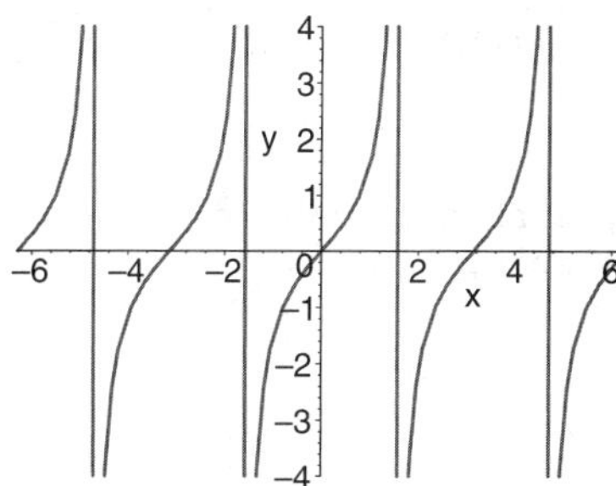

Maple draws almost vertical lines at the singularities. To specifiy a plot without these lines, use the discont=true option.

```
> plot( tan(x), x=-2*Pi..2*Pi, y=-4..4, discont=true );
```

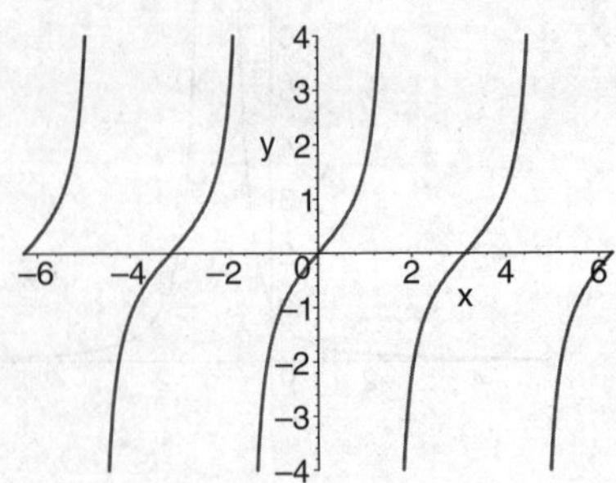

Multiple Functions

To graph more than one function in the same plot, give **plot** a list of functions.

```
> plot( [ x, x^2, x^3, x^4 ], x=-10..10, y=-10..10 );
```

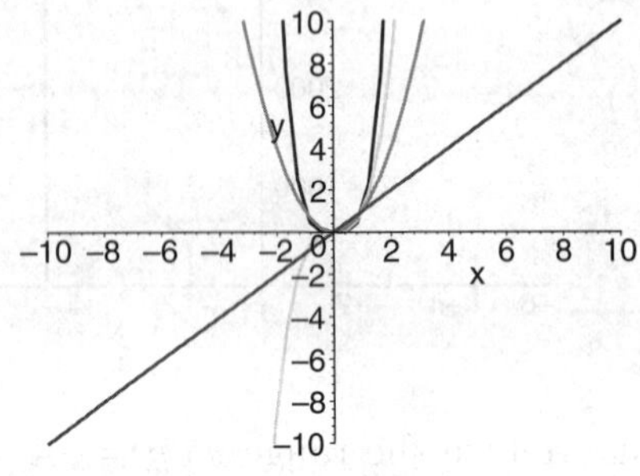


```
> f := x -> piecewise( x<0, cos(x), x>=0, 1+x^2 );
```

$$f := x \to \text{piecewise}(x < 0, \cos(x), 0 \le x, 1 + x^2)$$

```
> plot( [ f(x), diff(f(x), x), diff(f(x), x, x) ],
>    x=-2..2, discont=true );
```

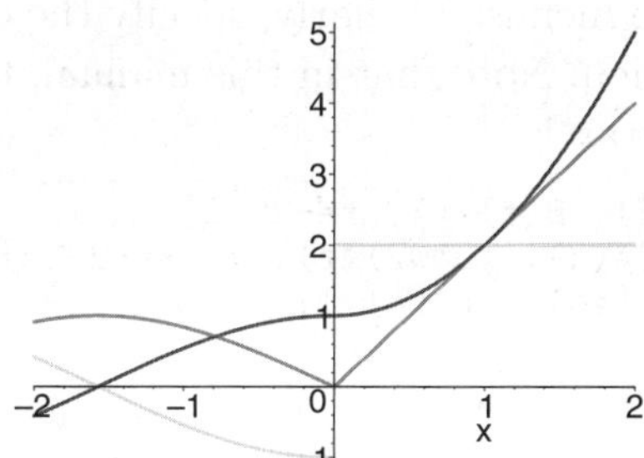

This technique also works for parametrized plots.

```
> plot( [ [ 2*cos(t), sin(t), t=0..2*Pi ],
>         [ t^2, t^3, t=-1..1 ] ], scaling=constrained );
```

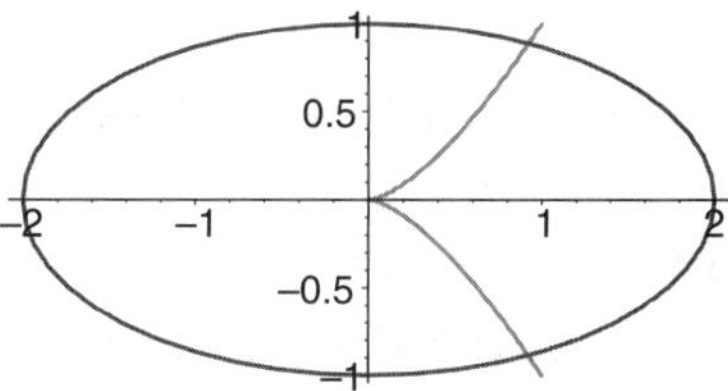

To distinguish between several graphs in the same plot, use different line styles such as solid, dashed, or dotted. Use the **linestyle** option where **linestyle=SOLID** for the first function, $\sin(x)/x$, and **linestyle=DOT** for the second function, $\cos(x)/x$.

```
> plot( [ sin(x)/x, cos(x)/x ], x=0..8*Pi, y=-0.5..1.5,
> linestyle=[SOLID,DOT] );
```

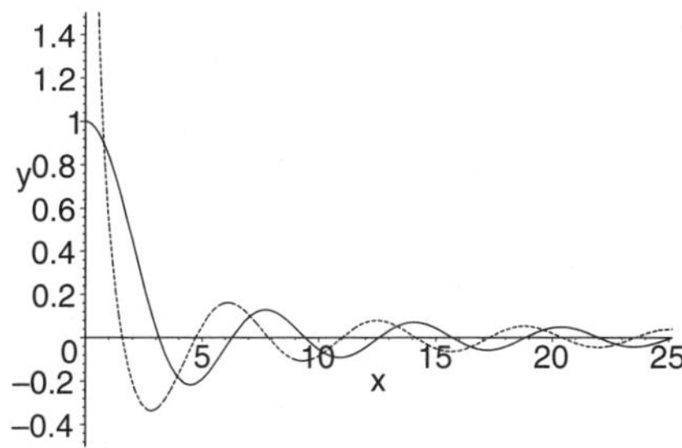

You can also change the line style by using the standard menus and the context-sensitive menus. Similarly, specify the colors of the graphs by using the `color` option. Note that in this manual, the lines appear in two different shades of gray.

```
> plot( [ [f(x), D(f)(x), x=-2..2],
>         [D(f)(x), (D@@2)(f)(x), x=-2..2] ],
>       color=[gold, plum] );
```

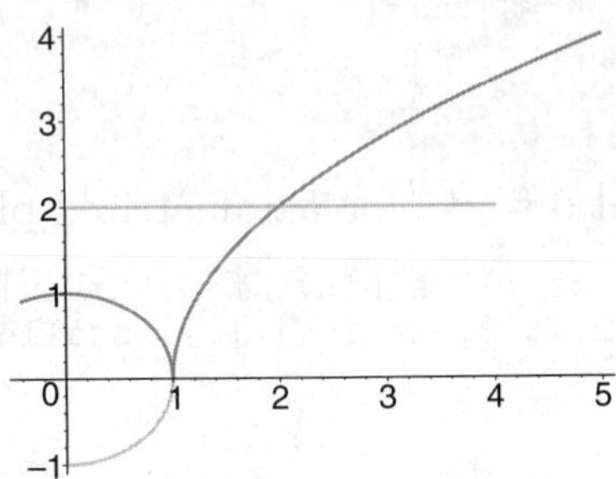

For more details on colors, refer to the `?plot,color` help page.

Plotting Data Points

To plot numeric data, call `pointplot` in the `plots` package with the data in a list of lists of the form

$$[[x_1, y_1], [x_2, y_2], \ldots, [x_n, y_n]].$$

If the list is long, assign it to a name.

```
> data_list:=[[-2,4],[-1,1],[0, 0],[1,1],[2,4],[3,9],[4,16]];
```

$$data\_list :=$$
$$[[-2, 4], [-1, 1], [0, 0], [1, 1], [2, 4], [3, 9], [4, 16]]$$

```
> pointplot(data_list);
```

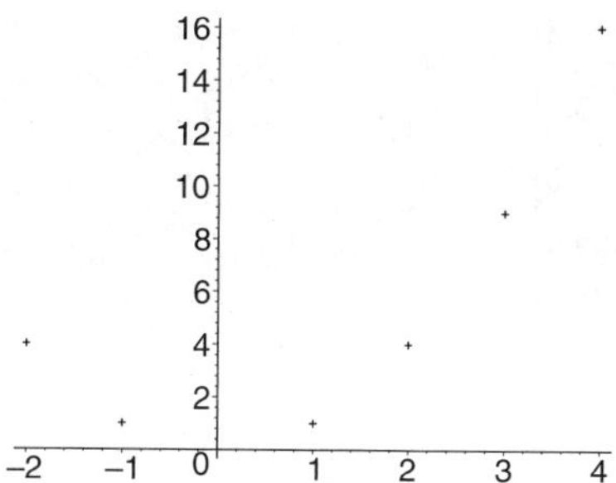

By default, Maple does not join the points with straight lines. Use the `style=line` option to plot the lines. You can also use the menus to draw lines.

```
> pointplot( data_list, style=line );
```

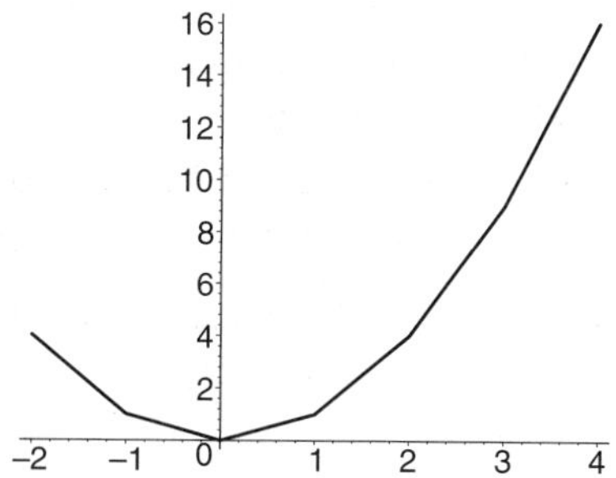

To change the appearance of the points, use the context-sensitive menu or the `symbol` and `symbolsize` options.

```
> data_list_2:=[[1,1], [2,2], [3,3], [4,4]];
```

$$data\_list\_2 := [[1, 1], [2, 2], [3, 3], [4, 4]]$$

```
> pointplot(data_list_2, style=point, symbol=cross,
> symbolsize=30);
```

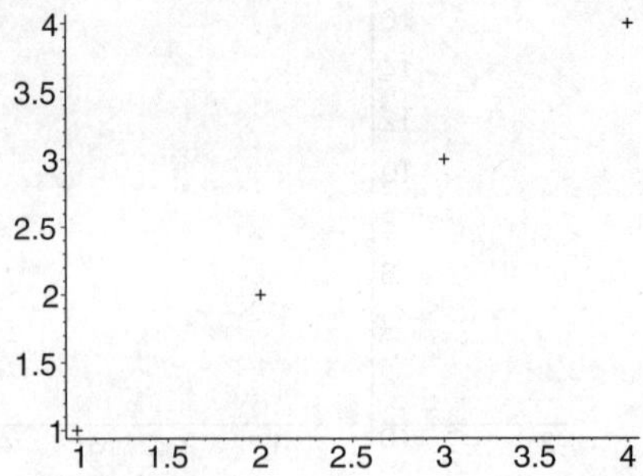

Use the CurveFitting package to fit a curve through several points, and then use the plot function to see the result. For more information, refer to the ?CurveFitting help page.

Refining Plots

Maple uses an adaptive plotting algorithm. It calculates the value of the function or expression at a modest number of approximately equidistant points in the specified plotting interval. Maple then computes more points within the subintervals that have a large amount of fluctuation. Occasionally, this adaptive algorithm does not produce a satisfactory plot.

```
> plot(sum((-1)^(i)*abs(x-i/10), i=0..50), x=-1..6);
```

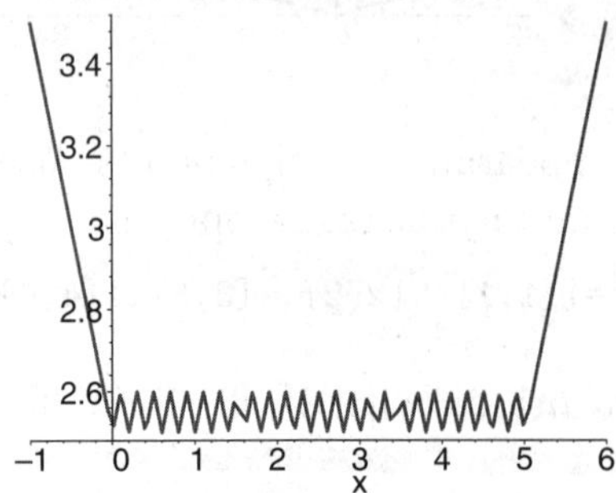

To refine this plot, indicate that Maple compute more points.

```
> plot(sum((-1)^(i)*abs(x-i/10), i=0..50), x=-1..6,
>       numpoints=500);
```

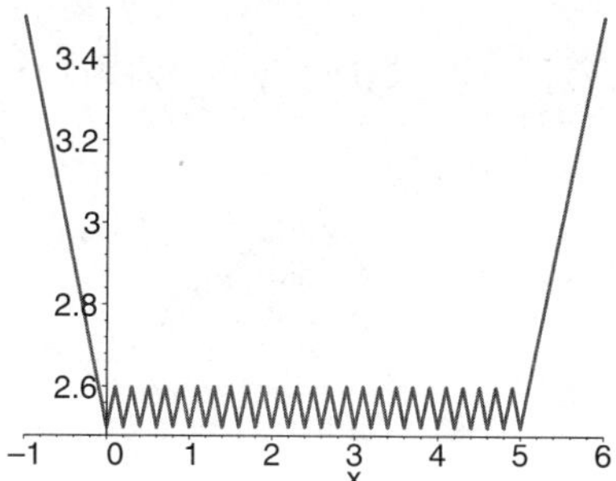

For further details and examples, refer to the `?plot` and `?plot,options` help pages.

5.2 Graphing in Three Dimensions

You can plot a function of two variables as a surface in three-dimensional space. This allows you to visualize the function. The syntax for `plot3d` is similar to that for `plot`.

Plot an explicit function, $z = f(x, y)$.

```
> plot3d( sin(x*y), x=-2..2, y=-2..2 );
```

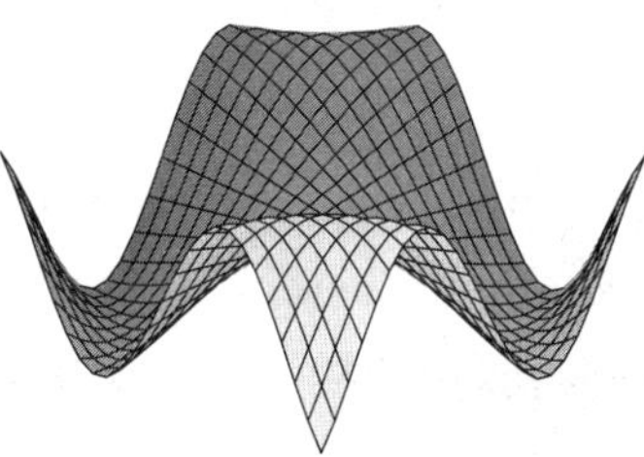

You can rotate the plot by dragging in the plot window. The menus allow you to change various characteristics of a plot.

As with the `plot` command, `plot3d` can graph user-defined functions.

```
> f := (x,y) -> sin(x) * cos(y);
```

$$f := (x,\, y) \to \sin(x)\cos(y)$$

```
> plot3d( f(x,y), x=0..2*Pi, y=0..2*Pi );
```

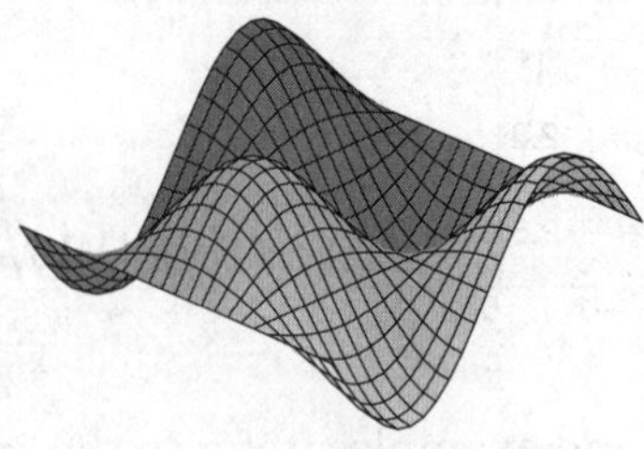

By default, Maple displays the graph as a shaded surface. To change the surface, use the context-sensitive menu or the `style` option. For example, `style=hidden` draws the graph as a hidden wireframe structure.

```
> plot3d( f(x,y), x=0..2*Pi, y=0..2*Pi, style=hidden );
```

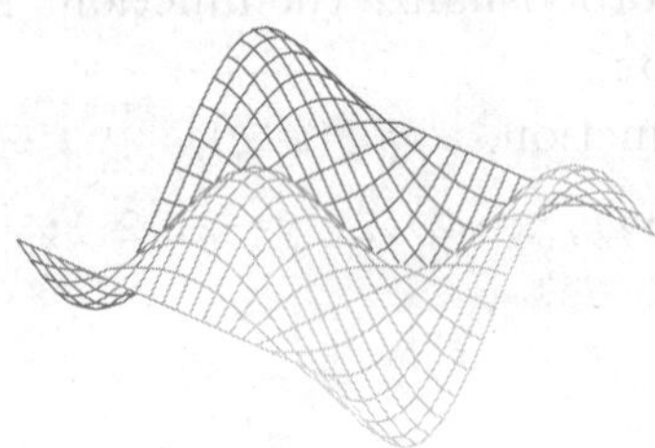

For a list of `style` options, refer to the `?plot3d,options` help page. The range of the second parameter can depend on the first parameter.

```
> plot3d( sqrt(x-y), x=0..9, y=-x..x );
```

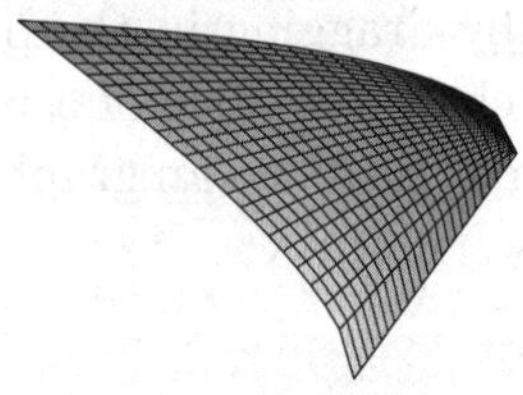

Parametric Plots

You cannot specify some surfaces explicitly as $z = f(x, y)$. The sphere is an example of such a plot. As for two-dimensional graphs (see section 5.1), one solution is a *parametric* plot. Make the three coordinates, x, y, and z, functions of two parameters, for example, s and t. You can specify parametric plots in three dimensions by using the following syntax.

```
plot3d( [ x-expr, y-expr, z-expr ],
    parameter1=range, parameter2=range )
```

Here are two examples.

```
> plot3d( [ sin(s), cos(s)*sin(t), sin(t) ],
>     s=-Pi..Pi, t=-Pi..Pi );
```

```
> plot3d( [ s*sin(s)*cos(t), s*cos(s)*cos(t), s*sin(t) ],
>     s=0..2*Pi, t=0..Pi );
```

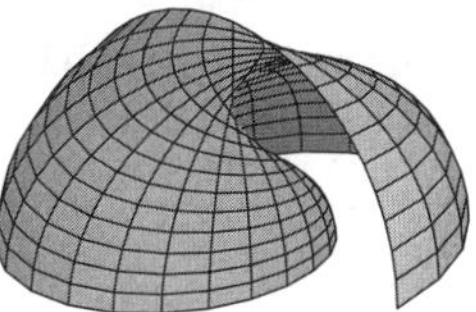

Spherical Coordinates

The Cartesian (ordinary) coordinate system is only one of many coordinate systems in three dimensions. In the spherical coordinate system, the three coordinates are the distance r to the origin, the angle θ in the xy-plane measured in the counterclockwise direction from the x-axis, and the angle ϕ measured from the z-axis.

Figure 4.2 The Spherical Coordinate System

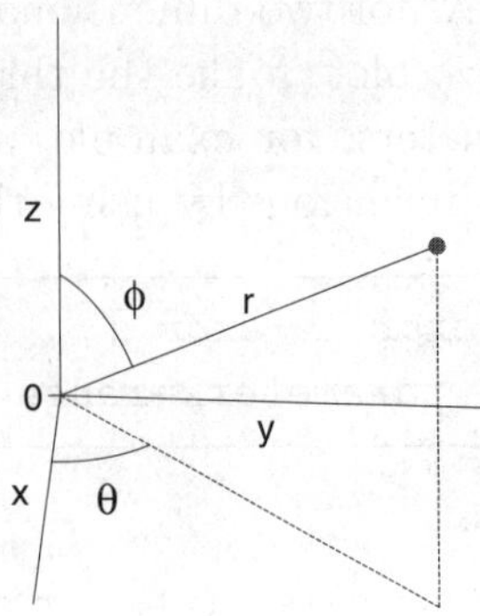

You can plot a function in spherical coordinates by using the `sphereplot` command in the `plots` package. To access the command with its short name, use `with(plots)`. To avoid listing all the commands in the `plots` package, use a colon, rather than a semicolon.

```
> with(plots):
```

Use the `sphereplot` command in the following manner.

```
sphereplot( r-expr, theta=range, phi=range )
```

The graph of $r = (4/3)^{\theta} \sin \phi$ looks like this:

```
> sphereplot( (4/3)^theta * sin(phi),
>     theta=-1..2*Pi, phi=0..Pi );
```

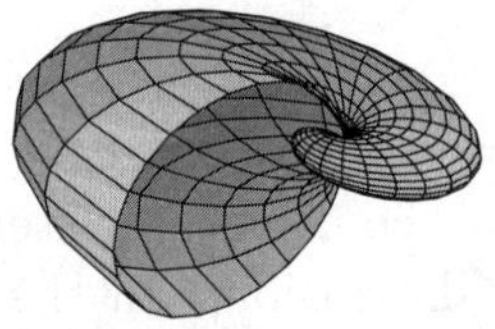

To plot a sphere in spherical coordinates, specify the radius, perhaps 1, let θ run around the equator, and let ϕ run from the North Pole ($\phi = 0$) to the South Pole ($\phi = \pi$).

```
> sphereplot( 1, theta=0..2*Pi, phi=0..Pi,
>   scaling=constrained );
```

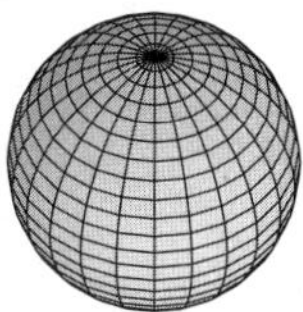

For more information on constrained versus unconstrained plotting, see **5.1 Graphing in Two Dimensions**.

The `sphereplot` command also accepts parametrized plots, that is, functions that define the radius and both angle-coordinates in terms of two parameters, for example, s and t. The syntax is similar to a parametrized plot in Cartesian (ordinary) coordinates. See this section, page 121.

```
sphereplot( [ r-expr, theta-expr, phi-expr ],
            parameter1=range, parameter2=range )
```

Here $r = \exp(s) + t$, $\theta = \cos(s + t)$, and $\phi = t^2$.

```
> sphereplot( [ exp(s)+t, cos(s+t), t^2 ],
>             s=0..2*Pi, t=-2..2 );
```

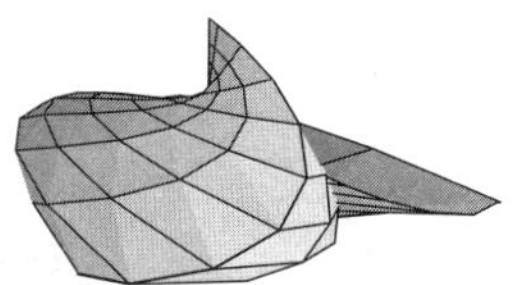

Cylindrical Coordinates

Specify a point in the *cylindrical coordinate system* using the three coordinates r, θ, and z. Here r and θ are polar coordinates (see section 5.1) in the xy-plane and z is the usual Cartesian z-coordinate.

Figure 4.3 The Cylindrical Coordinate System

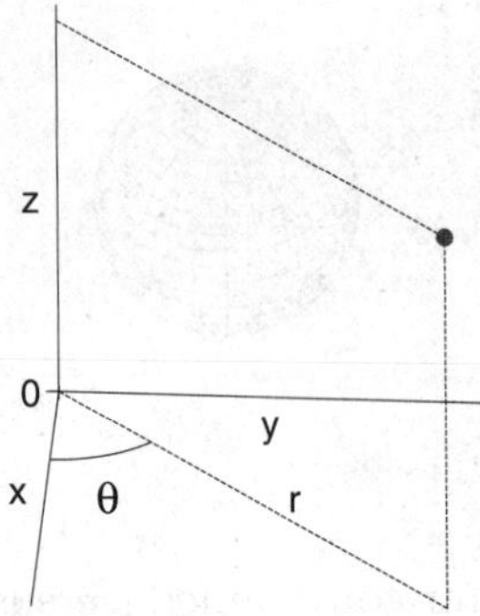

You can plot a function in cylindrical coordinates by using the **cylinderplot** command in the **plots** package.

```
> with(plots):
```

You can plot graphs in cylindrical coordinates by using the following syntax.

```
cylinderplot( r-expr, angle=range, z=range )
```

Here is a three-dimensional version of the spiral previously shown in **5.1 Graphing in Two Dimensions**.

```
> cylinderplot( theta, theta=0..4*Pi, z=-1..1 );
```

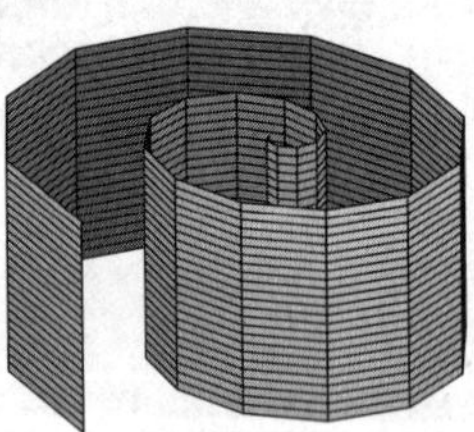

To plot a cone in cylindrical coordinates, let r equal z and let θ vary from 0 to 2π.

```
> cylinderplot( z, theta=0..2*Pi, z=0..1 );
```

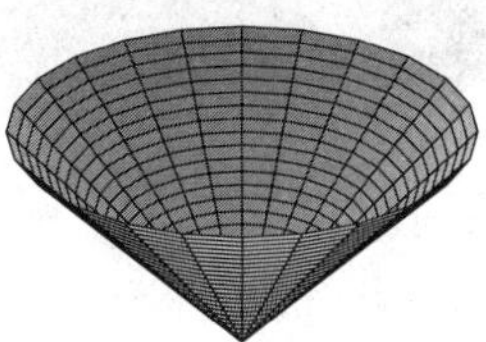

The cylinderplot command also accepts parametrized plots. The syntax is similar to that of parametrized plots in Cartesian (ordinary) coordinates. See this section, page 121.

```
cylinderplot( [ r-expr, theta-expr, z-expr ],
              parameter1=range, parameter2=range )
```

The following is a plot of $r = st$, $\theta = s$, and $z = \cos(t^2)$.

```
> cylinderplot( [s*t, s, cos(t^2)], s=0..Pi, t=-2..2 );
```

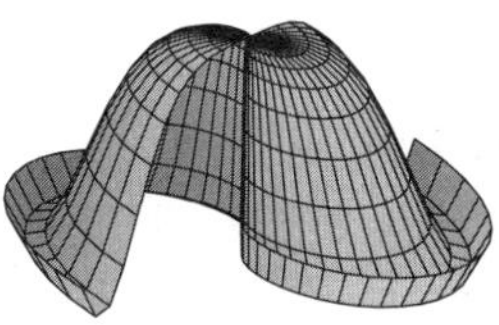

Refining Plots

To create a smoother or more precise plot, calculate more points. Use the grid option

```
grid=[m, n]
```

where m is the number of points for the first coordinate, and n is the number of points for the second coordinate.

```
> plot3d( sin(x)*cos(y), x=0..3*Pi, y=0..3*Pi, grid=[50,50] );
```

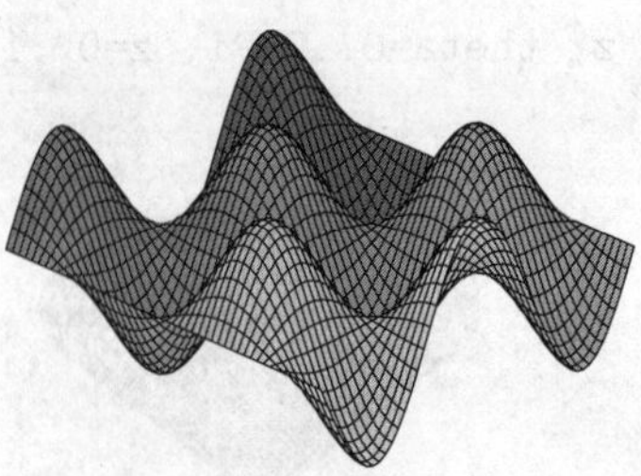

In the next example, a large number of points (100) for the first coordinate (theta) makes the spiral look smooth. However, the function does not change in the z-direction. Thus, a small number of points (5) is sufficient.

```
> cylinderplot( theta, theta=0..4*Pi, z=-1..1, grid=[100,5] );
```

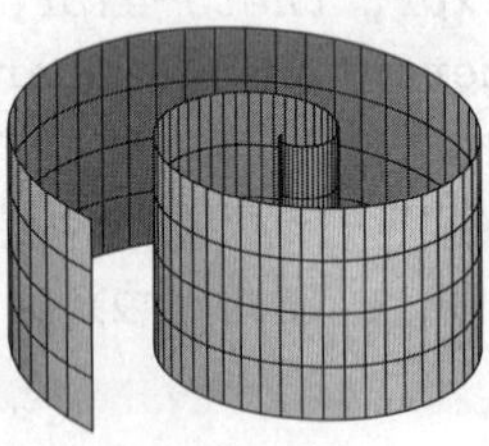

The default grid is approximately 25 by 25 points.

Shading and Lighting Schemes

Two methods for shading a surface in a three-dimensional plot are available.

- One or more distinctly colored light sources illuminate the surface
- The color of each point is a direct function of its coordinates

Maple has many preselected light source configurations, which give aesthetically pleasing results. You can choose from these light sources through the context-sensitive menu or with the lightmodel option. For coloring the surface directly, many predefined coloring functions are also available through the menus or with the shading option.

Simultaneous use of light sources and direct coloring can complicate the resulting coloring. Use either light sources *or* direct coloring. Here is a surface colored with **zgrayscale shading** and no lighting.

```
> plot3d( x*y^2/(x^2+y^4), x=-5..5,y=-5..5,
>     shading=zgrayscale, lightmodel=none );
```

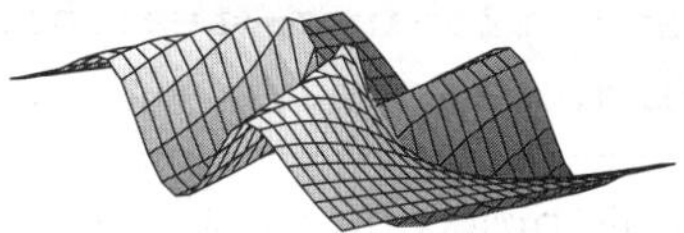

The same surface illuminated by lighting scheme **light1** and no **shading** follows.

```
> plot3d( x*y^2/(x^2+y^4), x=-5..5,y=-5..5,
>     shading=none, lightmodel=light1 );
```

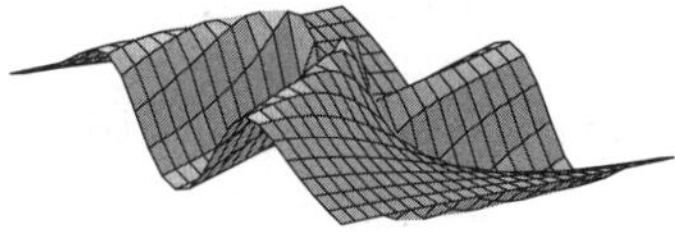

The plots appear in black and white in this book. Try them in Maple to see the effects in color.

5.3 Animation

Graphing is an excellent way to represent information. However, static plots do not always emphasize certain graphical behavior, such as the deformation of a bouncing ball, as effectively as their animated counterparts.

A Maple animation is a number of plot frames displayed in sequence, similar to the action of movie frames. The `animate` command is used for animations and is defined in the `plots` package. To access the command, use the short name after invoking the `with(plots)` command.

Animation in Two Dimensions

You can specify a two-dimensional animation by using this syntax.

```
animate(plotcommand, plotargs, t=a..b,...)
animate(plotcommand, plotargs, t=L,...)
```

- `plotcommand` - Maple procedure that generates a 2-D or 3-D plot
- `plotargs` - represents arguments to the plot command
- `t` - name of the parameter on which the animation is made
- `a,b` - real constants giving the range of the animation
- `L` - list of real or complex constants

The following is an example of an animation.

```
> with(plots):
```

```
Warning, the name changecoords has been redefined
```

```
> animate( plot, [sin(x*t), x=-10..10], t=1..2 );
```

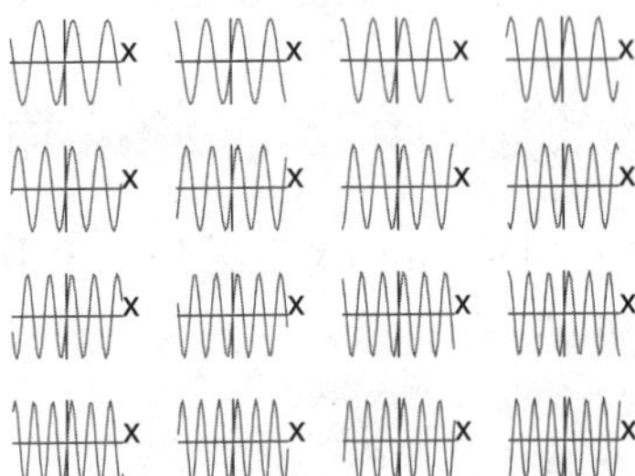

Playing an Animation To play an animation:

1. Select the plot by clicking it. The Maple worksheet Animation menu item is displayed.
2. From the **Animation** menu, select **Play**.

Specifying Frames By default, a two-dimensional animation consists of sixteen plots (`frames`). If the motion is not smooth, you can increase the number of frames. Note that computing many frames may require a lot of time and memory. The following command can be pasted into Maple to produce an animation with 50 frames.

```
> animate( plot, [sin(x*t), x=-10..10,] t=1..2, frames=50);
```

The usual `plot` options are also available. Enter the following example into Maple to view the animation.

```
> animate( plot, [sin(x*t), x=-10..10], t=1..2,
>     frames=50, numpoints=100 );
```

You can plot any two-dimensional animation as a three-dimensional static plot. For example, try plotting the animation of $\sin(xt)$ above as a surface.

```
> plot3d( sin(x*t), x=-10..10, t=1..2, grid=[50,100],
>     orientation=[135,45], axes=boxed , style=HIDDEN );
```

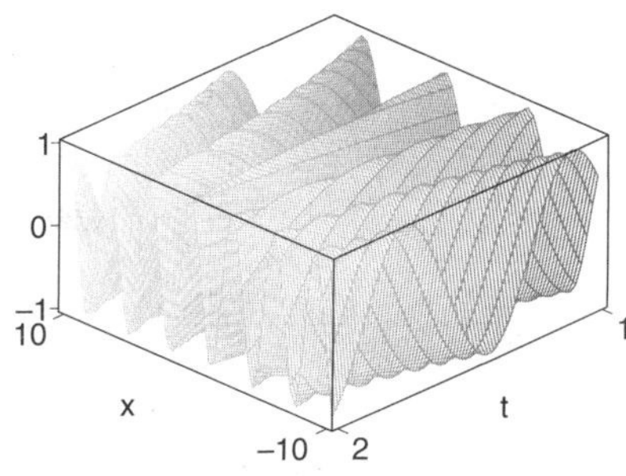

Selecting to use an animation or a plot may be a subjective preference, but it also depends on the concepts that the animation or plot is supposed to convey.

Animating Parametrized Graphs Animating parametrized graphs is also possible. For more information on parametrized graphs, see section 5.1.

```
> animate( plot,[ [a*cos(u), sin(u), u=0..2*Pi] ], a=0..2 );
```

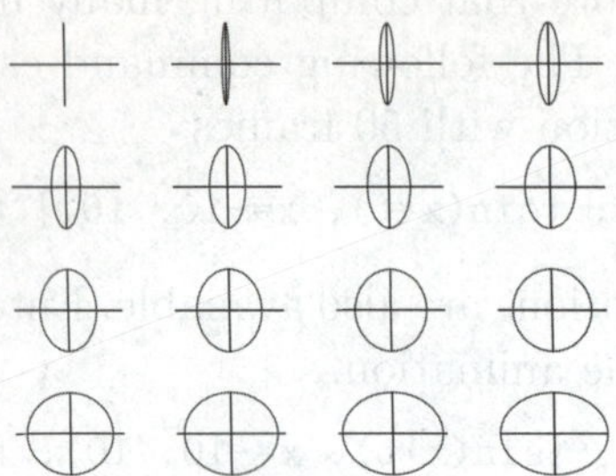

By using the coords option, animate uses a coordinate system other than the Cartesian (ordinary) system.

```
> animate( plot, [theta*t, theta=0..8*Pi, coords=polar], t=1..4 );
```

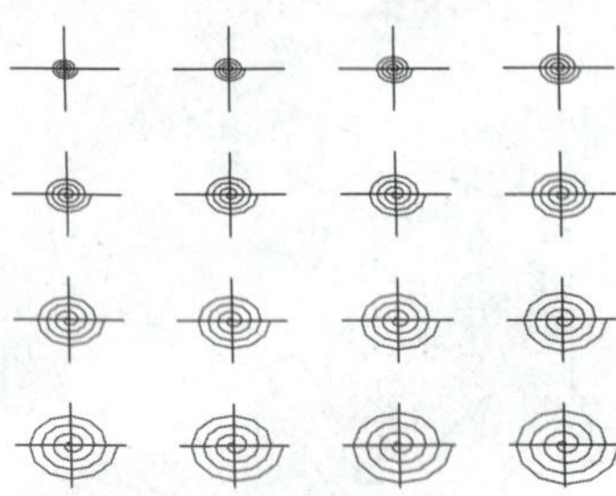

To view the actual animations, enter the commands for the animations in Maple.

Animation in Three Dimensions

You can use the animate command as follows.

```
animate(plotcommand, plotargs, t=a..b,...)
animate(plotcommand, plotargs, t=L,...)
```

- plotcommand - Maple procedure that generates a 2-D or 3-D plot
- plotargs - represents arguments to the plot command
- t - name of the parameter on which the animation is made

- a,b - real constants giving the range of the animation
- L - list of real or complex constants

The following is an example of a three-dimensional animation.

```
> animate( plot3d, [cos(t*x)*sin(t*y),
>             x=-Pi..Pi, y=-Pi..Pi], t=1..2 );
```

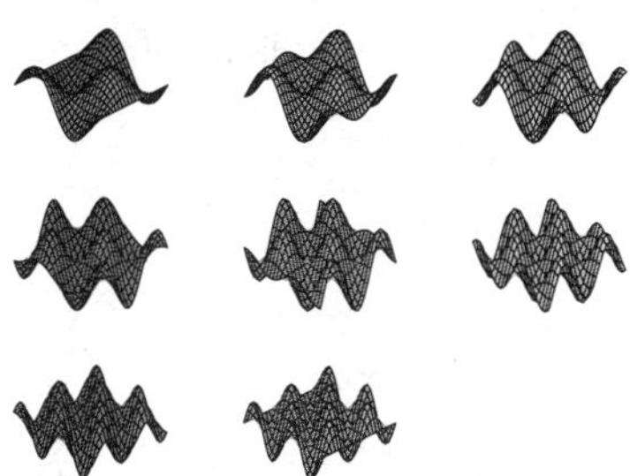

Specifying Frames By default, a three-dimensional animation consists of eight plots (`frames`). As with two-dimensional animations, the `frames` option determines the number of frames.

```
> animate( plot3d, [cos(t*x)*sin(t*y), x=-Pi..Pi, y=-Pi..Pi], t=1..2,
>     frames=16 );
```

Section 5.2 describes three-dimensional parametrized plots. You can also animate these.

```
> animate( plot3d,[ [s*time, t-time, s*cos(t*time)],
>     s=1..3, t=1..4], time=2..4, axes=boxed);
```

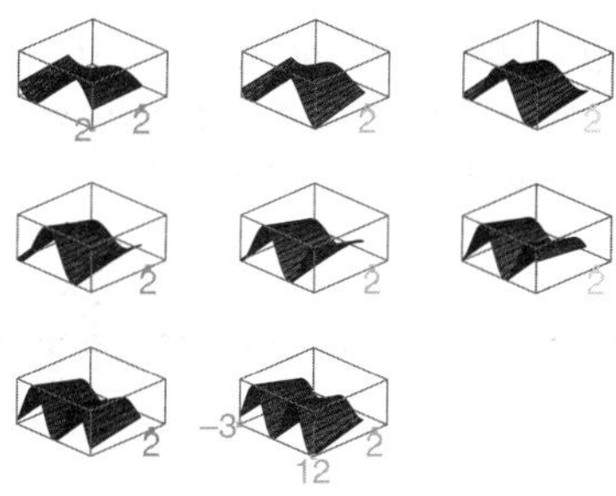

To animate a function in a coordinate system other than the Cartesian, use the `coords` option. Enter the following examples into Maple to view the animations. For spherical coordinates, use coords=spherical.

```
> animate( plot3d, [(1.3)^theta * sin(t*phi), theta=-1..2*Pi,
>     phi=0..Pi], t=1..8, coords=spherical );
```

For cylindrical coordinates, use coords=cylindrical.

```
> animate( plot3d, [sin(theta)*cos(z*t), theta=1..3, z=1..4],
>       t=1/4..7/2, coords=cylindrical );
```

For a list of the coordinate systems in Maple, refer to the ?plots,changecoords help page.

5.4 Annotating Plots

You can add text annotation to plots. The option title prints the specified title in the plot window, centered, and near the top.

```
> plot( sin(x), x=-2*Pi..2*Pi, title="Plot of Sine" );
```

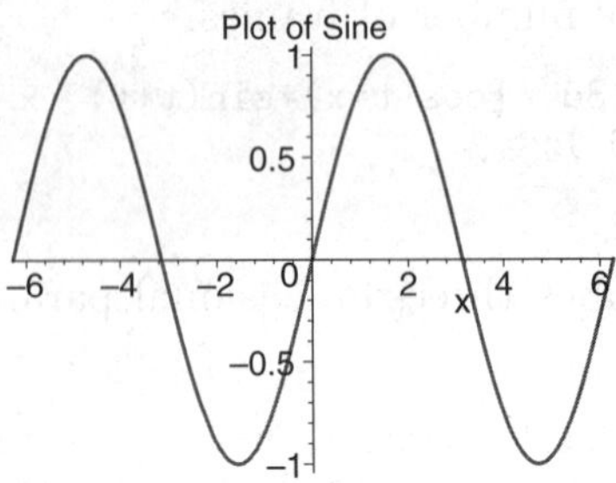

Important: When specifying the title, you must place double quotes (") around the text. Maple uses double quotes to delimit strings. Text that appears between double quotes is not processed further. To specify the font, style, and size of the title, use the titlefont option.

```
> with(plots):
```

```
Warning, the name changecoords has been redefined
```

```
> sphereplot( 1, theta=0..2*Pi, phi=0..Pi,
>    scaling=constrained, title="The Sphere",
>    titlefont=[HELVETICA, BOLD, 24] );
```

The Sphere

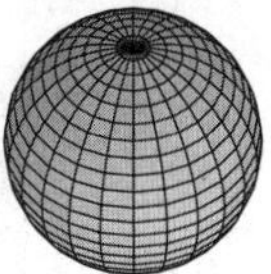

Labeling a Plot

You can label a plot using the following options.

- The `labels` option enables you to specify the labels on the axes
- The `labelsfont` option allows you to control the label font and style
- The `labeldirections` option enables you to place axis labels either vertically or horizontally.

Note that the labels do not have to match the variables in the expression you are plotting.

```
> plot( x^2, x=0..3, labels=["time","velocity"],
>          labeldirections=[horizontal,vertical] );
```

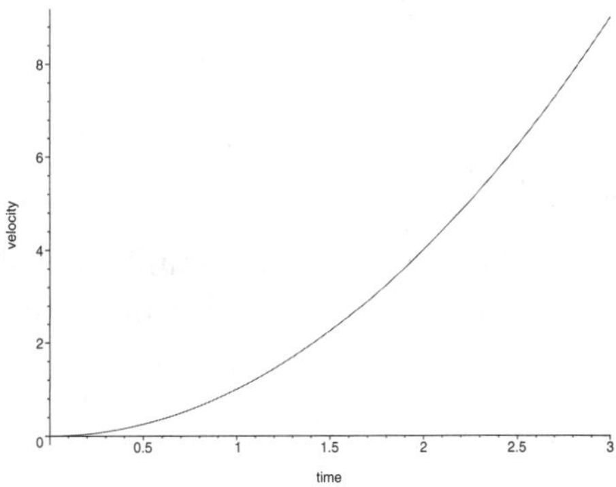

Printing Labels You can print labels only if your plot displays axes. For three-dimensional graphs, there are no axes by default. You must use the `axes` option.

```
> plot3d( sin(x*y), x=-1..1, y=-1..1,
>      labels=["length", "width", "height"], axes=FRAMED );
```

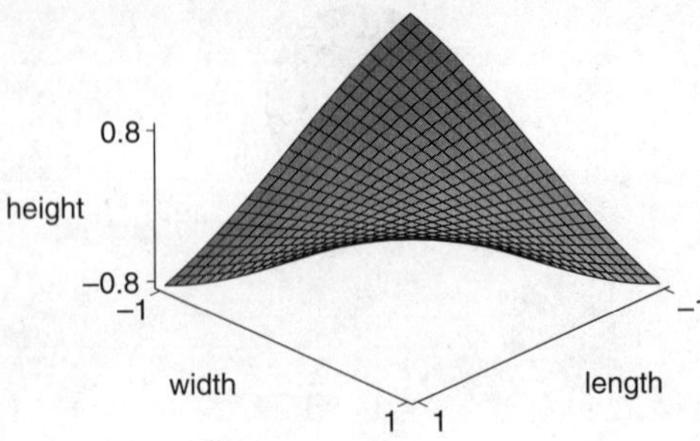

To add a text legend to your plot, use the **legend** option.

```
> plot( [sin(x), cos(x)], x=-3*Pi/2..3*Pi/2, linestyle=[1,4],
>      legend=["The Sine Function", "The Cosine Function"] );
```

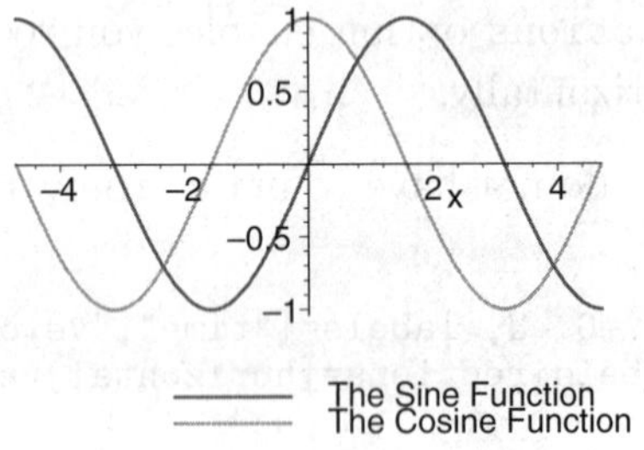

5.5 Composite Plots

Maple allows you to display several plots simultaneously after assigning names to the individual plots. Since plot structures are usually large, end the assignments with colons (rather than semicolons).

```
> my_plot := plot( sin(x), x=-10..10 ):
```

You can save the plot for future use, as you would any other expression.

Displaying an Assigned Plot To display the plot in the first example, use the `display` command defined in the `plots` package.

```
> with(plots):
```

```
> display( my_plot );
```

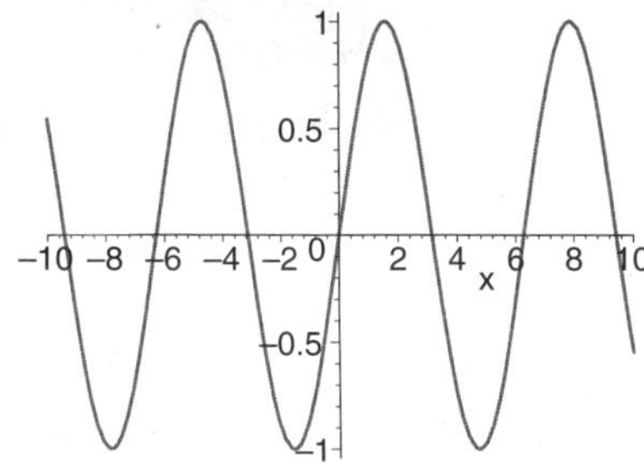

The display command can draw a union of multiple plots. Simply give a list of plots.

```
> a := plot( [ sin(t), exp(t)/20, t=-Pi..Pi ] ):
> b := polarplot( [ sin(t), exp(t), t=-Pi..Pi ] ):
```

```
> display( [a,b] );
```

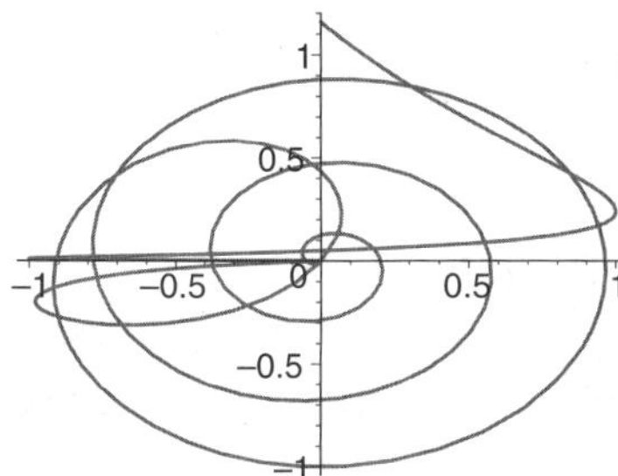

This technique allows you to display plots of different types in the same axes. You can also display three-dimensional plots and animations.

```
> c := sphereplot( 1, theta=0..2*Pi, phi=0..Pi ):
```

```
> d := cylinderplot( 0.5, theta=0..2*Pi, z=-2..2 ):
> display( [c,d], scaling=constrained );
```

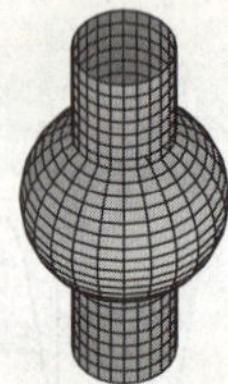

Enter the previous definition of b and the following Maple commands to view an animation and a plot in the same axes.

```
> e := animate( plot, [m*x, x=-1..1], m=-1..1 ):
> display( [b,e] );
```

Displaying Animations Simultaneously If you display two or more animations together, ensure that they have the same number of frames. Enter the following example into Maple to view two animations simultaneously.

```
> f := animate( plot3d, [sin(x+y+t), x=0..2*Pi, y=0..2*Pi], t=0..5,
>       frames=20 ):
> g := animate( plot3d, [t, x=0..2*Pi, y=0..2*Pi], t=-1.5..1.5,
>       frames=20):
> display( [f,g] );
```

Placing Text in Plots

The title and labels options to the plotting commands allow you to put titles and labels on your graphs. The textplot and textplot3d commands allow you to specify the exact positions of the text. The plots package contains these two commands.

```
> with(plots):
```

You can use textplot and textplot3d as follows.

```
textplot( [ x-coord, y-coord, "text" ] );
textplot3d( [ x-coord, y-coord, z-coord, "text"] );
```

For example,

The Sphere

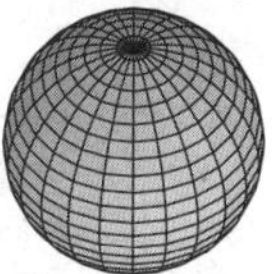

Labeling a Plot

You can label a plot using the following options.

- The `labels` option enables you to specify the labels on the axes
- The `labelsfont` option allows you to control the label font and style
- The `labeldirections` option enables you to place axis labels either vertically or horizontally.

Note that the labels do not have to match the variables in the expression you are plotting.

```
> plot( x^2, x=0..3, labels=["time","velocity"],
>           labeldirections=[horizontal,vertical] );
```

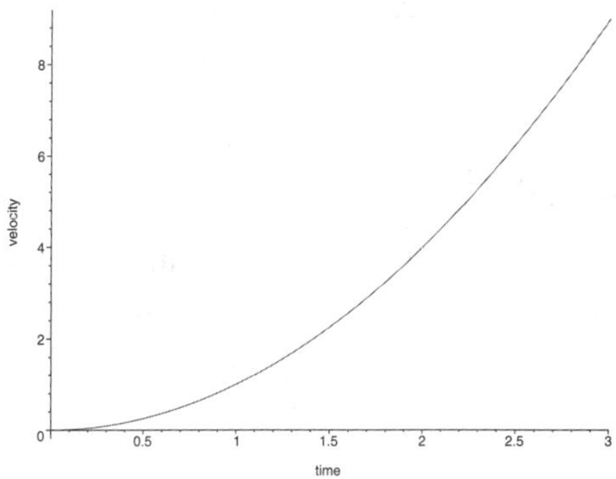

Printing Labels You can print labels only if your plot displays axes. For three-dimensional graphs, there are no axes by default. You must use the **axes** option.

```
> plot3d( sin(x*y), x=-1..1, y=-1..1,
>     labels=["length", "width", "height"], axes=FRAMED );
```

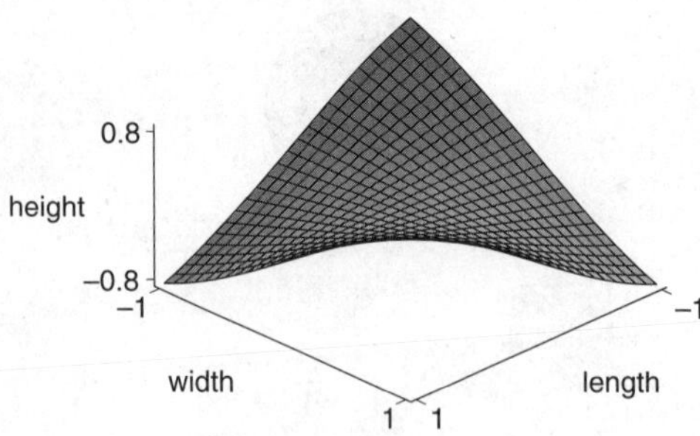

To add a text legend to your plot, use the legend option.

```
> plot( [sin(x), cos(x)], x=-3*Pi/2..3*Pi/2, linestyle=[1,4],
>      legend=["The Sine Function", "The Cosine Function"] );
```

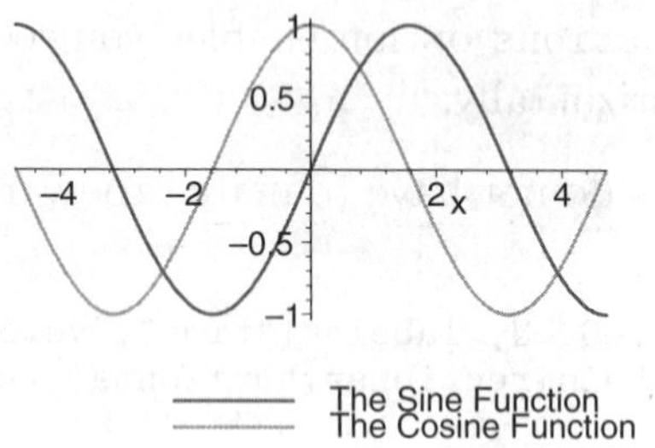

5.5 Composite Plots

Maple allows you to display several plots simultaneously after assigning names to the individual plots. Since plot structures are usually large, end the assignments with colons (rather than semicolons).

```
> my_plot := plot( sin(x), x=-10..10 ):
```

You can save the plot for future use, as you would any other expression.

Displaying an Assigned Plot To display the plot in the first example, use the display command defined in the plots package.

Color Plates

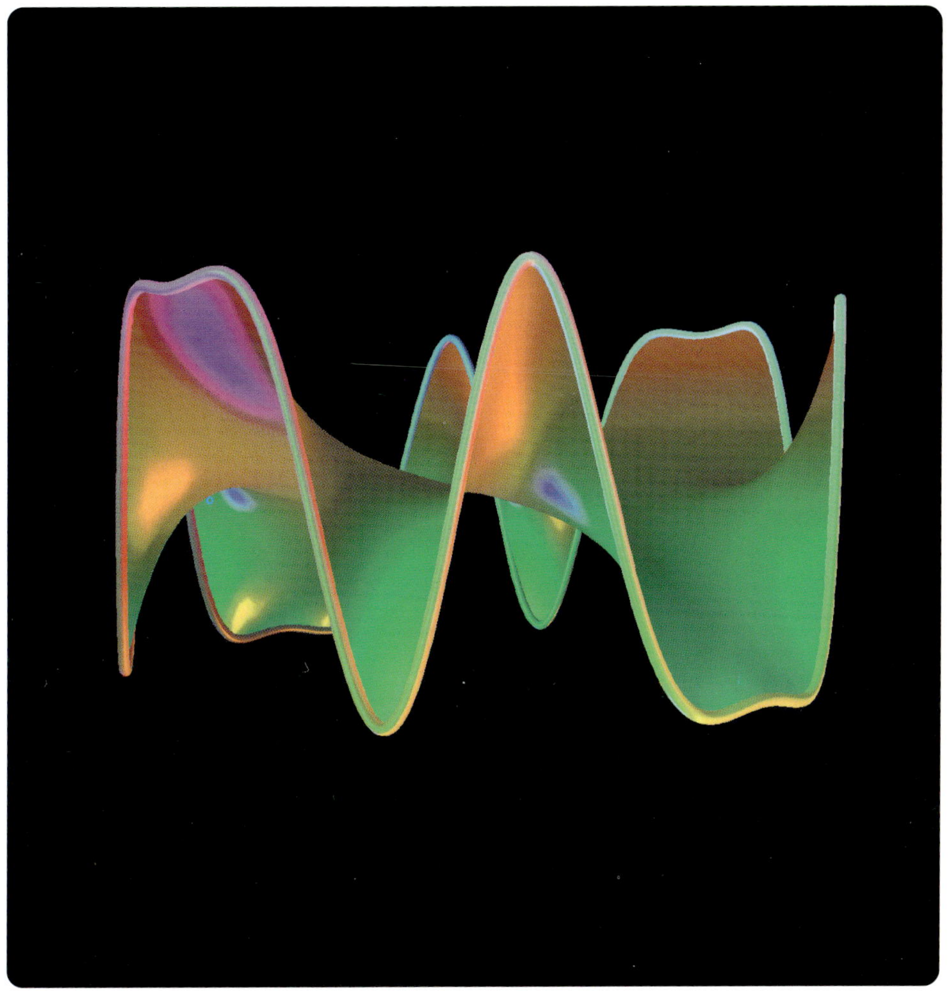

Plate 1: Dirichlet Problem for a Circle

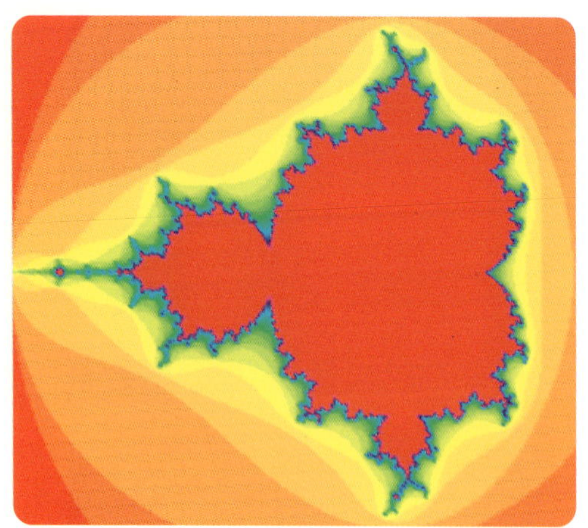

Plate 2: Mandelbrot Set

Plate 3: Origami Bird

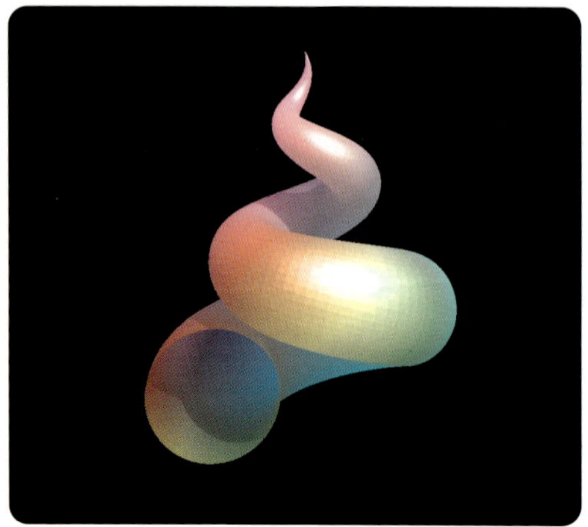

Plate 4: Conchoid

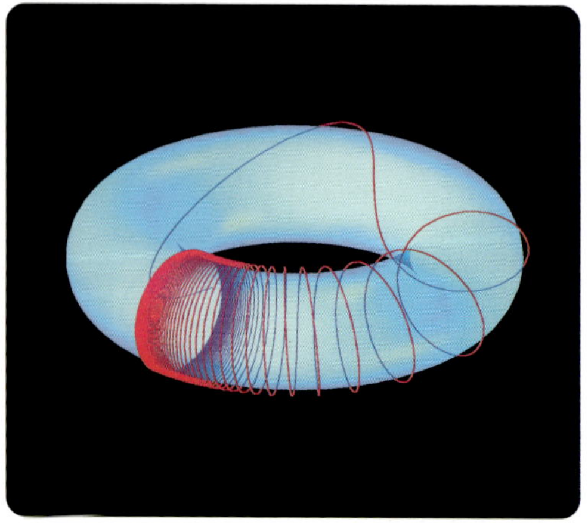

Plate 5: Gauss Map
Graphed on a Torus

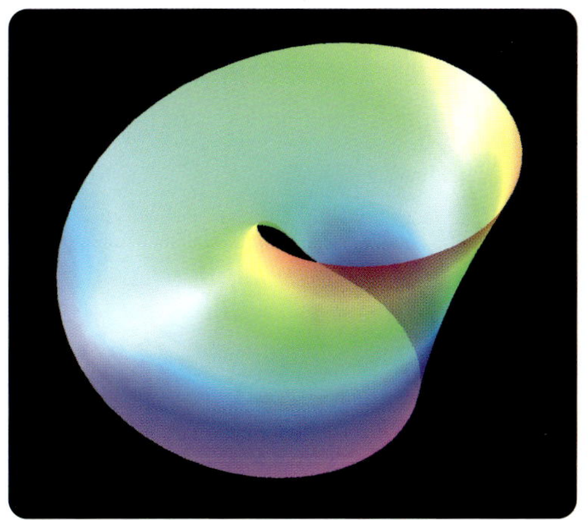

Plate 6: Moebius Strip

Plate 7: Icosahedron

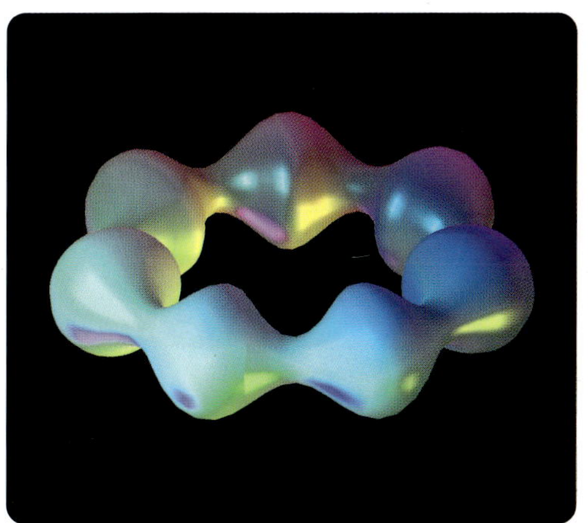

Plate 8: Parameterized Surface of Revolution

Plate 9: Snowmen

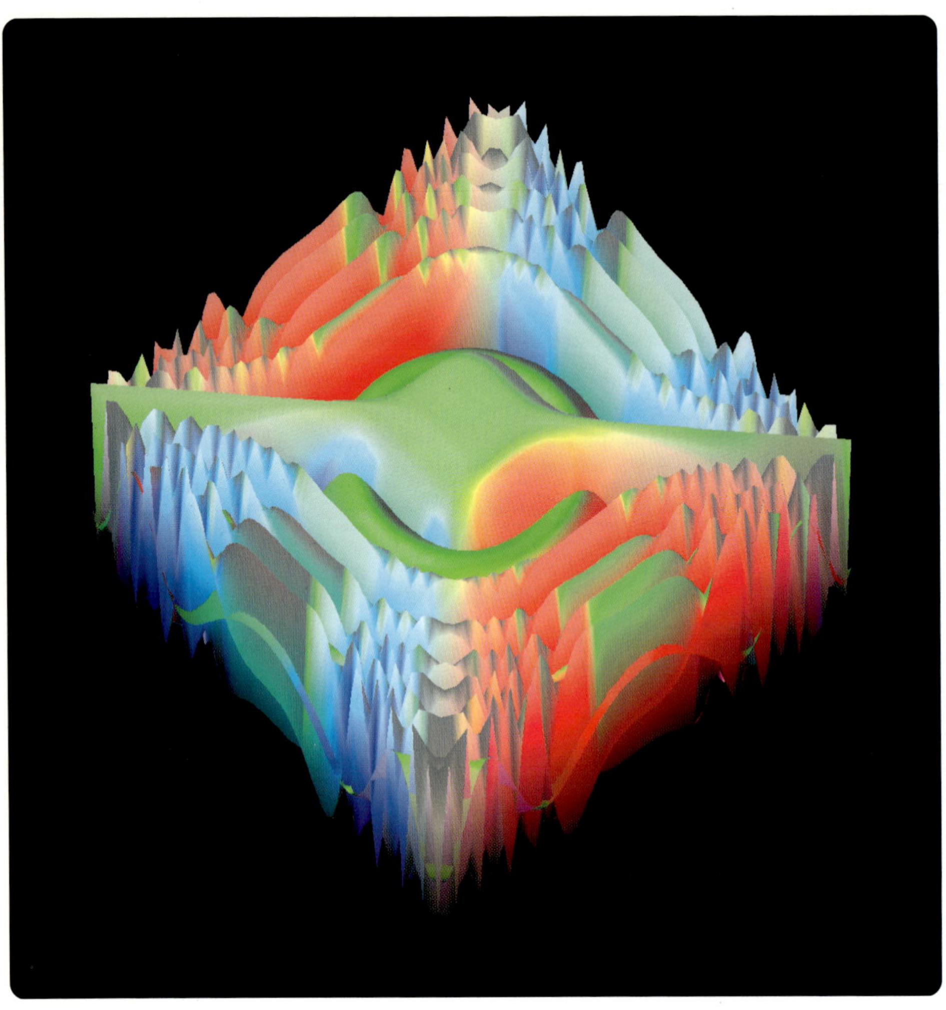

Plate 10: Function of Two Variables in Cartesian Coordinates

```
> a := plot( sin(x), x=-Pi..Pi ):
```

```
> b := textplot( [ Pi/2, 1.25, "Local Maximum" ] ):
> c := textplot( [ -Pi/2, -1.25, "Local Minimum" ] ):
> g := textplot( [ Pi/2, 1, "X" ] ):
> h := textplot( [ -Pi/2, -1, "X" ] ):
> display( [a,b,c,g,h] );
```

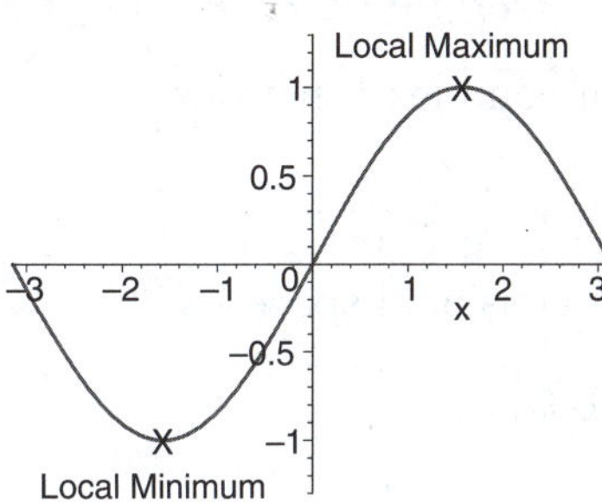

For details on controlling the placement of text, refer to the ?plots,textplot help page. To specify the font for textplot and textplot3d, use the font option. In the following plot, the origin, a saddle point, is labelled P.

```
> d := plot3d( x^2-y^2, x=-1..1, y=-1..1 ):
> e := textplot3d( [0, 0, 0, "P"],
>      font=[HELVETICA, OBLIQUE, 22], color=white ):
> display( [d,e], orientation=[68,45] );
```

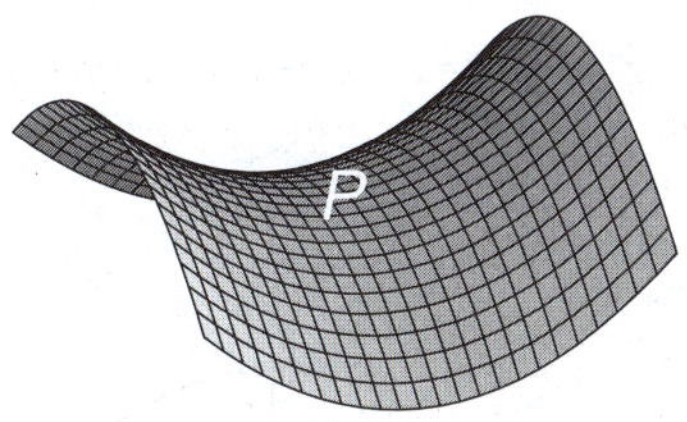

5.6 Special Types of Plots

The plots package contains many routines for producing special types of graphics. This section provides example commands for plotting the following.

- Implicity defined functions
- Inequalities
- Plots with logarithmic scales
- Density functions
- Contours as in a topographical map
- Conformal plots of complex functions
- Vector fields
- Curves in three-dimensional space
- Objects of type Matrix
- Root loci
- Vectors in two and three-dimensional space
- Plots in the visualization component of the `Student` package

For further explanation of a particular plot command, refer to `?plots,`*`command`*.

```
> with(plots):
```

Plot implicitly defined functions by using `implicitplot`.

```
> implicitplot( x^2+y^2=1, x=-1..1, y=-1..1, scaling=
>    constrained );
```

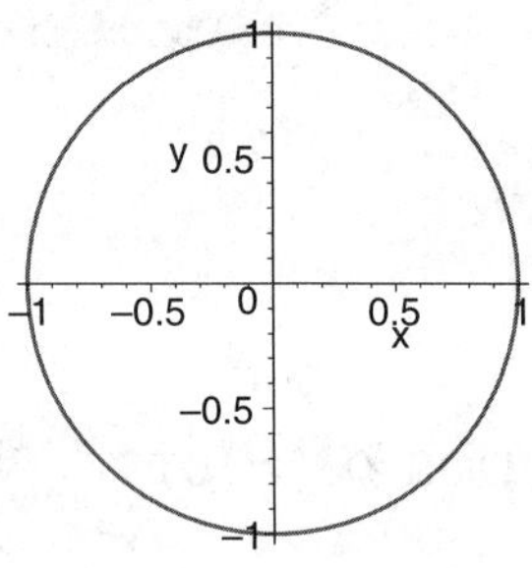

The following is a plot of the region satisfying the inequalities $x+y < 5$, $0 < x$, and $x \leq 4$.

```
> inequal( {x+y<5, 0<x, x<=4}, x=-1..5, y=-10..10,
>     optionsexcluded=(color=yellow) );
```

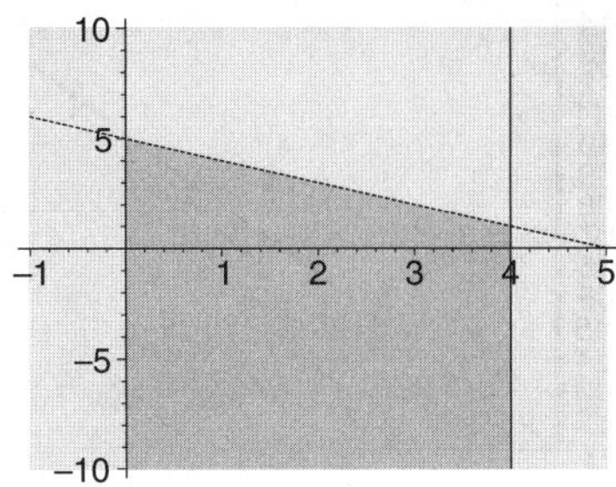

Here the vertical axis has a logarithmic scale.

```
> logplot( 10^x, x=0..10 );
```

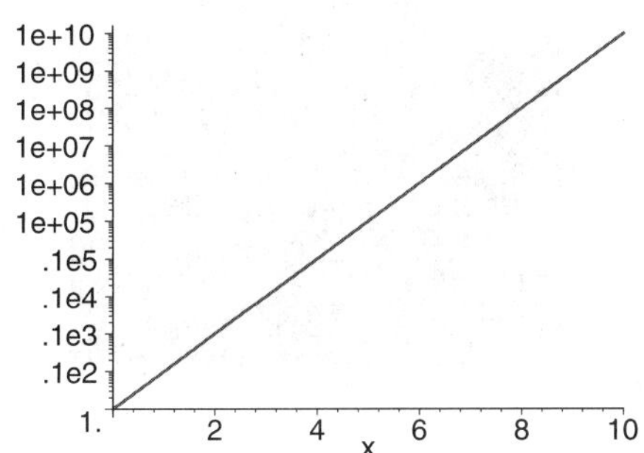

A `semilogplot` has a logarithmic horizontal axis.

```
> semilogplot( 2^(sin(x)), x=1..10 );
```

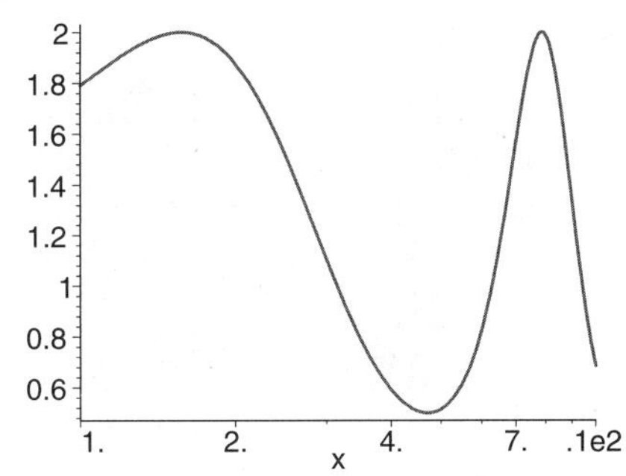

Maple can also create plots where both axes have logarithmic scales.

```
> loglogplot( x^17, x=1..7 );
```

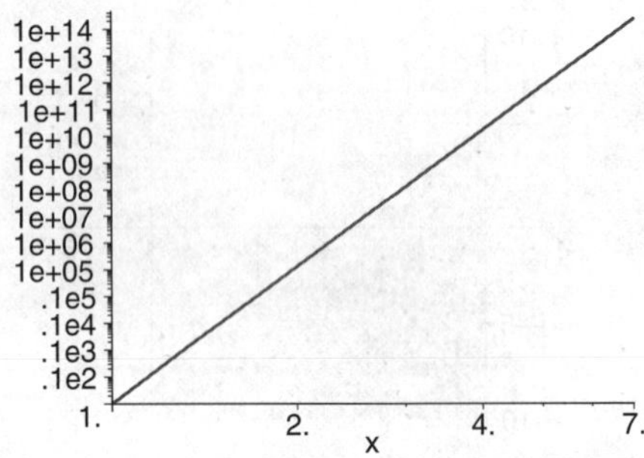

In a **densityplot**, lighter shading indicates a larger function value.

```
> densityplot( sin(x*y), x=-1..1, y=-1..1 );
```

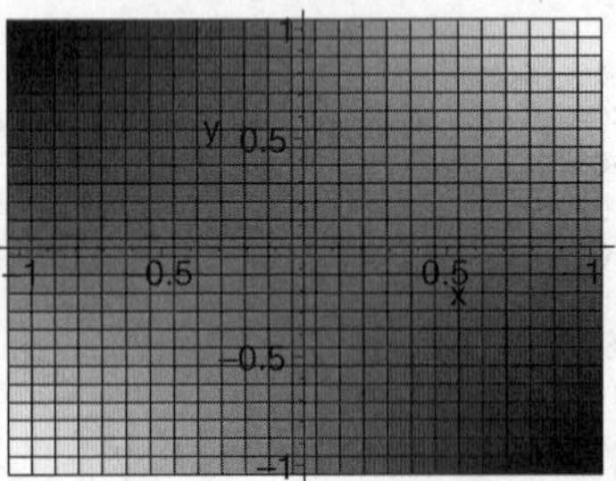

Along the following curves, $\sin(xy)$ is constant, as in a topographical map.

```
> contourplot(sin(x*y),x=-10..10,y=-10..10);
```

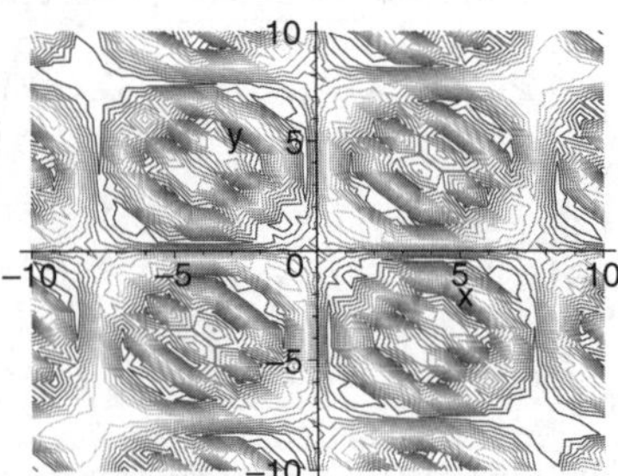

A rectangular grid in the complex plane becomes the following graph when you map it by $z \mapsto z^2$.

```
> conformal( z^2, z=0..2+2*I );
```

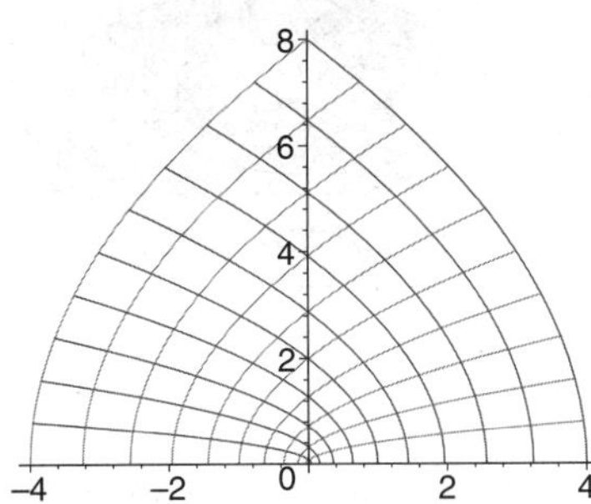

The **fieldplot** command draws the given vector for many values of x and y. That is, it plots a vector field, such as a magnetic field.

```
> fieldplot( [y*cos(x*y), x*cos(x*y)], x=-1..1, y=-1..1);
```

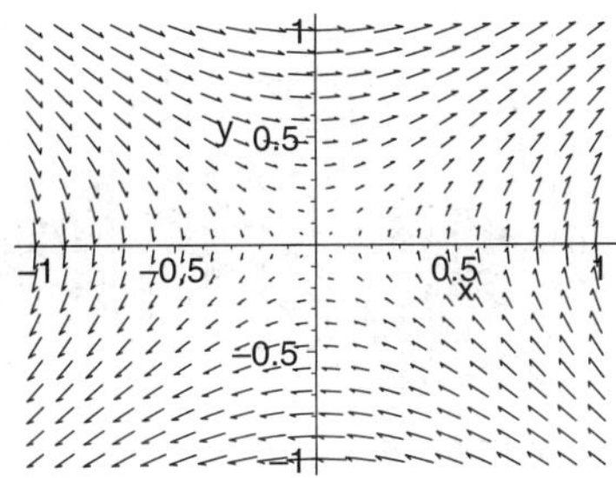

Maple can draw curves in three-dimensional space.

```
> spacecurve( [cos(t),sin(t),t], t=0..12 );
```

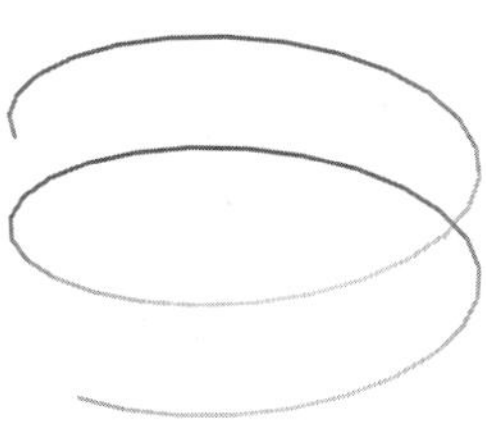

Here Maple inflates the previous spacecurve to form a tube.

```
> tubeplot( [cos(t),sin(t),t], t=0..4*Pi, radius=0.5 );
```

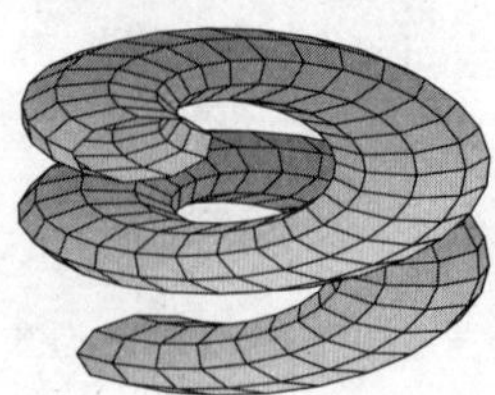

The `matrixplot` command plots the values of a object of type Matrix.

```
> A := LinearAlgebra[HilbertMatrix](8):
> B := LinearAlgebra[ToeplitzMatrix]([1,2,3,4,-4,-3,-2,-1],
>     symmetric):
> matrixplot( A+B, heights=histogram, axes=frame,
>     gap=0.25, style=patch);
```

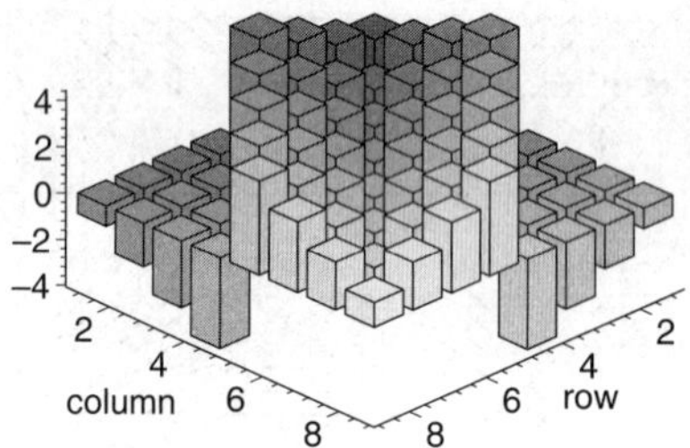

The following is a demonstration of a root locus plot.

```
> rootlocus( (s^5-1)/(s^2+1), s, -5..5, style=point,
>     adaptive=false );
```

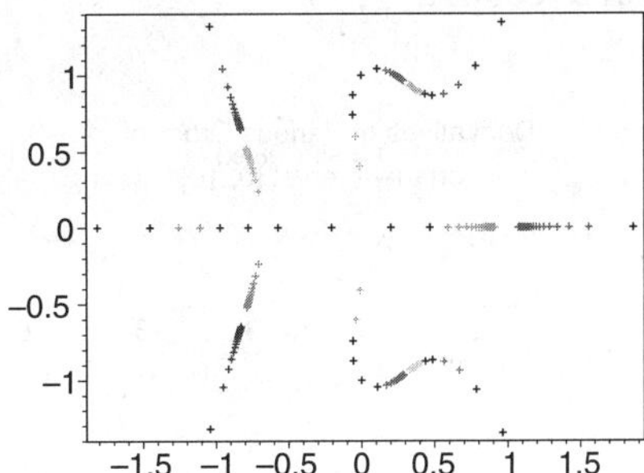

The **arrow** command plots arrows or vectors in two or three dimensions.

```
> plots[arrow]( [<2, 1>, <3, 2>], [<2, 5>, <1, 4>], difference,
>    scaling=constrained );
```

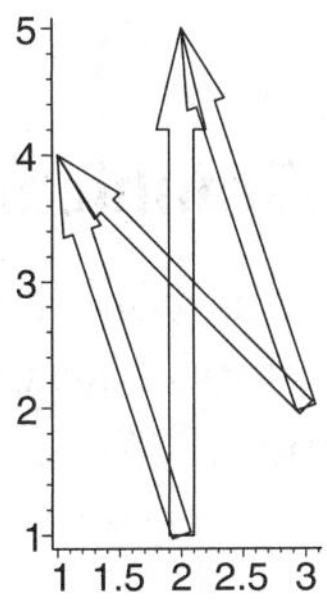

For a listing of other available plot types, enter **?plots** at the Maple prompt.

Visualization Component of the Student Package

The **Student** package is a collection of subpackages designed to assist with the teaching and learning of standard undergraduate mathematics. There are many routines for displaying functions, computations, and theorems. For example, in the **Student[Calculus1]** subpackage, the visualization routines are designed to assist in the understanding of basic calculus concepts. The following is an example of the **Student[Calculus1][DerivativePlot]** command.

The **DerivatePlot(f(x),x=a..b)** command plots an expression and its derivatives.

```
> with(Student[Calculus1]):
> f := proc() evalf(sqrt(rand()/10^12)) end proc:
> colors := proc() COLOR(RGB, f(), f(), f()) end proc:
```

```
> DerivativePlot(sin(0.98*x), x=0..10, order=1..20,
> derivativecolors=colors );
```

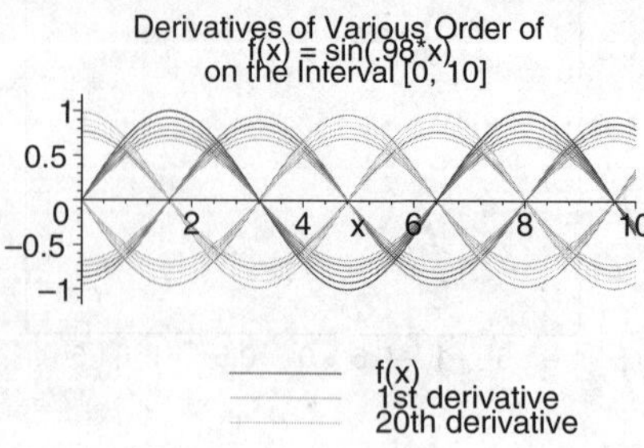

For a complete list of visualization routines in the `Student` subpackages, refer to the `?Student` help page and select a subpackage link.

5.7 Manipulating Graphical Objects

The `plottools` package contains commands for creating graphical objects and manipulating their plots. Use `with(plottools)` to access the commands using the short names.

```
> with(plottools):
```

Using the `display` Command

The objects in the `plottools` package do not automatically display. You must use the `display` command, defined in the `plots` package.

```
> with(plots):
> display( dodecahedron(), scaling=constrained, style=patch );
```

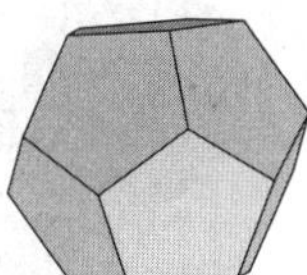

Sphere Before manipulating the following sphere, assign a name.

```
> s1 := sphere( [3/2,1/4,1/2], 1/4, color=red):
```

Note: In the sphere example, the assignment ends with a colon (:). If you use a semicolon (;), Maple displays a large plot structure.
To display the plot, use the `display` command.

```
> display( s1, scaling=constrained );
```

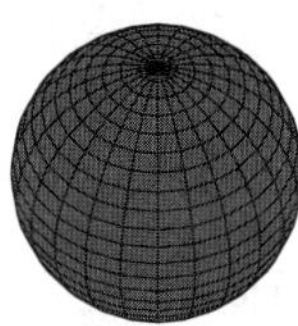

Place a second sphere in the picture and display the axes.

```
> s2 := sphere( [3/2,-1/4,1/2], 1/4, color=red):
> display( [s1, s2], axes=normal, scaling=constrained );
```

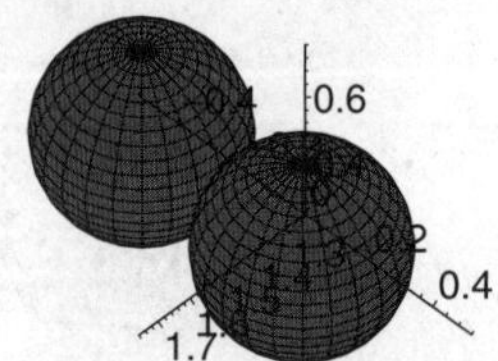

Cones You can also make cones with the `plottools` package.

```
> c := cone([0,0,0], 1/2, 2, color=khaki):
> display( c, axes=normal );
```

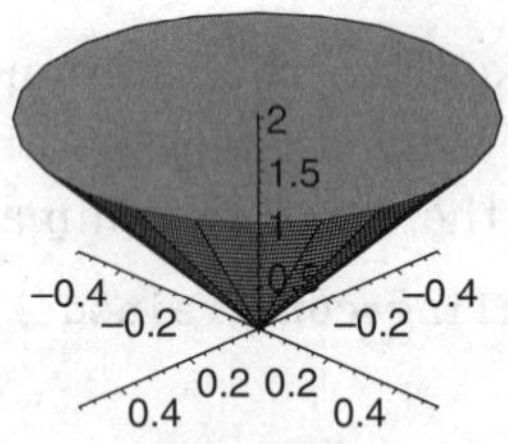

Rotation Experiment using Maple object rotation capabilities.

```
> c2 := rotate( c, 0, Pi/2, 0 ):
> display( c2, axes=normal );
```

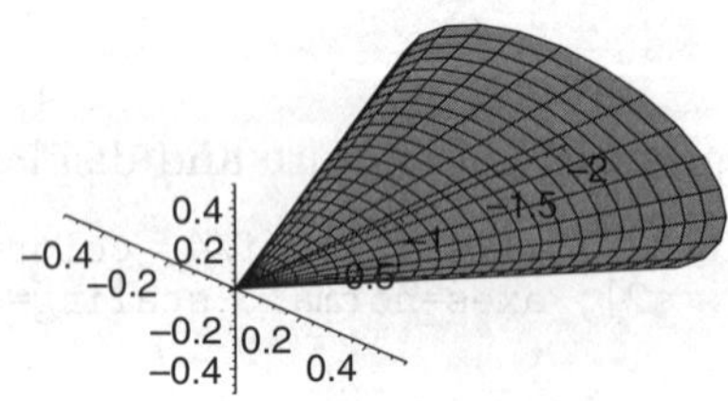

Translation You can also translate objects.

```
> c3 := translate( c2, 3, 0, 1/4 ):
> display( c3, axes=normal );
```

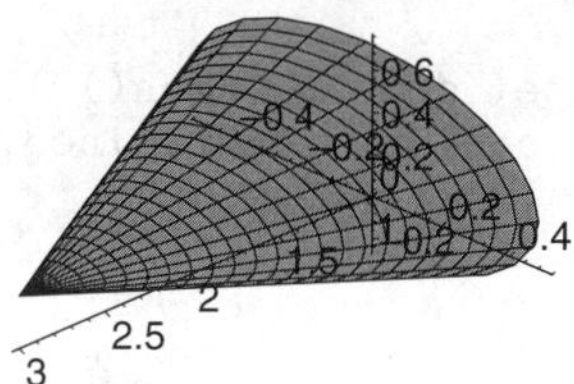

Hemisphere The `hemisphere` command makes a hemisphere. You can specify the radius and the coordinates of the center. Otherwise, leave an empty set of parentheses to accept the defaults.

```
> cup := hemisphere():
> display( cup );
```

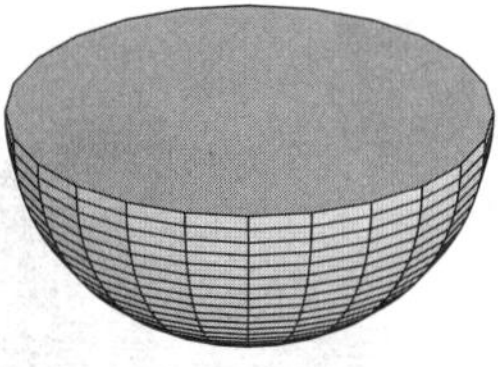

```
> cap := rotate( cup, Pi, 0, 0 ):
> display( cap );
```

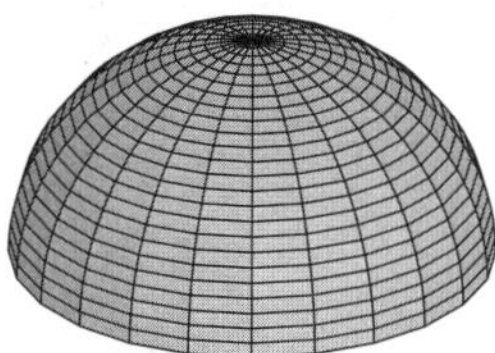

Dodecahedron All the sides of the dodecahedron mentioned earlier in this section are pentagons. If you raise the midpoint of each pentagon by using the `stellate` command, the term for the resulting object is *stellated* dodecahedron.

```
> a := stellate( dodecahedron() ):
> display( a, scaling=constrained, style=patch );
```

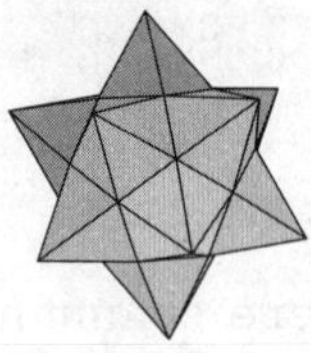

```
> stelhs := stellate(cap, 2):
> display( stelhs );
```

Instead of stellating the dodecahedron, you can cut out, for example, the inner three quarters of each pentagon.

```
> a := cutout( dodecahedron(), 3/4 ):
> display(  a, scaling=constrained, orientation=[45, 30] );
```

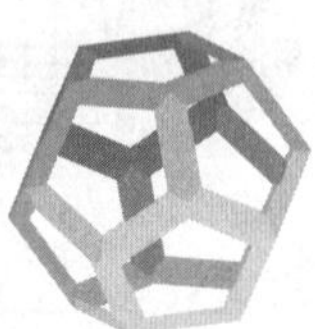

```
> hedgehog := [s1, s2, c3, stelhs]:
> display( hedgehog, scaling=constrained,
>     style=patchnogrid );
```

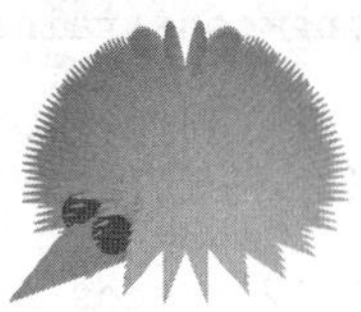

5.8 Code for Color Plates

Generating impressive graphics in Maple may require only a few lines of code as shown by the examples in this section. However, other graphics require many lines of code. Code for the color plates[1] that do not have code included in this section can be found in the Maple Application Center.

There are two ways to access the Maple Application Center.

- Open your Internet browser of choice and enter *http://www.mapleapps.com*
- From the **Help** menu, select **Maple on the Web**, and **Maple Application Center**.

To access color plate code not included:

1. Go to the Maple Application Center.
2. Scroll to the bottom of the page. In the **Maple Tools** section, click **Maple Color Plates**. The code is available in both HTML and Maple Worksheet formats.

Hundreds of graphics, including animations, are also available in the Maple Graphics Gallery and in the Maple Animation Gallery. To access these galleries, go to the Maple Application Center and click **Maple Graphics**.

[1]Several of the color plates provided were exported and rendered in POV-Ray™. As a result, exact duplication of these images may be difficult.

Note: On some computers, the `numpoints` options value may need to be decreased to generate the plot.

1. **Dirichlet Problem for a Circle**

```
> with(plots):
> setoptions3d(scaling=constrained, projection=0.5,
> style=patchnogrid):
> f1 := (x, y) -> 0.5*sin(10*x*y):
> f2 := t -> f1(cos(t), sin(t)):
> a0 := evalf(Int(f2(t), t=-Pi..Pi)/Pi):
> a := seq(evalf(Int(f2(t)*cos(n*t), t=-Pi..Pi)/Pi), n=1..50):
> b := seq(evalf(Int(f2(t)*sin(n*t), t=-Pi..Pi)/Pi), n=1..50):
> L := (r, s) -> a0/2+sum('r^n*(a[n]*cos(n*s)+b[n]*sin(n*s))',
> 'n'=1..50):
> q := plot3d([r*cos(s), r*sin(s), L(r, s)], r=0..1, s=0..2*Pi,
> color=[L(r, s), -L(r, s), 0.2], grid=[29, 100],
> numpoints=10000):
> p := tubeplot([cos(t), sin(t), f2(t), t=-Pi..Pi,
> radius=0.015], tubepoints=70, numpoints=1500):
> display3d({q, p}, orientation=[3, 89], lightmodel=light3);
```

2. **Mandelbrot Set**

   The Mandelbrot Set is one of the most complex objects in mathematics given the chaotic nature that surrounds the image. Code for this graphic is available at the Maple Application Center.

3. **Origami Bird**

   The Origami Bird can be displayed as a simple graphic as well as a Maple animation. Code for the graphic and the animation are available at the Maple Application Center.

4. **Conchoid**

   Code for this and other seashells is available at the Maple Application Center.

5. **Gauss Map Graphed on a Torus**

```
> with(plots):
> sp := [rho*cos(2*Pi*t), rho*sin(2*Pi*t), 0, radius=b]:
> pc := n -> [ (rho-r*cos(2*Pi*t))*cos(2*Pi/(n+t)),
>              (rho-r*cos(2*Pi*t))*sin(2*Pi/(n+t)),
>              -r*sin(2*Pi*t)]:
> rho, r, b := 3, 1.1, 1:
> s := spacecurve( {seq(pc(k),  k=1..50)}, t=0..1, thickness=2,
> color=blue, view=[-4.4..4.4, -4.4..4.4, -2.2..2.2]):
> s2 := tubeplot( sp, t=0..1, tubepoints=150,
> view=[-4.4..4.4, -4.4..4.4, -2.2..2.2], style=PATCHNOGRID,
> color=cyan):
```

```
> display( {s,s2}, scaling=CONSTRAINED, orientation=[50,65],
> transparency=0.8, shading=ZHUE, lightmodel=light1);
```

6. **Moebius Strip**

```
> moebius := plot3d([4+x*cos(1/2*y), y, x*sin(1/2*y)],
> x=-Pi..Pi, y=-0..2*Pi, coords=cylindrical, style=patchnogrid,
> grid=[60,60], orientation=[35,135], lightmodel=light4,
> shading=zhue, scaling=constrained, transparency=0.3):
> plots[display](moebius);
```

7. **Icosahedron**

```
> with(geom3d):
> icosahedron(p1, point(o, 0, 0, 0), 1):
> stellate(p2, p1, 4):
> p := draw(p2):
> q := plottools[homothety](p,3):
> plots[display]([p,q], scaling=constrained, style=patchnogrid,
> lightmodel=light4, shading=xyz, orientation=[-107,81]);
```

To view other variations, change the height value in the `stellate` command.

8. **Parameterized Surface of Revolution**

```
> r1 := 2 + sin(7*t):
> z1 := r1*cos(s):
> r2 := 8+r1*sin(s):
> plot3d([r2*sin(t), r2*cos(t), z1], s=0..2*Pi, t=0..2*Pi,
> grid=[80, 80], axes=none, style=patchnogrid, lightmodel=light1,
> shading=XYZ, scaling=constrained, orientation=[100,50]);
```

9. **Snowmen**

The Snowmen graphic is an animation. Code for this animation is available at the Maple Application Center.

10. **Function of Two Variables in Cartesian Coordinates**

```
> plot3d({sin(x^2+y^2), 2*cos(x^3+y^3)}, x=-3..3, y=-3..3,
> style=patch, grid=[70, 70], axes=none, shading=zgreyscale,
> style=patchnogrid, scaling=constrained, orientation=[50,30],
> lightmodel=light1);
```

5.9 Interactive Plot Builder

Maple allows you to build plots interactively. The interactive plot builder is invoked by using the context-sensitive menu or the `plots[interactive]` command.

Using the Graphical User Interface To Activate Interactive Plot Builder The following provides instructions for using the graphical user interface to build plots.

To activate the interactive plot builder:

1. Right-click the output of an executed Maple input command. A pop-up menu appears.
2. Select **Plots**, **PlotBuilder**. The **Interactive Plot Builder** dialog appears.
3. From the check box list, select a plot type. For example, for a two-dimensional plot, select the **2-D plot** check box.
4. To continue, click **Next**. Based on the check box selection, the corresponding dialog opens. For example, if you selected the **2-D plot** check box, the **2-D Plot** dialog appears.
5. From the various drop-down fields, select the appropriate feature for your plot. For example, to create a dash-line plot, click the **dash** option from the **Line** drop-down list.

   Note: To reset the plot options in the plot dialog, click the **Reset** button. To return to a previous dialog, click the **Back** button.
6. Once you have selected various options, click the **Plot** button. Maple generates the plot and displays it in the worksheet. The Maple command, including options you selected, are displayed in the worksheet.

Using the Command-Line Interactive Plot Builder The `plots[interactive]` command is part of the `plots` package. To build plots, use the `interactive` command followed by the expression in parentheses. Follow the instructions in the subsequently displayed dialogs.

```
> with(plots):
> interactive(sin(x)+1);
```

After executing the command, the **Interactive Plot Builder** dialog is displayed. Form this point, the instructions for using the graphical user interface apply, beginning with step 3 in the previous procedure.

5.10 Conclusion

This chapter examined Maple two- and three-dimensional plotting capabilities, involving explicitly, parametrically, and implicitly given functions. Cartesian, polar, spherical, and cylindrical are a few of the many coordinate systems that Maple can handle. Furthermore, you can animate a graph and shade it in a variety of ways for a clearer understanding of its nature.

Use the commands found in the `plots` package to display various graphs of functions and expressions. Some of the special plot types that you can create using these commands include contour, density, and logarithmic plots. The commands within the `plottools` package create and manipulate objects. Such commands, for instance, allow you to translate, rotate, and even stellate a graphical object. The interactive plot builder facilitates specifying and displaying plots by providing a graphical user interface.

5.10 Conclusion

6 Evaluation and Simplification

Expression manipulation serves many purposes, for example, converting output expressions into a familiar form to check answers or into a specific form needed by certain Maple routines. The issue of simplification is difficult in symbolic mathematics. What is simple in one context may not be in another context—each individual context can have its own definition of a simple form.

Working with Expressions in Maple

Maple provides a set of tools for working with expressions, for performing both mathematical and structural manipulations.

- Mathematical manipulations correspond to a standard mathematical process, for example, factoring a polynomial, or rationalizing the denominator of a rational expression.
- Structural manipulation tools allow you to access and modify parts of the Maple data structures that represent expressions and other types of objects.

In This Chapter

- Mathematical manipulations
- Assumptions
- Structural manipulations
- Evaluation rules

6.1 Mathematical Manipulations

Solving equations by hand usually involves performing a sequence of algebraic manipulations. You can also perform these steps using Maple.

```
> eq := 4*x + 17 = 23;
```

$$eq := 4\,x + 17 = 23$$

To solve this equation, you must subtract 17 from both sides of the equation. Subtract the equation 17=17 from eq. Enclose the unnamed equation in parentheses.

```
> eq - ( 17 = 17 );
```

$$4\,x = 6$$

Divide through by 4. Note that you do not have to use 4=4 in this case.

```
> % / 4;
```

$$x = \frac{3}{2}$$

The following sections focus on more sophisticated manipulations.

Expanding Polynomials as Sums

Sums are generally easier to comprehend than products, so you may find it useful to expand a polynomial as a sum of products. The expand command has this capability.

```
> poly := (x+1)*(x+2)*(x+5)*(x-3/2);
```

$$poly := (x+1)\,(x+2)\,(x+5)\,(x-\frac{3}{2})$$

```
> expand( poly );
```

$$x^4 + \frac{13}{2}\,x^3 + 5\,x^2 - \frac{31}{2}\,x - 15$$

The expand command expands the numerator of a rational expression.

```
> expand( (x+1)*(y^2-2*y+1) / z / (y-1) );
```

$$\frac{x\,y^2}{z\,(y-1)} - 2\,\frac{x\,y}{z\,(y-1)} + \frac{x}{z\,(y-1)} + \frac{y^2}{z\,(y-1)} - 2\,\frac{y}{z\,(y-1)} + \frac{1}{z\,(y-1)}$$

Note: To convert an expression containing fractions into a single rational expression and then cancel common factors, use the `normal` command. See this section, page 165.

Expansion Rules The `expand` command also recognizes expansion rules for many standard mathematical functions.

```
> expand( sin(2*x) );
```

$$2\sin(x)\cos(x)$$

```
> ln( abs(x^2)/(1+abs(x)) );
```

$$\ln(\frac{|x|^2}{1+|x|})$$

```
> expand(%);
```

$$2\ln(|x|) - \ln(1+|x|)$$

The `combine` command recognizes the same rules but applies them in the opposite direction. For information on combining terms, see this section, page 164.

You can specify subexpressions that you do *not* want to expand, as an argument to `expand`.

```
> expand( (x+1)*(y+z) );
```

$$x\,y + x\,z + y + z$$

```
> expand( (x+1)*(y+z), x+1 );
```

$$(x+1)\,y + (x+1)\,z$$

You can expand an expression over a special domain.

```
> poly := (x+2)^2*(x-2)*(x+3)*(x-1)^2*(x-1);
```

$$poly := (x+2)^2\,(x-2)\,(x+3)\,(x-1)^3$$

```
> expand( poly );
```

$$x^7 + 2\,x^6 - 10\,x^5 - 12\,x^4 + 37\,x^3 + 10\,x^2 - 52\,x + 24$$

```
> % mod 3;
```

$$x^7 + 2\,x^6 + 2\,x^5 + x^3 + x^2 + 2\,x$$

However, using the Expand command is more efficient.

```
> Expand( poly ) mod 3;
```

$$x^7 + 2\,x^6 + 2\,x^5 + x^3 + x^2 + 2\,x$$

When you use Expand with mod, Maple performs all intermediate calculations in modulo arithmetic. You can also write your own expand subroutines. For more details, refer to the ?expand help page.

Collecting the Coefficients of Like Powers

An expression like $x^2+2x+1-ax+b-cx^2$ is easier to read if you collect the coefficients of x^2, x, and the constant terms, by using the collect command.

```
> collect( x^2 + 2*x + 1 - a*x + b - c*x^2, x );
```

$$(1-c)\,x^2 + (2-a)\,x + b + 1$$

The second argument to the collect command specifies on which variable it should base the collection.

```
> poly := x^2 + 2*y*x - 3*y + y^2*x^2;
```

$$poly := x^2 + 2\,y\,x - 3\,y + y^2\,x^2$$

```
> collect( poly, x );
```

$$(1 + y^2)\,x^2 + 2\,y\,x - 3\,y$$

```
> collect( poly, y );
```

$$y^2\,x^2 + (2\,x - 3)\,y + x^2$$

You can collect on variables or unevaluated function calls.

```
> trig_expr := sin(x)*cos(x) + sin(x) + y*sin(x);
```

$$\mathit{trig\_expr} := \sin(x)\cos(x) + \sin(x) + y\sin(x)$$

```
> collect( trig_expr, sin(x) );
```

$$(\cos(x) + 1 + y)\sin(x)$$

```
> DE := diff(f(x),x,x)*sin(x) - diff(f(x),x)*sin(f(x))
>     + sin(x)*diff(f(x),x) + sin(f(x))*diff(f(x),x,x);
```

$$DE := (\tfrac{d^2}{dx^2}\,\mathrm{f}(x))\sin(x) - (\tfrac{d}{dx}\,\mathrm{f}(x))\sin(\mathrm{f}(x)) + \sin(x)\,(\tfrac{d}{dx}\,\mathrm{f}(x)) \\ + \sin(\mathrm{f}(x))\,(\tfrac{d^2}{dx^2}\,\mathrm{f}(x))$$

```
> collect( DE, diff );
```

$$(-\sin(\mathrm{f}(x)) + \sin(x))\,(\frac{d}{dx}\,\mathrm{f}(x)) + (\sin(x) + \sin(\mathrm{f}(x)))\,(\frac{d^2}{dx^2}\,\mathrm{f}(x))$$

You cannot collect on sums or products.

```
> big_expr := z*x*y + 2*x*y + z;
```

$$\mathit{big\_expr} := z\,x\,y + 2\,y\,x + z$$

```
> collect( big_expr, x*y );
Error, (in collect) cannot collect y*x
```

Instead, make a substitution before you collect. In the preceding case, substituting a dummy name for x*y, then collecting on the dummy name produces the desired result.

```
> subs( x=xyprod/y, big_expr );
```

$$z\,xyprod + 2\,xyprod + z$$

```
> collect( %, xyprod );
```

$$(z + 2)\,xyprod + z$$

```
> subs( xyprod=x*y, % );
```

$$(z + 2)\,y\,x + z$$

Section **6.3 Structural Manipulations** explains the use of the subs command.

If you are collecting coefficients of more than one variable simultaneously, two options are available, the *recursive* and *distributed forms.* The recursive form initially collects in the first specified variable, then in the next, and so on. The default is the recursive form.

```
> poly := x*y + z*x*y + y*x^2 - z*y*x^2 + x + z*x;
```

$$poly := y\,x + z\,x\,y + y\,x^2 - z\,y\,x^2 + x + z\,x$$

```
> collect( poly, [x,y] );
```

$$(1 - z)\,y\,x^2 + ((1 + z)\,y + 1 + z)\,x$$

The distributed form collects the coefficients of all variables at the same time.

```
> collect( poly, [x,y], distributed );
```

$$(1 + z)\,x + (1 + z)\,y\,x + (1 - z)\,y\,x^2$$

The collect command does not sort the terms. Use the sort command to sort. See this section, page 171.

Factoring Polynomials and Rational Functions

To write a polynomial as a product of terms of smallest possible degree, use the `factor` command.

```
> factor( x^2-1 );
```

$$(x-1)(x+1)$$

```
> factor( x^3+y^3 );
```

$$(x+y)(x^2-y\,x+y^2)$$

You can also factor rational functions. The `factor` command factors both the numerator and the denominator, then removes common terms.

```
> rat_expr := (x^16 - y^16) / (x^8 - y^8);
```

$$rat\_expr := \frac{x^{16}-y^{16}}{x^8-y^8}$$

```
> factor( rat_expr );
```

$$x^8+y^8$$

```
> rat_expr := (x^16 - y^16) / (x^7 - y^7);
```

$$rat\_expr := \frac{x^{16}-y^{16}}{x^7-y^7}$$

```
> factor(rat_expr);
```

$$\frac{(x+y)(x^2+y^2)(x^4+y^4)(x^8+y^8)}{x^6+y\,x^5+y^2\,x^4+y^3\,x^3+y^4\,x^2+y^5\,x+y^6}$$

Specifying the Algebraic Number Field The `factor` command factors a polynomial over the ring implied by the coefficients. The following polynomial has integer coefficients, so the terms in the factored form have integer coefficients.

```
> poly := x^5 - x^4 - x^3 + x^2 - 2*x + 2;
```

$$poly := x^5 - x^4 - x^3 + x^2 - 2\,x + 2$$

```
> factor( poly );
```

$$(x-1)\,(x^2-2)\,(x^2+1)$$

In this next example, the coefficients include $\sqrt{2}$. Note the differences in the result.

```
> expand( sqrt(2)*poly );
```

$$\sqrt{2}\,x^5 - \sqrt{2}\,x^4 - \sqrt{2}\,x^3 + \sqrt{2}\,x^2 - 2\,\sqrt{2}\,x + 2\,\sqrt{2}$$

```
> factor( % );
```

$$\sqrt{2}\,(x^2+1)\,(x+\sqrt{2})\,(x-\sqrt{2})\,(x-1)$$

You can explicitly extend the coefficient field by giving a second argument to `factor`.

```
> poly := x^4 - 5*x^2 + 6;
```

$$poly := x^4 - 5\,x^2 + 6$$

```
> factor( poly );
```

$$(x^2-2)\,(x^2-3)$$

```
> factor( poly, sqrt(2) );
```

$$(x^2-3)\,(x+\sqrt{2})\,(x-\sqrt{2})$$

```
> factor( poly, { sqrt(2), sqrt(3) } );
```

$$(x+\sqrt{2})\,(x-\sqrt{2})\,(x+\sqrt{3})\,(x-\sqrt{3})$$

You can also specify the extension by using `RootOf`. Here `RootOf(x^2-2)` represents any solution to $x^2 - 2 = 0$, that is either $\sqrt{2}$ or $-\sqrt{2}$.

```
> factor( poly, RootOf(x^2-2) );
```

$$(x^2 - 3)\,(x + \mathrm{RootOf}(\_Z^2 - 2))\,(x - \mathrm{RootOf}(\_Z^2 - 2))$$

For more information on performing calculations in an algebraic number field, refer to the `?evala` help page.

Factoring in Special Domains Use the `Factor` command to factor an expression over the integers modulo p for some prime p. The syntax is similar to that of the `Expand` command.

```
> Factor( x^2+3*x+3 ) mod 7;
```

$$(x + 4)\,(x + 6)$$

The `Factor` command also allows algebraic field extensions.

```
> Factor( x^3+1 ) mod 5;
```

$$(x + 1)\,(x^2 + 4\,x + 1)$$

```
> Factor( x^3+1, RootOf(x^2+x+1) ) mod 5;
```

$$(x + \mathrm{RootOf}(\_Z^2 + \_Z + 1))$$
$$(x + 4\,\mathrm{RootOf}(\_Z^2 + \_Z + 1) + 4)\,(x + 1)$$

For details about the algorithm used, factoring multivariate polynomials, or factoring polynomials over an algebraic number field, refer to the `?Factor` help page.

Removing Rational Exponents

In general, it is preferred to represent rational expressions without fractional exponents in the denominator. The `rationalize` command removes roots from the denominator of a rational expression by multiplying by a suitable factor.

```
> 1 / ( 2 + root[3](2) );
```

$$\frac{1}{2 + 2^{(1/3)}}$$

```
> rationalize( % );
```

$$\frac{2}{5} - \frac{1}{5}\,2^{(1/3)} + \frac{1}{10}\,2^{(2/3)}$$

```
> (x^2+5) / (x + x^(5/7));
```

$$\frac{x^2+5}{x+x^{(5/7)}}$$

```
> rationalize( % );
```

$$(x^2+5)\,(x^{(6/7)} - x^{(12/7)} - x^{(4/7)} + x^{(10/7)} + x^{(2/7)} - x^{(8/7)} + x^2)$$
$$/(x^3+x)$$

The result of rationalize is often larger than the original.

Combining Terms

The combine command applies a number of transformation rules for various mathematical functions.

```
> combine( sin(x)^2 + cos(x)^2 );
```

$$1$$

```
> combine( sin(x)*cos(x) );
```

$$\frac{1}{2}\sin(2\,x)$$

```
> combine( exp(x)^2 * exp(y) );
```

$$e^{(2\,x+y)}$$

```
> combine( (x^a)^2 );
```

$$x^{(2\,a)}$$

To see how combine arrives at the result, give infolevel[combine] a positive value.

```
> infolevel[combine] := 1;
```

$$infolevel_{combine} := 1$$

```
> expr := Int(1, x) + Int(x^2, x);
```

$$expr := \int 1\,dx + \int x^2\,dx$$

```
> combine( expr );
```

```
combine:   combining with respect to   linear
combine:   combining with respect to   linear
combine:   combining with respect to   linear
combine:   combining with respect to   cmbpwr
combine:   combining with respect to   power
combine:   combining with respect to   power
combine:   combining with respect to   power
combine:   combining with respect to   cmbplus
combine:   combining with respect to   cmbpwr
combine:   combining with respect to   power
combine:   combining with respect to   cmbpwr
combine:   combining with respect to   power
combine:   combining with respect to   power
combine:   combining with respect to   power
```

$$\int x^2 + 1\,dx$$

The `expand` command applies most of these transformation rules in the other direction. See this section, page 156.

Factored Normal Form

If an expression contains fractions, convert the expression into one large fraction, and cancel common factors in the numerator and denominator. The `normal` command performs this process, which often leads to simpler expressions.

```
> normal( x + 1/x );
```

$$\frac{x^2 + 1}{x}$$

```
> expr := x/(x+1) + 1/x + 1/(1+x);
```

$$expr := \frac{x}{x+1} + \frac{1}{x} + \frac{1}{x+1}$$

```
> normal( expr );
```

$$\frac{x+1}{x}$$

```
> expr := (x^2 - y^2) / (x-y)^3;
```

$$expr := \frac{x^2 - y^2}{(x-y)^3}$$

```
> normal( expr );
```

$$\frac{x+y}{(x-y)^2}$$

```
> expr := (x - 1/x) / (x-2);
```

$$expr := \frac{x - \frac{1}{x}}{x-2}$$

```
> normal( expr );
```

$$\frac{x^2 - 1}{x\,(x-2)}$$

Use the second argument **expanded** if you want **normal** to expand the numerator and the denominator.

```
> normal( expr, expanded );
```

$$\frac{x^2 - 1}{x^2 - 2\,x}$$

The `normal` command acts recursively over functions, sets, and lists.

```
> normal( [ expr, exp(x+1/x) ] );
```

$$[\frac{x^2-1}{x\,(x-2)},\, e^{(\frac{x^2+1}{x})}]$$

```
> big_expr := sin( (x*(x+1)-x)/(x+2) )^2
>             + cos( (x^2)/(-x-2) )^2;
```

$$big\_expr := \sin(\frac{(x+1)\,x-x}{x+2})^2 + \cos(\frac{x^2}{-x-2})^2$$

```
> normal( big_expr );
```

$$\sin(\frac{x^2}{x+2})^2 + \cos(\frac{x^2}{x+2})^2$$

Note from the previous example that **normal** does not simplify trigonometric expressions, only rational polynomial functions.

A Special Case Normal may return an expression in expanded form that is not as simple as the factored form.

```
> expr := (x^25-1) / (x-1);
```

$$expr := \frac{x^{25}-1}{x-1}$$

```
> normal( expr );
```

$$1 + x^2 + x + x^{11} + x^{12} + x^4 + x^3 + x^5 + x^{16} + x^7 + x^6 + x^{14} + x^{19} + x^{17} + x^{15} + x^{18} + x^9 + x^8 + x^{10} + x^{24} + x^{22} + x^{23} + x^{21} + x^{20} + x^{13}$$

To cancel the common $(x-1)$ term from the numerator and the denominator without expanding the numerator, use `factor`. See this section, page 161.

```
> factor(expr);
```

$$(x^4 + x^3 + x^2 + x + 1)\,(x^{20} + x^{15} + x^{10} + x^5 + 1)$$

Simplifying Expressions

The results of Maple simplification calculations can be very complicated. The `simplify` command tries to find a simpler expression by applying a list of manipulations.

```
> expr := 4^(1/2) + 3;
```

$$expr := \sqrt{4} + 3$$

```
> simplify( expr );
```

$$5$$

```
> expr := cos(x)^5 + sin(x)^4 + 2*cos(x)^2
>      - 2*sin(x)^2 - cos(2*x);
```

$$expr := \cos(x)^5 + \sin(x)^4 + 2\cos(x)^2 - 2\sin(x)^2 - \cos(2\,x)$$

```
> simplify( expr );
```

$$\cos(x)^4\,(\cos(x) + 1)$$

Simplification rules are recognized for trigonometric expressions, logarithmic and exponential expressions, radical expressions, expressions with powers, `RootOf` expressions, and various special functions.

If you specify a particular simplification rule as an argument to the `simplify` command, then it uses only that simplification rule (or that class of rules).

```
> expr := ln(3*x) + sin(x)^2 + cos(x)^2;
```

$$expr := \ln(3\,x) + \sin(x)^2 + \cos(x)^2$$

```
> simplify( expr, trig );
```

$$\ln(3\,x) + 1$$

```
> simplify( expr, ln );
```

$$\ln(3) + \ln(x) + \sin(x)^2 + \cos(x)^2$$

```
> simplify( expr );
```

$$\ln(3) + \ln(x) + 1$$

For a list of built-in simplification rules, refer to the `?simplify` help page.

Simplification with Assumptions

Maple may not perform a simplification as you would. Although you know that a variable has special properties, Maple treats the variable in a more general way.

```
> expr := sqrt( (x*y)^2 );
```

$$expr := \sqrt{x^2\, y^2}$$

```
> simplify( expr );
```

$$\sqrt{x^2\, y^2}$$

The option `assume=`*`property`* specifies that `simplify` assume that all the unknowns in the expression have that *property*.

```
> simplify( expr, assume=real );
```

$$|x\, y|$$

```
> simplify( expr, assume=positive );
```

$$x\, y$$

You can also use the general assume facility to place assumptions on individual variables. See **6.2 Assumptions**.

Simplification with Side Relations

Sometimes you can simplify an expression using your own special-purpose transformation rule. The `simplify` command allows you do to this by means of *side relations*.

```
> expr := x*y*z + x*y + x*z + y*z;
```

$$expr := x\,y\,z + x\,y + x\,z + y\,z$$

```
> simplify( expr, { x*z=1 } );
```

$$x\,y + y\,z + y + 1$$

You can give one or more side relations in a set or list. The `simplify` command uses the given equations as additional allowable simplifications.

Specifying the order in which `simplify` performs the simplification provides another level of control.

```
> expr := x^3 + y^3;
```

$$expr := x^3 + y^3$$

```
> siderel := x^2 + y^2 = 1;
```

$$siderel := x^2 + y^2 = 1$$

```
> simplify( expr, {siderel}, [x,y] );
```

$$y^3 - x\,y^2 + x$$

```
> simplify( expr, {siderel}, [y,x] );
```

$$x^3 - y\,x^2 + y$$

- In the first case, Maple makes the substitution $x^2 = 1 - y^2$ in the expression, then attempts to make substitutions for y^2 terms. Not finding any, it stops.
- In the second case, Maple makes the substitution $y^2 = 1 - x^2$ in the expression, then attempts to make substitutions for x^2 terms. Not finding any, it stops.

The `simplify` routine is based on Gröbner basis manipulations of polynomials. For more information, refer to the `?simplify,siderels` help page.

Sorting Algebraic Expressions

Maple prints the terms of a polynomial in the order the polynomial was first created. To sort the polynomial by decreasing degree, use the `sort` command.

```
> poly := 1 + x^4 - x^2 + x + x^3;
```

$$poly := 1 + x^4 - x^2 + x + x^3$$

```
> sort( poly );
```

$$x^4 + x^3 - x^2 + x + 1$$

Note that `sort` reorders algebraic expressions in place, replacing the original polynomial with the sorted copy.

```
> poly;
```

$$x^4 + x^3 - x^2 + x + 1$$

Sorting Multivariate Polynomials You can sort multivariate polynomials in two ways, by total degree or by lexicographic order.

- The default method is total degree, which sorts terms into descending order of degree.
- If two terms have the same degree, it sorts those terms by lexicographic order (in other words, `[a,b]` specifies that a comes before b and so forth).

```
> sort( x+x^3 + w^5 + y^2 + z^4, [w,x,y,z] );
```

$$w^5 + z^4 + x^3 + y^2 + x$$

```
> sort( x^3*y + y^2*x^2, [x,y] );
```

$$x^3\,y + x^2\,y^2$$

```
> sort( x^3*y + y^2*x^2 + x^4, [x,y] );
```

$$x^4 + x^3\,y + x^2\,y^2$$

Note that the order of the variables in the list determines the ordering of the expression.

```
> sort( x^3*y + y^2*x^2, [x,y] );
```

$$x^3\,y + x^2\,y^2$$

```
> sort( x^3*y + y^2*x^2, [y,x] );
```

$$y^2\,x^2 + y\,x^3$$

To sort the entire expression by *lexicographic ordering*, use the `plex` option with the `sort` command.

```
> sort( x + x^3 + w^5 + y^2 + z^4, [w,x,y,z], plex );
```

$$w^5 + x^3 + x + y^2 + z^4$$

Again, the order of the unknowns in the call to `sort` determines the ordering.

```
> sort( x + x^3 + w^5 + y^2 + z^4, [x,y,z,w], plex );
```

$$x^3 + x + y^2 + z^4 + w^5$$

The `sort` command can also sort lists. See **6.3 Structural Manipulations**.

Converting Between Equivalent Forms

You can write many mathematical functions in several equivalent forms. For example, you can express $\sin(x)$ in terms of the exponential function. The `convert` command can perform this and many other types of conversions. For more information, refer to the `?convert` help page.

```
> convert( sin(x), exp );
```

$$\frac{-1}{2}\,I\,(e^{(x\,I)} - \frac{1}{e^{(x\,I)}})$$

```
> convert( cot(x), sincos );
```

$$\frac{\cos(x)}{\sin(x)}$$

```
> convert( arccos(x), ln );
```

$$-I\ln(x+\sqrt{-x^2+1}\,I)$$

```
> convert( binomial(n,k), factorial );
```

$$\frac{n!}{k!\,(n-k)!}$$

The `parfrac` argument indicates partial fractions.

```
> convert( (x^5+1) / (x^4-x^2), parfrac, x );
```

$$x+\frac{1}{x-1}-\frac{1}{x^2}$$

You can also use **convert** to find a fractional *approximation* to a floating-point number.

```
> convert( .3284879342, rational );
```

$$\frac{19615}{59713}$$

Note that conversions are not necessarily mutually inverse.

```
> convert( tan(x), exp );
```

$$\frac{-I\,((e^{(x\,I)})^2-1)}{(e^{(x\,I)})^2+1}$$

```
> convert( %, trig );
```

$$\frac{-I\,((\cos(x)+\sin(x)\,I)^2-1)}{(\cos(x)+\sin(x)\,I)^2+1}$$

The `simplify` command reveals that this expression is $\sin(x)/\cos(x)$, that is, $\tan(x)$.

```
> simplify( % );
```

$$\frac{\sin(x)}{\cos(x)}$$

You can also use the `convert` command to perform structural manipulations on Maple objects. See **6.3 Structural Manipulations**.

6.2 Assumptions

There are two means of imposing assumptions on unknowns.

- To globally change the properties of unknowns, use the `assume` facility.
- To perform a single operation under assumptions on unknowns, use the `assuming` command.

The `assume` facility and `assuming` command are discussed in the following subsections. For more information on these commands, refer to the `?assume` and `?assuming` help pages.

The assume Facility

The *assume facility* is a set of routines for dealing with properties of unknowns. The `assume` command allows improved simplification of symbolic expressions, especially with multiple-valued functions, for example, the square root.

```
> sqrt(a^2);
```

$$\sqrt{a^2}$$

Maple cannot simplify this, as the result is different for positive and negative values of a. Stating an assumption about the value of a allows Maple to simplify the expression.

```
> assume( a>0 );
> sqrt(a^2);
```

$$a\tilde{}$$

The tilde (~) on a variable indicates that an assumption has been made about it. New assumptions replace old ones.

```
> assume( a<0 );
> sqrt(a^2);
```

$$-a\tilde{}$$

Using the `about` Command Use the `about` command to get information about the assumptions on an unknown.

```
> about(a);

Originally a, renamed a~:
  is assumed to be: RealRange(-infinity,Open(0))
```

Using the `additionally` Command Use the `additionally` command to make additional assumptions about unknowns.

```
> assume(m, nonnegative);
> additionally( m<=0 );
> about(m);

Originally m, renamed m~:
  is assumed to be: 0
```

Many functions make use of the assumptions on an unknown. The `frac` command returns the fractional part of a number.

```
> frac(n);
```

$$\mathrm{frac}(n)$$

```
> assume(n, integer);
> frac(n);
```

$$0$$

The following limit depends on b.

```
> limit(b*x, x=infinity);
```

$$\mathrm{signum}(b)\,\infty$$

```
> assume( b>0 );
> limit(b*x, x=infinity);
```

$$\infty$$

Command Operation Details You can use `infolevel` to have Maple report the details of command operations.

```
> infolevel[int] := 2;
```

$$infolevel_{int} := 2$$

```
> int( exp(c*x), x=0..infinity );
```

```
int/cook/nogo1:
Given Integral
Int(exp(c*x),x = 0 .. infinity)
Fits into this pattern:
Int(exp(-Ucplex*x^S1-U2*x^S2)*x^N*ln(B*x^DL)^M*cos(C1*x^R)/
((A0+A1*x^D)^P),x = t1 .. t2)
Definite integration: Can't determine if the integral is convergent.
Need to know the sign of --> -c
Will now try indefinite integration and then take limits.
int/indef1:   first-stage indefinite integration
int/indef2:   second-stage indefinite integration
int/indef2:   applying derivative-divides
int/indef1:   first-stage indefinite integration
int/definite/contour:   contour integration
```

$$\lim_{x \to \infty} \frac{e^{(c\,x)} - 1}{c}$$

The `int` command must know the sign of `c` (or rather the sign of `-c`).

```
> assume( c>0 );
> int( exp(c*x), x=0..infinity );
```

```
int/cook/nogo1:
Given Integral
Int(exp(x),x = 0 .. infinity)
Fits into this pattern:
Int(exp(-Ucplex*x^S1-U2*x^S2)*x^N*ln(B*x^DL)^M*cos(C1*x^R)/
((A0+A1*x^D)^P),x = t1 .. t2)
int/cook/IIntd1:
--> U must be <= 0 for converging integral
--> will use limit to find if integral is +infinity
--> or - infinity or undefined
```

$$\infty$$

Logarithms are multiple-valued. For general complex values of x, $\ln(e^x)$ is different from x.

```
> ln( exp( 3*Pi*I ) );
```

$$\pi I$$

Therefore, Maple does not simplify the following expression unless it is known to be correct, for example, when x is real.

```
> ln(exp(x));
```

$$\ln(e^x)$$

```
> assume(x, real);
> ln(exp(x));
```

$$x\tilde{}$$

Testing the Properities of Unknowns You can use the is command to directly test the properties of unknowns.

```
> is( c>0 );
```

true

```
> is(x, complex);
```

true

```
> is(x, real);
```

true

In this next example, Maple still assumes that the variable a is negative.

```
> eq := xi^2 = a;
```

$$eq := \xi^2 = a\tilde{}$$

```
> solve( eq, {xi} );
```

$$\{\xi = \sqrt{-a\tilde{}}\, I\}, \{\xi = -I\, \sqrt{-a\tilde{}}\}$$

To remove assumptions that you make on a name, simply unassign the name. However, the expression eq still refers to a~.

```
> eq;
```

$$\xi^2 = a\tilde{}$$

You must remove the assumption on a *inside* eq before you remove the assumption on a. First, remove the assumptions on a inside eq.

```
> eq := subs( a='a', eq );
```

$$eq := \xi^2 = a$$

Then, unassign a.

```
> a := 'a';
```

$$a := a$$

If you require an assumption to hold for only one evaluation, then you can use the assuming command, described in the following subsection. When using the assuming command, you do not need to remove the assumptions on unknowns and equations.

The assuming Command

To perform a single evaluation under assumptions on the name(s) in an expression, use the assuming command. Its use is equivalent to imposing assumptions by using the assume facility, evaluating the expression, then removing the assumptions from the expression and names. This facilitates experimenting with the evaluation of an expression under different assumptions.

```
> about(a);
```

```
a:
  nothing known about this object
```

```
> sqrt(a^2) assuming a<0;
```

$$-a$$

```
> about(a);
```

```
a:
  nothing known about this object
```

```
> sqrt(a^2) assuming a>0;
```

$$a$$

You can evaluate an expression under an assumption on all names in an expression

```
> sqrt((a*b)^2) assuming positive;
```

$$a\,b\tilde{}$$

or assumptions on specific names.

```
> ln(exp(x)) + ln(exp(y)) assuming x::real, y::complex;
```

$$x\tilde{} + \ln(e^y)$$

Using the Double Colon In the previous example, the double colon (`::`) indicates a property assignment. In general, it is used for type checking. For more information, refer to the `?type` help page.

6.3 Structural Manipulations

Structural manipulations include selecting and changing parts of an object. They use knowledge of the structure or internal representation of an object rather than working with the expression as a purely mathematical expression. In the special cases of lists and sets, selecting an element is straightforward. The concept of what constitutes the parts of a general expression is more difficult. However, many of the commands that manipulate lists and sets also apply to general expressions.

```
> L := { Z, Q, R, C, H, O };
```

$$L := \{O, R, Z, Q, C, H\}$$

```
> L[3];
```

$$Z$$

Mapping a Function onto a List or Set

To apply a function or command to each of the elements rather than to the object as a whole, use the `map` command.

```
> f( [a, b, c] );
```

$$\mathrm{f}([a, b, c])$$

```
> map( f, [a, b, c] );
```

$$[\mathrm{f}(a), \mathrm{f}(b), \mathrm{f}(c)]$$

```
> map( expand, { (x+1)*(x+2), x*(x+2) } );
```

$$\{x^2 + 3\,x + 2, x^2 + 2\,x\}$$

```
> map( x->x^2, [a, b, c] );
```

$$[a^2, b^2, c^2]$$

If you give `map` more than two arguments, it passes the extra argument(s) to the function.

```
> map( f, [a, b, c], p, q );
```

$$[f(a, p, q), f(b, p, q), f(c, p, q)]$$

```
> map( diff, [ (x+1)*(x+2), x*(x+2) ], x );
```

$$[2x + 3, 2x + 2]$$

Using the map2 Command The map2 command is closely related to map. Whereas map sequentially replaces the first argument of a function, the map2 command replaces the second argument to a function.

```
> map2( f, p, [a,b,c], q, r );
```

$$[f(p, a, q, r), f(p, b, q, r), f(p, c, q, r)]$$

You can use map2 to list all the partial derivatives of an expression.

```
> map2( diff, x^y/z, [x,y,z] );
```

$$[\frac{x^y\, y}{x\, z}, \frac{x^y \ln(x)}{z}, -\frac{x^y}{z^2}]$$

You can use map2 in conjunction with the map command. For an example, see the ?map help page.

Using the seq Command You can use the seq command to generate sequences resembling the output from map. In this example, seq generates a sequence by applying the function f to the elements of a set and a list.

```
> seq( f(i), i={a,b,c} );
```

$$f(a), f(b), f(c)$$

```
> seq( f(p, i, q, r), i=[a,b,c] );
```

$$f(p, a, q, r), f(p, b, q, r), f(p, c, q, r)$$

Another example is Pascal's Triangle.

```
> L := [ seq( i, i=0..5 ) ];
```

$$L := [0, 1, 2, 3, 4, 5]$$

```
> [ seq( [ seq( binomial(n,m), m=L ) ], n=L ) ];
```

$$[[1, 0, 0, 0, 0, 0], [1, 1, 0, 0, 0, 0], [1, 2, 1, 0, 0, 0], [1, 3, 3, 1, 0, 0], [1, 4, 6, 4, 1, 0], [1, 5, 10, 10, 5, 1]]$$

```
> map( print, % );
```

$$[1, 0, 0, 0, 0, 0]$$

$$[1, 1, 0, 0, 0, 0]$$

$$[1, 2, 1, 0, 0, 0]$$

$$[1, 3, 3, 1, 0, 0]$$

$$[1, 4, 6, 4, 1, 0]$$

$$[1, 5, 10, 10, 5, 1]$$

$$[]$$

Using the `add` and `mul` Commands The `add` and `mul` commands work like `seq` except that they generate sums and products, respectively, instead of sequences.

```
> add( i^2, i=[5, y, sin(x), -5] );
```

$$50 + y^2 + \sin(x)^2$$

Note: The `map`, `map2`, `seq`, `add`, and `mul` commands can also act on general expressions.

Choosing Elements from a List or Set

You can select certain elements from a list or a set, if you have a boolean-valued function that determines which elements to select. The following boolean-valued function returns `true` if its argument is larger than three.

```
> large := x -> is(x > 3);
```

$$\mathit{large} := x \to \mathrm{is}(3 < x)$$

Use the `select` command to choose the elements in a list or set that satisfy `large`.

```
> L := [ 8, 2.95, Pi, sin(9) ];
```

$$L := [8, 2.95, \pi, \sin(9)]$$

```
> select( large, L );
```

$$[8, \pi]$$

Using the `remove` Command The `remove` command removes the elements from `L` that satisfy `large` and displays as output the remaining elements.

```
> remove( large, L );
```

$$[2.95, \sin(9)]$$

Using the `selectremove` Command To perform operations of both the `select` and `remove` commands simultaneously, use the `selectremove` command.

```
> selectremove( large, L);
```

$$[8, \pi], [2.95, \sin(9)]$$

Using the `type` Command Use the `type` command to determine the type of an expression.

```
> type( 3, numeric );
```

$$true$$

```
> type( cos(1), numeric );
```

$$false$$

The syntax of `select` here passes the third argument, `numeric`, to the `type` command.

```
> select( type, L, numeric );
```

$$[8, 2.95]$$

For more information on types and using `select` and `remove` on a general expression, see this section, pages 190–196.

Merging Two Lists

Sometimes you need to merge two lists. Here is a list of x-values and a list of y-values.

```
> X := [ seq( ithprime(i), i=1..6 ) ];
```

$$X := [2, 3, 5, 7, 11, 13]$$

```
> Y := [ seq( binomial(6, i), i=1..6 ) ];
```

$$Y := [6, 15, 20, 15, 6, 1]$$

To plot the y-values against the x-values, construct a list of lists: `[ [x1,y1], [x2,y2], ... ]`. That is, for each pair of values, construct a two-element list.

```
> pair := (x,y) -> [x, y];
```

$$\mathit{pair} := (x, y) \to [x, y]$$

Using the `zip` Command The `zip` command can merge the lists `X` and `Y` according to the binary function `pair`.

```
> P := zip( pair, X, Y );
```

$$P := [[2, 6], [3, 15], [5, 20], [7, 15], [11, 6], [13, 1]]$$

```
> plot( P );
```

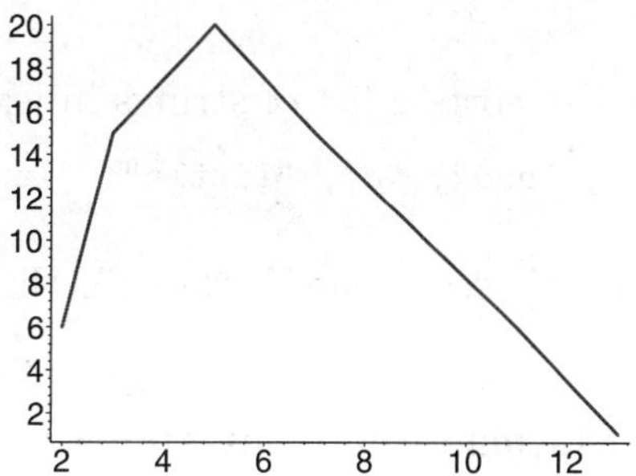

If the two lists have different length, then zip returns a list the size of the shorter one.

```
> zip( (x,y) -> x.y, [a,b,c,d,e,f], [1,2,3] );
```

$$[a,\ 2\,b,\ 3\,c]$$

You can specify a fourth argument to zip. Then zip returns a list the size of the longer input list, using the fourth argument for the missing values.

```
> zip( (x,y) -> x.y, [a,b,c,d,e,f], [1,2,3], 99 );
```

$$[a,\ 2\,b,\ 3\,c,\ 99\,d,\ 99\,e,\ 99\,f]$$

```
> zip( igcd, [7657,342,876], [34,756,213,346,123], 6! );
```

$$[1,\ 18,\ 3,\ 2,\ 3]$$

The zip command can also merge vectors. For more information, refer to the ?zip help page.

Sorting Lists

A list is a fundamental order-preserving data structure in Maple. The elements in a list remain in the order used in creating the list. You can create a copy of a list sorted in another order by using the sort command. The sort command sorts lists, among other things, in ascending order. It sorts a list of numbers in numerical order.

```
> sort( [1,3,2,4,5,3,6,3,6] );
```

$$[1, 2, 3, 3, 3, 4, 5, 6, 6]$$

The `sort` command also sorts a list of strings in lexicographic order.

```
> sort( ["Mary", "had", "a", "little", "lamb"] );
```

$$[\text{“Mary”}, \text{“a”}, \text{“had”}, \text{“lamb”}, \text{“little”}]$$

Session Dependent Machine Addresses If a list contains both numbers and strings, or expressions different from numbers and strings, `sort` uses the machine addresses, which are session dependent.

```
> sort( [x, 1, "apple"] );
```

$$[1, x, \text{“apple”}]$$

```
> sort( [-5, 10, sin(34)] );
```

$$[10, \sin(34), -5]$$

Note that to Maple, π is not numeric.

```
> sort( [4.3, Pi, 2/3] );
```

$$[\pi, \frac{2}{3}, 4.3]$$

You can specify a boolean function to define an ordering for a list. The boolean function must take two arguments and return `true` if the first argument precedes the second. You can use this to sort a list of numbers in descending order.

```
> sort( [3.12, 1, 1/2], (x,y) -> evalb( x>y ) );
```

$$[3.12, 1, \frac{1}{2}]$$

Using the `is` Command The `is` command can compare constants like π and $\sin(5)$ with pure numbers.

```
> bf := (x,y) -> is( x < y );
```

$$bf := (x,\, y) \to \mathrm{is}(x < y)$$

```
> sort( [4.3, Pi, 2/3, sin(5)], bf );
```

$$[\sin(5),\, \frac{2}{3},\, \pi,\, 4.3]$$

You can also sort strings by length.

```
> shorter := (x,y) -> evalb( length(x) < length(y) );
```

$$\mathit{shorter} := (x,\, y) \to \mathrm{evalb}(\mathrm{length}(x) < \mathrm{length}(y))$$

```
> sort( ["Mary", "has", "a", "little", "lamb"], shorter );
```

$$[\text{“a”},\, \text{“has”},\, \text{“lamb”},\, \text{“Mary”},\, \text{“little”}]$$

Sorting Mixed List of Strings and Numbers Maple does not have a built-in method for sorting lists of mixed strings and numbers, other than by machine address. To sort a mixed list of strings and numbers, you can do the following.

```
> big_list := [1,"d",3,5,2,"a","c","b",9];
```

$$\mathit{big\_list} := [1,\, \text{“d”},\, 3,\, 5,\, 2,\, \text{“a”},\, \text{“c”},\, \text{“b”},\, 9]$$

Make two lists from the original, one consisting of numbers and one consisting of strings.

```
> list1 := select( type, big_list, string );
```

$$\mathit{list1} := [\text{“d”},\, \text{“a”},\, \text{“c”},\, \text{“b”}]$$

```
> list2 := select( type, big_list, numeric );
```

$$\mathit{list2} := [1,\, 3,\, 5,\, 2,\, 9]$$

Then sort the two lists independently.

```
> list1 := sort(list1);
```

$$list1 := [\text{"a"}, \text{"b"}, \text{"c"}, \text{"d"}]$$

```
> list2 := sort(list2);
```

$$list2 := [1, 2, 3, 5, 9]$$

Finally, stack the two lists together.

```
> sorted_list := [ op(list1), op(list2) ];
```

$$sorted\_list := [\text{"a"}, \text{"b"}, \text{"c"}, \text{"d"}, 1, 2, 3, 5, 9]$$

Note: The `sort` command can also sort algebraic expressions. See **6.1 Mathematical Manipulations**.

The Parts of an Expression

To manipulate the details of an expression, you must select the individual parts. Three easy cases for doing this involve equations, ranges, and fractions.

Using the `lhs` and `rhs` Commands The `lhs` command selects the left-hand side of an equation.

```
> eq := a^2 + b^ 2 = c^2;
```

$$eq := a^2 + b^2 = c^2$$

```
> lhs( eq );
```

$$a^2 + b^2$$

The `rhs` command similarly selects the right-hand side.

```
> rhs( eq );
```

$$c^2$$

The `lhs` and `rhs` commands also work on ranges.

```
> lhs( 2..5 );
```

$$2$$

```
> rhs( 2..5 );
```

$$5$$

```
> eq := x = -2..infinity;
```

$$eq := x = -2..\infty$$

```
> lhs( eq );
```

$$x$$

```
> rhs( eq );
```

$$-2..\infty$$

```
> lhs( rhs(eq) );
```

$$-2$$

```
> rhs( rhs(eq) );
```

$$\infty$$

Using the `numer` and `demom` Commands The `numer` and `denom` commands extract the numerator and denominator, respectively, from a fraction.

```
> numer( 2/3 );
```

$$2$$

```
> denom( 2/3 );
```

$$3$$

```
> fract := ( 1+sin(x)^3-y/x) / ( y^2 - 1 + x );
```

$$fract := \frac{1 + \sin(x)^3 - \frac{y}{x}}{y^2 - 1 + x}$$

```
> numer( fract );
```

$$x + \sin(x)^3\, x - y$$

```
> denom( fract );
```

$$x\,(y^2 - 1 + x)$$

Using the `whattype`, `op`, and `nops` Commands Consider the expression

```
> expr := 3 + sin(x) + 2*cos(x)^2*sin(x);
```

$$expr := 3 + \sin(x) + 2\cos(x)^2 \sin(x)$$

The `whattype` command identifies `expr` as a sum.

```
> whattype( expr );
```

$$+$$

Use the `op` command to list the terms of a sum or, in general, the operands of an expression.

```
> op( expr );
```

$$3,\ \sin(x),\ 2\cos(x)^2 \sin(x)$$

The expression `expr` consists of three terms. Use the `nops` command to count the number of operands in an expression.

```
> nops( expr );
```

$$3$$

You can select, for example, the third term as follows.

```
> term3 := op(3, expr);
```

$$term3 := 2\cos(x)^2 \sin(x)$$

The expression **term3** is a product of three factors.

```
> whattype( term3 );
```

$$*$$

```
> nops( term3 );
```

$$3$$

```
> op( term3 );
```

$$2, \cos(x)^2, \sin(x)$$

Retrieve the second factor in **term3** in the following manner.

```
> factor2 := op(2, term3);
```

$$factor2 := \cos(x)^2$$

It is an exponentiation.

```
> whattype( factor2 );
```

$$\hat{}$$

The expression **factor2** has two operands.

```
> op( factor2 );
```

$$\cos(x), 2$$

The first operand is a function and has only one operand.

```
> op1 := op(1, factor2);
```

$$op1 := \cos(x)$$

```
> whattype( op1 );
```

$$function$$

```
> op( op1 );
```

$$x$$

The name `x` is a symbol.

```
> whattype( op(op1) );
```

$$symbol$$

Since you did not assign a value to x, it has only one operand, namely itself.

```
> nops( x );
```

$$1$$

```
> op( x );
```

$$x$$

You can represent the result of finding the operands of the operands of an expression as a picture called an *expression tree*. The following is an expression tree for `expr`.

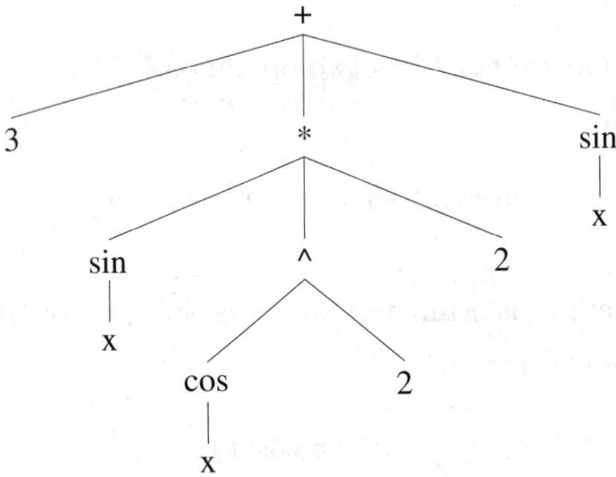

The operands of a list or set are the elements.

```
> op( [a,b,c] );
```

$$a, b, c$$

```
> op( {d,e,f} );
```

$$e, d, f$$

This section (page 180) describes how the `map` command applies a function to all the elements of a list or set. The functionality of `map` extends to general expressions.

```
> map( f, x^2 );
```

$$\mathrm{f}(x)^{\mathrm{f}(2)}$$

The `select` and `remove` commands, described in this section (pages 182–184) also work on general expressions.

```
> large := z -> evalb( is(z>3) = true );
```

$$large := z \to \mathrm{evalb}(\mathrm{is}(3 < z) = true)$$

```
> remove( large, 5+8*sin(x) - exp(9) );
```

$$8\sin(x) - e^9$$

Maple has many commands that can be used as the boolean function in a call to `select` or `remove`. The `has` command determines whether an expression contains a certain subexpression.

```
> has( x*exp(cos(t^2)), t^2 );
```

$$true$$

```
> has( x*exp(cos(t^2)), cos );
```

$$true$$

Some of the solutions to the following set of equations contain `RootOf`s.

```
> sol := { solve( { x^2*y^2 = b*y, x^2-y^2 = a*x },
>                 {x,y} ) };
```

$$sol := \{\{y = 0,\, x = 0\},\, \{y = 0,\, x = a\}, \{ \\ x = \mathrm{RootOf}(\_Z^6 - b^2 - a\,\_Z^5), \\ y = \frac{b}{\mathrm{RootOf}(\_Z^6 - b^2 - a\,\_Z^5)^2}\}\}$$

To select solutions, use `select` and `has`.

```
> select( has, sol, RootOf );
```

$$\{\{x = \mathrm{RootOf}(\_Z^6 - b^2 - a\,\_Z^5), \\ y = \frac{b}{\mathrm{RootOf}(\_Z^6 - b^2 - a\,\_Z^5)^2}\}\}$$

You can also select or remove subexpressions by type. The `type` command determines if an expression is of a certain type.

```
> type( 3+x, `+` );
```

$$true$$

In this example, the `select` command passes its third argument, `` `+` ``, to `type`.

```
> expr := ( 3+x ) * x^2 * sin( 1+sqrt(Pi) );
```

$$expr := (3 + x)\, x^2 \sin(1 + \sqrt{\pi})$$

```
> select( type, expr, `+` );
```

$$3 + x$$

The `hastype` command determines if an expression contains a subexpression of a certain type.

```
> hastype( sin( 1+sqrt(Pi) ), `+` );
```

$$true$$

Use the combination `select(hastype,...)` to select the operands of an expression that contain a certain type.

```
> select( hastype, expr, '+' );
```

$$(3+x)\sin(1+\sqrt{\pi})$$

To find the subexpressions of a certain type rather than the operands that contain them, use the `indets` command.

```
> indets( expr, '+' );
```

$$\{3+x,\, 1+\sqrt{\pi}\}$$

The two `RootOf`s in `sol` above are of type `RootOf`. Since the two `RootOf`s are identical, the set that `indets` returns contains only one element.

```
> indets( sol, RootOf );
```

$$\{\mathrm{RootOf}(\_Z^6 - b^2 - a\,\_Z^5)\}$$

Not all commands are their own type, as is `RootOf`, but you can use the structured type `specfunc(`*`type`*`, `*`name`*`)`. This type matches the function *name* with arguments of type *type*.

```
> type( diff(y(x), x), specfunc(anything, diff) );
```

$$true$$

You can use this to find all the derivatives in a large differential equation.

```
> DE := expand( diff( cos(y(t)+t)*sin(t*z(t)), t ) )
>     + diff(x(t), t);
```

$$DE := -\sin(t\,z(t))\sin(y(t))\cos(t)\left(\tfrac{d}{dt}y(t)\right)$$
$$-\sin(t\,z(t))\sin(y(t))\cos(t)$$
$$-\sin(t\,z(t))\cos(y(t))\sin(t)\left(\tfrac{d}{dt}y(t)\right)$$
$$-\sin(t\,z(t))\cos(y(t))\sin(t)+\cos(t\,z(t))\cos(y(t))\cos(t)\,z(t)$$
$$+\cos(t\,z(t))\cos(y(t))\cos(t)\,t\left(\tfrac{d}{dt}z(t)\right)$$
$$-\cos(t\,z(t))\sin(y(t))\sin(t)\,z(t)$$
$$-\cos(t\,z(t))\sin(y(t))\sin(t)\,t\left(\tfrac{d}{dt}z(t)\right)+\left(\tfrac{d}{dt}x(t)\right)$$

```
> indets( DE, specfunc(anything, diff) );
```

$$\{\frac{d}{dt}x(t),\ \frac{d}{dt}y(t),\ \frac{d}{dt}z(t)\}$$

The following operands of `DE` contain the derivatives.

```
> select( hastype, DE, specfunc(anything, diff) );
```

$$-\sin(t\,z(t))\sin(y(t))\cos(t)\left(\tfrac{d}{dt}y(t)\right)$$
$$-\sin(t\,z(t))\cos(y(t))\sin(t)\left(\tfrac{d}{dt}y(t)\right)$$
$$+\cos(t\,z(t))\cos(y(t))\cos(t)\,t\left(\tfrac{d}{dt}z(t)\right)$$
$$-\cos(t\,z(t))\sin(y(t))\sin(t)\,t\left(\tfrac{d}{dt}z(t)\right)+\left(\tfrac{d}{dt}x(t)\right)$$

`DE` has only one operand that is itself a derivative.

```
> select( type, DE, specfunc(anything, diff) );
```

$$\frac{d}{dt}x(t)$$

Maple recognizes many types. For a list, refer to the `?type` help page. For more information on structured types, such as `specfunc`, refer to the `?type,structured` help page.

Substitution

Often you want to substitute a value for a variable (that is, evaluate an expression at a point). For example, if you need to solve the problem, "If $f(x) = \ln(\sin(xe^{\cos(x)}))$, find $f'(2)$," then you must substitute the value 2 for x in the derivative. The `diff` command finds the derivative.

```
> y := ln( sin( x * exp(cos(x)) ) );
```

$$y := \ln(\sin(x\, e^{\cos(x)}))$$

```
> yprime := diff( y, x );
```

$$yprime := \frac{\cos(x\, e^{\cos(x)})\,(e^{\cos(x)} - x\sin(x)\, e^{\cos(x)})}{\sin(x\, e^{\cos(x)})}$$

Use the `eval` command to substitute a value for `x` in `yprime`.

```
> eval( yprime, x=2 );
```

$$\frac{\cos(2\, e^{\cos(2)})\,(e^{\cos(2)} - 2\sin(2)\, e^{\cos(2)})}{\sin(2\, e^{\cos(2)})}$$

The `evalf` command returns a floating-point approximation of the result.

```
> evalf( % );
```

$$-0.1388047428$$

The command makes syntactical substitutions, not mathematical substitutions. This means that you can make substitutions for any subexpression.

```
> subs( cos(x)=3, yprime );
```

$$\frac{\cos(x\, e^3)\,(e^3 - x\sin(x)\, e^3)}{\sin(x\, e^3)}$$

But you are limited to subexpressions as Maple identifies them.

```
> expr := a * b * c * a^b;
```

$$expr := a\, b\, c\, a^b$$

```
> subs( a*b=3, expr );
```

$$a\, b\, c\, a^b$$

The expr expression is a product of four factors.

```
> op( expr );
```

$$a,\ b,\ c,\ a^b$$

The product a*b is not a factor in expr. You can make the substitution a*b=3 in three ways: solve the subexpression for one of the variables,

```
> subs( a=3/b, expr );
```

$$3\,c\,(\frac{3}{b})^b$$

use a side relation to simplify,

```
> simplify( expr, { a*b=3 } );
```

$$3\,c\,a^b$$

or use the algsubs command, which performs algebraic substitutions.

```
> algsubs( a*b=3, expr);
```

$$3\,c\,a^b$$

Note that in the first case all occurrences of a have been replaced by 3/b. Whereas, in the second and third cases both variables a and b remain in the result.

You can make several substitutions with one call to subs.

```
> expr := z * sin( x^2 ) + w;
```

$$expr := z\sin(x^2) + w$$

```
> subs( x=sqrt(z), w=Pi, expr );
```

$$z\sin(z) + \pi$$

The subs command makes the substitutions from left to right.

```
> subs( z=x, x=sqrt(z), expr );
```

$$\sqrt{z}\sin(z) + w$$

If you give a set or list of substitutions, **subs** makes those substitutions simultaneously.

```
> subs( { x=sqrt(Pi), z=3 }, expr );
```

$$3\sin(\pi) + w$$

Note that in general you must explicitly evaluate the result of a call to subs.

```
> eval( % );
```

$$w$$

Use the **subsop** command to substitute for a specific operand of an expression.

```
> expr := 5^x;
```

$$expr := 5^x$$

```
> op( expr );
```

$$5, x$$

```
> subsop( 1=t, expr );
```

$$t^x$$

The zeroth operand of a function is typically the name of the function.

```
> expr := cos(x);
```

$$expr := \cos(x)$$

```
> subsop( 0=sin, expr );
```

$$\sin(x)$$

For information about the operands of an expression, see this section, pages 188–193.

Changing the Type of an Expression

To convert an expression to another type, use the convert command. Consider the Taylor series for $\sin(x)$.

```
> f := sin(x);
```

$$f := \sin(x)$$

```
> t := taylor( f, x=0 );
```

$$t := x - \frac{1}{6}x^3 + \frac{1}{120}x^5 + \mathrm{O}(x^6)$$

For example, you cannot plot a series, you must use convert(..., polynom) to convert it into a polynomial approximation first.

```
> p := convert( t, polynom );
```

$$p := x - \frac{1}{6}x^3 + \frac{1}{120}x^5$$

Similarly, the title of a plot must be a string, not a general expression. You can use convert(..., string) to convert an expression to a string.

```
> p_txt := convert( p, string );
```

$$p\_txt := \text{"x-1/6*x^3+1/120*x^ 5"}$$

```
> plot( p, x=-4..4, title=p_txt );
```

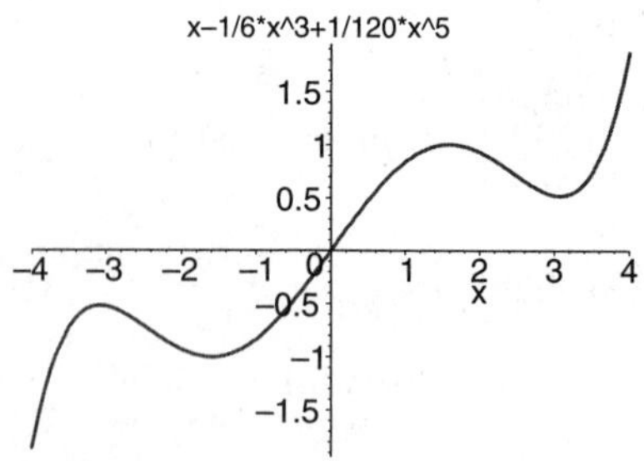

The `cat` command concatenates all its arguments to create a new string.

```
> ttl := cat( convert( f, string ),
>             " and its Taylor approximation ",
>             p_txt );
```

ttl := "sin(x) and its Taylor approximation x-1/6*x^\
3+1/120*x^5"

```
> plot( [f, p], x=-4..4, title=ttl );
```

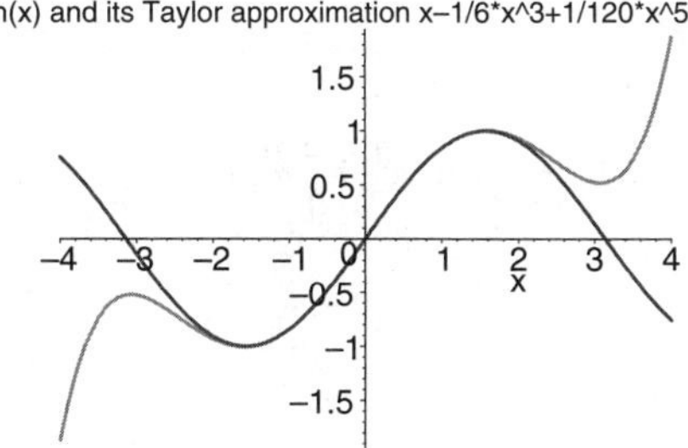

You can also convert a list to a set or a set to a list.

```
> L := [1,2,5,2,1];
```

$$L := [1, 2, 5, 2, 1]$$

```
> S := convert( L, set );
```

$$S := \{1, 2, 5\}$$

```
> convert( S, list );
```

$$[1, 2, 5]$$

The `convert` command can perform many other structural and mathematical conversions. For more information, refer to the `?convert` help page.

6.4 Evaluation Rules

In a symbolic mathematics program such as Maple you encounter the issue of *evaluation*. If you assign the value `y` to `x`, the value `z` to `y`, and the value 5 to `z`, then to what should `x` evaluate?

Levels of Evaluation

Maple, in most cases, does full evaluation of names. That is, when you use a name or symbol, Maple checks if the name or symbol has an assigned value. If it has a value, Maple substitutes the value for the name. If this value itself has an assigned value, Maple performs a substitution again, and so on, recursively, until no more substitutions are possible.

```
> x := y;
```

$$x := y$$

```
> y := z;
```

$$y := z$$

```
> z := 5;
```

$$z := 5$$

Maple evaluates `x` fully. That is, Maple substitutes `y` for `x`, `z` for `y`, and then 5 for `z`.

```
> x;
```

$$5$$

You can use the `eval` command to control the level of evaluation of an expression. If you call `eval` with one argument, then `eval` evaluates that argument fully.

```
> eval(x);
```

$$5$$

A second argument to `eval` specifies how far you want to evaluate the first argument.

```
> eval(x, 1);
```

$$y$$

```
> eval(x, 2);
```

$$z$$

```
> eval(x, 3);
```

$$5$$

The main exceptions to the rule of full evaluation are special data structures like tables, matrices, and procedures, and the behavior of local variables inside a procedure.

Last-Name Evaluation

The data structures `array`, `table`, `matrix`, and `proc` have a special evaluation behavior called *last-name evaluation*.

```
> x := y;
```

$$x := y$$

```
> y := z;
```

$$y := z$$

```
> z := array( [ [1,2], [3,4] ] );
```

$$z := \begin{bmatrix} 1 & 2 \\ 3 & 4 \end{bmatrix}$$

Maple substitutes `y` for `x` and `z` for `y`. Because evaluation of the last name, `z`, produces an array, one of the four special structures, `z` is unevaluated.

```
> x;
```

$$z$$

Maple uses last-name evaluation for arrays, tables, matrices, and procedures to retain compact representations of unassigned table entries (for example, T[3]) and unevaluated commands (for example, sin(x)). For more information on last-name evaluation, refer to the ?last_name_eval help page. You can force full evaluation by calling eval explicitly.

```
> eval(x);
```

$$\begin{bmatrix} 1 & 2 \\ 3 & 4 \end{bmatrix}$$

```
> add2 := proc(x,y) x+y; end proc;
```

$$add2 := \textbf{proc}(x,\ y)\ x + y\,\textbf{end proc}$$

```
> add2;
```

$$add2$$

You can force full evaluation by using eval or print.

```
> eval(add2);
```

$$\textbf{proc}(x,\ y)\ x + y\,\textbf{end proc}$$

Note that full evaluation of Maple library procedures, by default, suppresses the code in the procedure. To illustrate this, examine the erfi command.

```
> erfi;
```

$$\mathit{erfi}$$

```
> eval(erfi);
```

$$\textbf{proc}(x{::}algebraic)\ \ldots\ \textbf{end proc}$$

Set the interface variable verboseproc to 2, and then try again.

```
> interface( verboseproc=2 );
> eval(erfi);
```

```
proc(x::algebraic)
optionsystem,‘Copyright (c) 1996 Waterloo Maple\
 Inc. All rights reserved.‘;
   try return _Remember('procname'(args))
   catch :
   end try;
   if nargs ≠ 1 then
      error “expecting 1 argument, got %1”, nargs
   elif type(x, 'complex(float)') then evalf('erfi'(x))
   elif type(x, '∞') then
      if type(x, 'cx_infinity') then undefined + undefined * I
      elif type(x, 'undefined') then
         NumericTools : − ThrowUndefined(x)
      elif type(x, 'extended_numeric') then x
      elif type(ℜ(x), '∞') then ∞ + ∞ * I
      else CopySign(I, ℑ(x))
      end if
   elif type(x, 'undefined') then
      NumericTools : − ThrowUndefined(x, 'preserve' = 'axes')
   elif type(x, ‘ * ‘) and member(I, {op(x)}) then erf(−I * x) * I
   elif type(x, 'complex(numeric)') and csgn(x) < 0 then
      − erfi(−x)
   eliftype(x, ‘ * ‘) and type(op(1, x), 'complex(numeric)')
    and csgn(op(1, x)) < 0then − erfi(−x)
   elif type(x, ‘ + ‘) and traperror(sign(x)) = −1 then − erfi(−x)
   else 'erfi'(x)
   end if
end proc
```

The default value of `verboseproc` is 1.

```
> interface( verboseproc=1 );
```

The `?interface` help page explains the possible settings of `verboseproc` and the other `interface` variables.

One-Level Evaluation

Local variables of a procedure use one-level evaluation. That is, if you assign a local variable, then the result of evaluation is the value most recently assigned directly to that variable.

```
> test:=proc()
>     local x, y, z;
>     x := y;
>     y := z;
>     z := 5;
>     x;
> end proc:
> test();
```

$$y$$

Compare this evaluation with the similar interactive example in this section on page 202. Full evaluation within a procedure is rarely necessary and can lead to inefficiency. If you require full evaluation within a procedure, use `eval`.

Commands with Special Evaluation Rules

The `assigned` and `evaln` Commands The functions `assigned` and `evaln` evaluate their arguments only to the level at which they become names.

```
> x := y;
```

$$x := y$$

```
> y := z;
```

$$y := z$$

```
> evaln(x);
```

$$x$$

The `assigned` command checks if a name has a value assigned to it.

```
> assigned( x );
```

$$true$$

$$
\begin{array}{l}
\textbf{proc}(x{::}\mathit{algebraic}) \\
\textbf{option}\mathit{system}, \text{`}\mathit{Copyright\ (c)\ 1996\ Waterloo\ Maple}\backslash \\
\ \mathit{Inc.\ All\ rights\ reserved.}\text{`}; \\
\quad \textbf{try}\,\textbf{return}\ \_\text{Remember}(\text{'procname'}(\text{args})) \\
\quad \textbf{catch}: \\
\quad \textbf{end try}; \\
\quad \textbf{if}\,\text{nargs} \neq 1\,\textbf{then} \\
\qquad \textbf{error}\ \text{“expecting 1 argument, got }\%1\text{”, nargs} \\
\quad \textbf{elif}\,\text{type}(x, \text{'complex}(\mathit{float})\text{'})\,\textbf{then}\,\text{evalf}(\text{'}\mathit{erfi}\text{'}(x)) \\
\quad \textbf{elif}\,\text{type}(x, \text{'}\infty\text{'})\,\textbf{then} \\
\qquad \textbf{if}\,\text{type}(x, \text{'}\mathit{cx\_infinity}\text{'})\,\textbf{then}\,\mathit{undefined} + \mathit{undefined} * I \\
\qquad \textbf{elif}\,\text{type}(x, \text{'}\mathit{undefined}\text{'})\,\textbf{then} \\
\qquad\quad \mathit{NumericTools} : -\mathit{ThrowUndefined}(x) \\
\qquad \textbf{elif}\,\text{type}(x, \text{'}\mathit{extended\_numeric}\text{'})\,\textbf{then}\,x \\
\qquad \textbf{elif}\,\text{type}(\Re(x), \text{'}\infty\text{'})\,\textbf{then}\,\infty + \infty * I \\
\qquad \textbf{else}\,\text{CopySign}(I, \Im(x)) \\
\qquad \textbf{end if} \\
\quad \textbf{elif}\,\text{type}(x, \text{'}\mathit{undefined}\text{'})\,\textbf{then} \\
\qquad \mathit{NumericTools} : -\mathit{ThrowUndefined}(x, \text{'}\mathit{preserve}\text{'} = \text{'}\mathit{axes}\text{'}) \\
\quad \textbf{elif}\,\text{type}(x, \text{`}*\text{`})\ \textbf{and}\ \text{member}(I, \{\text{op}(x)\})\,\textbf{then}\,\text{erf}(-I * x) * I \\
\quad \textbf{elif}\,\text{type}(x, \text{'complex}(\mathit{numeric})\text{'})\ \textbf{and}\ \text{csgn}(x) < 0\,\textbf{then} \\
\qquad -\text{erfi}(-x) \\
\quad \textbf{elif}\text{type}(x, \text{`}*\text{`})\ \textbf{and}\ \text{type}(\text{op}(1, x), \text{'complex}(\mathit{numeric})\text{'}) \\
\quad\ \textbf{and}\ \text{csgn}(\text{op}(1, x)) < 0\textbf{then}\ -\text{erfi}(-x) \\
\quad \textbf{elif}\,\text{type}(x, \text{`}+\text{`})\ \textbf{and}\ \text{traperror}(\text{sign}(x)) = -1\ \textbf{then}\ -\text{erfi}(-x) \\
\quad \textbf{else}\,\text{'}\mathit{erfi}\text{'}(x) \\
\quad \textbf{end if} \\
\textbf{end proc}
\end{array}
$$

The default value of `verboseproc` is 1.

```
> interface( verboseproc=1 );
```

The `?interface` help page explains the possible settings of `verboseproc` and the other `interface` variables.

One-Level Evaluation

Local variables of a procedure use one-level evaluation. That is, if you assign a local variable, then the result of evaluation is the value most recently assigned directly to that variable.

```
> test:=proc()
>    local x, y, z;
>       x := y;
>       y := z;
>       z := 5;
>       x;
> end proc:
> test();
```

$$y$$

Compare this evaluation with the similar interactive example in this section on page 202. Full evaluation within a procedure is rarely necessary and can lead to inefficiency. If you require full evaluation within a procedure, use `eval`.

Commands with Special Evaluation Rules

The `assigned` and `evaln` Commands The functions `assigned` and `evaln` evaluate their arguments only to the level at which they become names.

```
> x := y;
```

$$x := y$$

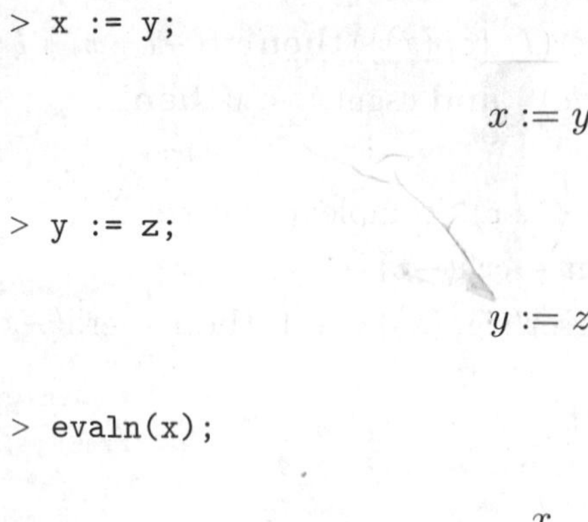

```
> y := z;
```

$$y := z$$

```
> evaln(x);
```

$$x$$

The `assigned` command checks if a name has a value assigned to it.

```
> assigned( x );
```

$$true$$

The seq Command The seq command for creating expression sequences does not evaluate its arguments. Therefore, seq can use a variable with an assigned value as a counting variable.

```
> i := 2;
```

$$i := 2$$

```
> seq( i^2, i=1..5 );
```

$$1, 4, 9, 16, 25$$

```
> i;
```

$$2$$

Contrast this with the behavior of sum.

```
> sum( i^2, i=1..5 );
Error, (in sum) summation variable previously assigned,
second argument evaluates to 2 = 1 .. 5
```

You can solve this problem by using right single quotes, as shown in the next section.

Quotation and Unevaluation

The Maple language supports the use of quotes to delay evaluation one level. Surrounding a name in right single quotes (') prevents Maple from evaluating the name. Hence, right single quotes are referred to as *unevaluation quotes.*

```
> i := 4;
```

$$i := 4$$

```
> i;
```

$$4$$

```
> 'i';
```

$$i$$

Use this method to avoid the following problem.

```
> i;
```

$$4$$

```
> sum( i^2, i=1..5 );
```

```
Error, (in sum) summation variable previously assigned,
second argument evaluates to 4 = 1 .. 5
```

```
> sum( 'i^2', 'i'=1..5 );
```

$$55$$

```
> i;
```

$$4$$

Full evaluation of a quoted expression removes one level of quotes.

```
> x := 0;
```

$$x := 0$$

```
> '''x'+1'';
```

$$''x' + 1'$$

```
> %;
```

$$'x' + 1$$

```
> %;
```

$$x + 1$$

```
> %;
```

$$1$$

Important: Quoting an expression delays evaluation, but does not prevent automatic simplifications and arithmetic.

```
> '1-1';
```

$$0$$

```
> 'p+q-i-p+3*q';
```

$$4\,q - i$$

If you enclose a simple variable in right single quotes, the result is the name of the variable. You can use this method to unassign a variable.

```
> x := 1;
```

$$x := 1$$

```
> x;
```

$$1$$

```
> x := 'x';
```

$$x := x$$

```
> x;
```

$$x$$

However, in general, you must use `evaln`.

```
> i := 4;
```

$$i := 4$$

```
> a[i] := 9;
```

$$a_4 := 9$$

Note that 'a[i]' is a[i] not a[4].

```
> 'a[i]';
```

$$a_i$$

You must use evaln to unassign a[i].

```
> evaln( a[i] );
```

$$a_4$$

```
> a[i] := evaln( a[i] );
```

$$a_4 := a_4$$

Using Quoted Variables as Function Arguments

Some Maple commands use names as a way to return information in addition to the standard return value. The divide command assigns the quotient to the global name, q.

```
> divide( x^2-1, x-1, 'q' );
```

$$true$$

```
> q;
```

$$x + 1$$

Use a quoted name to ensure that you are not passing a variable with an assigned value into the procedure. You can avoid the need for quotes if you ensure that the name you use has no previously assigned value.

```
> q := 2;
```

$$q := 2$$

```
> divide( x^2-y^2, x-y, q );
Error, wrong number (or type) of parameters in function
divide
```

```
> q := evaln(q);
```

$$q := q$$

```
> divide( x^2-y^2, x-y, q );
```

$$true$$

```
> q;
```

$$x + y$$

Note: The `rem`, `quo`, `irem`, and `iquo` commands behave in a similar manner.

Concatenation of Names

Concatenation is a way to form new variable names based on others.

```
> a||b;
```

$$ab$$

The concatenation operator, "||", in a name causes evaluation of the right-hand side of the operator, but not the left.

```
> a := x;
```

$$a := x$$

```
> b := 2;
```

$$b := 2$$

```
> a||b;
```

$$a2$$

```
> c := 3;
```

$$c := 3$$

```
> a||b||c;
```

$$a23$$

If a name does not evaluate to a single symbol, Maple does not evaluate a concatenation.

```
> a := x;
```

$$a := x$$

```
> b := y+1;
```

$$b := y + 1$$

```
> new_name := a||b;
```

$$new\_name := a||(y + 1)$$

```
> y := 3;
```

$$y := 3$$

```
> new_name;
```

$$a4$$

You can use concatenated names to assign and create expressions.

```
> i := 1;
```

$$i := 1$$

```
> b||i := 0;
```

$$b1 := 0$$

You must use right single quotes.

```
> sum( 'a||k' * x^k, k=0..8 );
```

$$a0 + a1\,x + a2\,x^2 + a3\,x^3 + a4\,x^4 + a5\,x^5 + a6\,x^6 + a7\,x^7 + a8\,x^8$$

If you do not use right single quotes, Maple evaluates `a||k` to `ak`.

```
> sum( a||k * x^k, k=0..8 );
```

$$ak + ak\,x + ak\,x^2 + ak\,x^3 + ak\,x^4 + ak\,x^5 + ak\,x^6 + ak\,x^7 + ak\,x^8$$

You can also use concatenation to form title strings for plots.

6.5 Conclusion

In this chapter, you have seen how to perform many kinds of expression manipulations, from adding two equations to selecting individual parts of a general expression. In general, no rule specifies which form of an expression is the simplest. The commands in this chapter allow you to convert an expression to many forms, often the ones *you* would consider simplest. If not, you can use side relations to specify your own simplification rules, or assumptions to specify properties of unknowns.

You have also seen that Maple, in most cases, uses full evaluation of variables. Some exceptions exist, which include last-name evaluation for certain data structures, one-level evaluation for local variables in a procedure, and delayed evaluation for names in right single quotes.

7 Solving Calculus Problems

This chapter provides examples of how Maple can help you present and solve problems from calculus.

In This Chapter

- Introductory Calculus
- Ordinary Differential Equations
- Partial Differential Equations

7.1 Introductory Calculus

This section contains examples of how to illustrate ideas and solve problems from calculus. The `Student[Calculus1]` package contains many commands that are especially useful in this area.

The Derivative

This section illustrates the graphical meaning of the derivative: the slope of the tangent line. Then it shows you how to find the set of inflection points for a function.

Define the function $f\colon x \mapsto \exp(\sin(x))$ in the following manner.

```
> f := x -> exp( sin(x) );
```

$$f := x \to e^{\sin(x)}$$

Find the derivative of f evaluated at $x_0 = 1$.

```
> x0 := 1;
```

$$x0 := 1$$

p_0 and p_1 are two points on the graph of f.

```
> p0 := [ x0, f(x0) ];
```

$$p0 := [1, e^{\sin(1)}]$$

```
> p1 := [ x0+h, f(x0+h) ];
```

$$p1 := [1 + h, e^{\sin(1+h)}]$$

The NewtonQuotient command from the Student[Calculus] package finds the slope of the secant line through p_0 and p_1.

```
> with(Student[Calculus1]):
```

Use NewtonQuotient command to find the expression for the slope.

```
> m := NewtonQuotient(f(x), x=x0, h=h);
```

$$m := \frac{e^{\sin(1+h)} - e^{\sin(1)}}{h}$$

If $h = 1$, the slope is

```
> eval(%, h=1);
```

$$e^{\sin(2)} - e^{\sin(1)}$$

The evalf command gives a floating-point approximation.

```
> evalf( % );
```

$$0.162800903$$

As h tends to zero, the secant slope values seem to converge.

```
> slopes := seq( NewtonQuotient( f(x), x=1.0, h=1.0/10^i ),
>               i=0..5);
```

$$slopes := 0.1628009030, 1.182946800, 1.246939100,$$
$$1.252742000, 1.253310000, 1.253300000$$

The following is the equation of the secant line.

```
> y - p0[2] = m * ( x - p0[1] );
```

$$y - e^{\sin(1)} = \frac{\left(e^{\sin(1+h)} - e^{\sin(1)}\right)(x-1)}{h}$$

The `isolate` command converts the equation to slope–intercept form.

```
> isolate( %, y );
```

$$y = \frac{\left(e^{\sin(1+h)} - e^{\sin(1)}\right)(x-1)}{h} + e^{\sin(1)}$$

You must convert the equation to a function.

```
> secant := unapply( rhs(%), x );
```

$$secant := x \to \frac{\left(e^{\sin(1+h)} - e^{\sin(1)}\right)(x-1)}{h} + e^{\sin(1)}$$

You can now plot the secant and the function for different values of h. First, make a sequence of plots.

```
> S := seq( plot( [f(x), secant(x)], x=0..4,
>                 view=[0..4, 0..4] ),
>           h=[1.0, 0.1, .01, .001, .0001, .00001] ):
```

The `display` command from the `plots` package can display the plots in sequence, that is, as an animation.

```
> with(plots):
```

```
Warning, the name changecoords has been redefined
```

```
> display( S, insequence=true, view=[0..4, 0..4] );
```

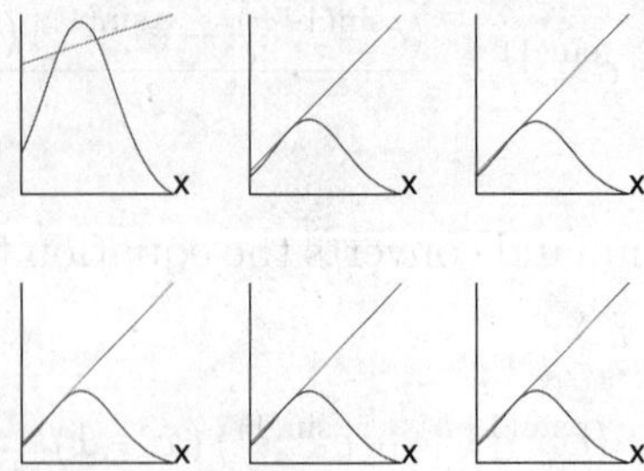

In the limit as h tends to zero, the slope is

```
> Limit( m, h=0 );
```

$$\lim_{h \to 0} \frac{e^{\sin(1+h)} - e^{\sin(1)}}{h}$$

The value of this limit is

```
> value( % );
```

$$e^{\sin(1)} \cos(1)$$

This answer is, of course, the value of $f'(x0)$. To see this, first define the function $f1$ to be the first derivative of f. Since f is a function, use D.

Important: The D operator computes derivatives of functions, while **diff** computes derivatives of expressions. For more information, refer to the **?operators,D** help page.

```
> f1 := D(f);
```

$$f1 := x \to \cos(x)\, e^{\sin(x)}$$

As expected, $f1(x0)$ equals the previous limit.

```
> f1(x0);
```

$$e^{\sin(1)} \cos(1)$$

In this case, the second derivative exists.

```
> diff( f(x), x, x );
```

$$-\sin(x)\, e^{\sin(x)} + \cos(x)^2\, e^{\sin(x)}$$

Define the function $f2$ to be the second derivative of f.

```
> f2 := unapply( %, x );
```

$$f2 := x \to -\sin(x)\, e^{\sin(x)} + \cos(x)^2\, e^{\sin(x)}$$

When you plot f and its first and second derivatives, f is increasing whenever $f1$ is positive, and f is concave down whenever $f2$ is negative.

```
> plot( [f(x), f1(x), f2(x)], x=0..10 );
```

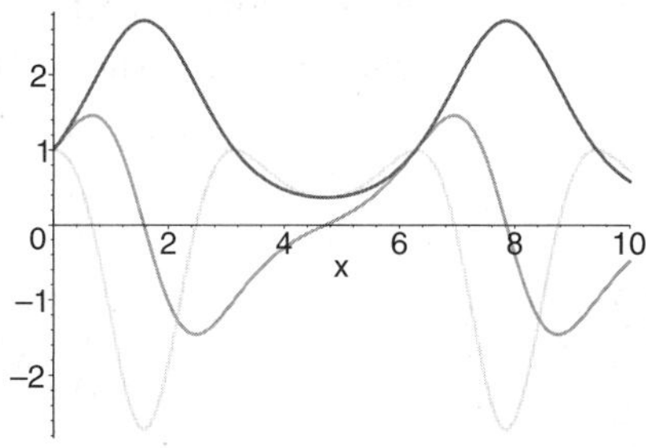

The graph of f has an inflection point where the second derivative changes sign, and the second derivative can change sign at the values of x where $f2(x)$ is zero.

```
> sol := { solve( f2(x)=0, x ) };
```

$$sol := \left\{\arctan\left(2\,\frac{\frac{1}{2}\sqrt{5}-\frac{1}{2}}{\sqrt{-2+2\sqrt{5}}}\right), -\arctan\left(2\,\frac{\frac{1}{2}\sqrt{5}-\frac{1}{2}}{\sqrt{-2+2\sqrt{5}}}\right)+\pi,\right.$$
$$\arctan(-\frac{1}{2}\sqrt{5}-\frac{1}{2}, \frac{1}{2}\sqrt{-2-2\sqrt{5}}),$$
$$\left.\arctan(-\frac{1}{2}\sqrt{5}-\frac{1}{2}, -\frac{1}{2}\sqrt{-2-2\sqrt{5}})\right\}$$

Two of these solutions are complex.

```
> evalf( sol );
```

$$\{0.6662394321, 2.475353222,$$
$$-1.570796327 + 1.061275064\,I,$$
$$-1.570796327 - 1.061275064\,I\}$$

In this example, only the real solutions are of interest. Use the `select` command to select the real constants from the solution set.

```
> infl := select( type, sol, realcons );
```

$$\mathit{infl} := \left\{\arctan\left(2\,\frac{\frac{1}{2}\sqrt{5}-\frac{1}{2}}{\sqrt{-2+2\sqrt{5}}}\right), -\arctan\left(2\,\frac{\frac{1}{2}\sqrt{5}-\frac{1}{2}}{\sqrt{-2+2\sqrt{5}}}\right)+\pi\right\}$$

```
> evalf( infl );
```

$$\{0.6662394321, 2.475353222\}$$

Observe that $f2$ actually does change sign at these x-values. The set of inflection points is given by the following.

```
> { seq( [x, f(x)], x=infl ) };
```

$$\left\{\left[\arctan\left(2\,\frac{\frac{1}{2}\sqrt{5}-\frac{1}{2}}{\sqrt{-2+2\sqrt{5}}}\right),\ e^{\left(2\,\frac{1/2\sqrt{5}-1/2}{\sqrt{-2+2\sqrt{5}}\sqrt{1+4\,\frac{(1/2\sqrt{5}-1/2)^2}{-2+2\sqrt{5}}}}\right)}\right],\right.$$

$$\left.\left[-\arctan\left(2\,\frac{\frac{1}{2}\sqrt{5}-\frac{1}{2}}{\sqrt{-2+2\sqrt{5}}}\right)+\pi,\ e^{\left(2\,\frac{1/2\sqrt{5}-1/2}{\sqrt{-2+2\sqrt{5}}\sqrt{1+4\,\frac{(1/2\sqrt{5}-1/2)^2}{-2+2\sqrt{5}}}}\right)}\right]\right\}$$

```
> evalf( % );
```

$$\{[0.6662394321,\ 1.855276958],$$
$$[2.475353222,\ 1.855276958]\}$$

Since f is periodic, it has, of course, infinitely many inflection points. You can obtain these by shifting the two inflection points above horizontally by integer multiples of 2π.

A Taylor Approximation

This section illustrates how you can use Maple to analyze the error term in a Taylor approximation. The following is Taylor's formula.

```
> taylor( f(x), x=a );
```

$$\mathrm{f}(a)+\mathrm{D}(f)(a)\,(x-a)+\frac{1}{2}\,(\mathrm{D}^{(2)})(f)(a)\,(x-a)^2+\frac{1}{6}\,(\mathrm{D}^{(3)})(f)(a)$$
$$(x-a)^3+\frac{1}{24}\,(\mathrm{D}^{(4)})(f)(a)\,(x-a)^4+\frac{1}{120}\,(\mathrm{D}^{(5)})(f)(a)\,(x-a)^5+$$
$$\mathrm{O}((x-a)^6)$$

You can use it to find a polynomial approximation of a function f near $x = a$.

```
> f := x -> exp( sin(x) );
```

$$f := x \to e^{\sin(x)}$$

```
> a := Pi;
```

$$a := \pi$$

```
> taylor( f(x), x=a );
```

$$1 - (x - \pi) + \frac{1}{2}(x - \pi)^2 - \frac{1}{8}(x - \pi)^4 + \frac{1}{15}(x - \pi)^5 + \mathrm{O}((x - \pi)^6)$$

Before you can plot the Taylor approximation, you must convert it from a series to a polynomial.

```
> poly := convert( %, polynom );
```

$$poly := 1 - x + \pi + \frac{1}{2}(x - \pi)^2 - \frac{1}{8}(x - \pi)^4 + \frac{1}{15}(x - \pi)^5$$

Plot the function f along with poly.

```
> plot( [f(x), poly], x=0..10, view=[0..10, 0..3] );
```

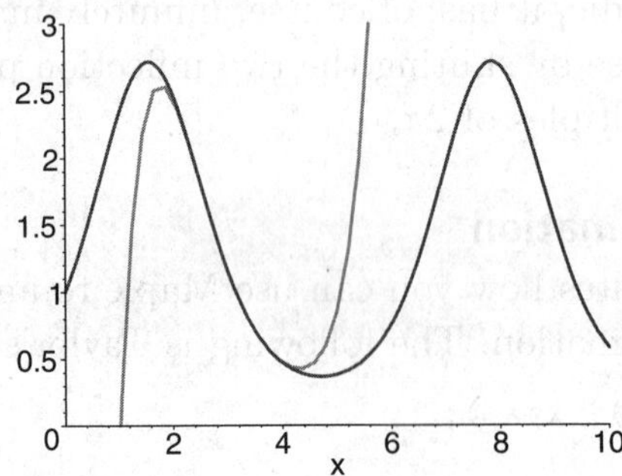

The expression $(1/6!)f^{(6)}(\xi)(x-a)^6$ gives the error of the approximation, where ξ is some number between x and a. The sixth derivative of f is

```
> diff( f(x), x$6 );
```

$$-\sin(x)\, e^{\sin(x)} + 16\cos(x)^2\, e^{\sin(x)} - 15\sin(x)^2\, e^{\sin(x)}$$
$$+ 75\sin(x)\cos(x)^2\, e^{\sin(x)} - 20\cos(x)^4\, e^{\sin(x)} - 15\sin(x)^3\, e^{\sin(x)}$$
$$+ 45\sin(x)^2\cos(x)^2\, e^{\sin(x)} - 15\sin(x)\cos(x)^4\, e^{\sin(x)}$$
$$+ \cos(x)^6\, e^{\sin(x)}$$

The use of the sequence operator \$ in the previous command allows you to abbreviate the calling sequence. Otherwise, you are required to enter `,` `x` six times to calculate the sixth derivative. Define the function $f6$ to be that derivative.

```
> f6 := unapply( %, x );
```

$$f6 := x \to -\sin(x)\, e^{\sin(x)} + 16\cos(x)^2\, e^{\sin(x)} - 15\sin(x)^2\, e^{\sin(x)} + 75\sin(x)\cos(x)^2\, e^{\sin(x)} - 20\cos(x)^4\, e^{\sin(x)} - 15\sin(x)^3\, e^{\sin(x)} + 45\sin(x)^2\cos(x)^2\, e^{\sin(x)} - 15\sin(x)\cos(x)^4\, e^{\sin(x)} + \cos(x)^6\, e^{\sin(x)}$$

The following is the error in the approximation.

```
> err := 1/6! * f6(xi) * (x - a)^6;
```

$$err := \frac{1}{720}(-\sin(\xi)\, e^{\sin(\xi)} + 16\cos(\xi)^2\, e^{\sin(\xi)} - 15\sin(\xi)^2\, e^{\sin(\xi)} + 75\sin(\xi)\cos(\xi)^2\, e^{\sin(\xi)} - 20\cos(\xi)^4\, e^{\sin(\xi)} - 15\sin(\xi)^3\, e^{\sin(\xi)} + 45\sin(\xi)^2\cos(\xi)^2\, e^{\sin(\xi)} - 15\sin(\xi)\cos(\xi)^4\, e^{\sin(\xi)} + \cos(\xi)^6\, e^{\sin(\xi)})(x-\pi)^6$$

The previous plot indicates that the error is small (in absolute value) for x between 2 and 4.

```
> plot3d( abs( err ), x=2..4, xi=2..4,
>     style=patch, axes=boxed );
```

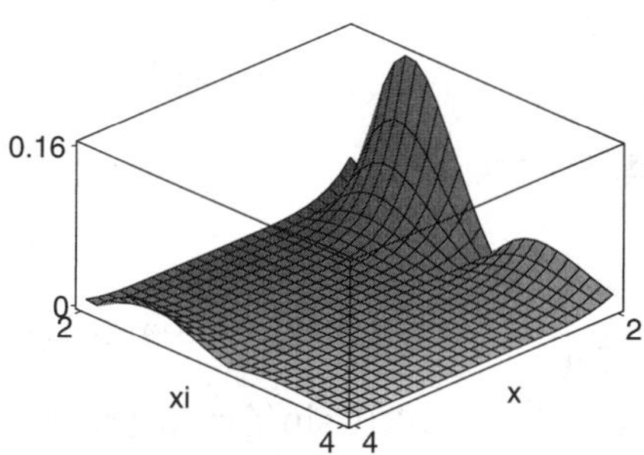

To find the size of the error, you need a full analysis of the expression `err` for x between 2 and 4 and ξ between a and x, that is, on the two closed regions bounded by $x = 2$, $x = 4$, $\xi = a$, and $\xi = x$. The `curve` command from the `plottools` package can illustrate these two regions.

```
> with(plots): with(plottools):

Warning, the name changecoords has been redefined
Warning, the name arrow has been redefined

> display( curve( [ [2,2], [2,a], [4,a], [4,4], [2,2] ] ),
>          labels=[x, xi] );
```

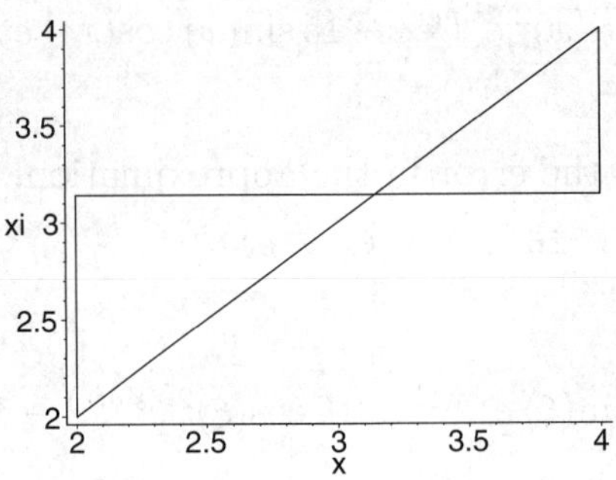

The partial derivatives of **err** help you find extrema of **err** inside the two regions. Then you must to check the four boundaries. The two partial derivatives of **err** are

```
> err_x := diff(err, x);
```

$$
\begin{aligned}
err\_x &:= \frac{1}{120}(-\sin(\xi)\, e^{\sin(\xi)} + 16\cos(\xi)^2\, e^{\sin(\xi)} \\
&- 15\sin(\xi)^2\, e^{\sin(\xi)} + 75\sin(\xi)\cos(\xi)^2\, e^{\sin(\xi)} - 20\cos(\xi)^4\, e^{\sin(\xi)} \\
&- 15\sin(\xi)^3\, e^{\sin(\xi)} + 45\sin(\xi)^2\cos(\xi)^2\, e^{\sin(\xi)} \\
&- 15\sin(\xi)\cos(\xi)^4\, e^{\sin(\xi)} + \cos(\xi)^6\, e^{\sin(\xi)})(x-\pi)^5
\end{aligned}
$$

```
> err_xi := diff(err, xi);
```

$$
\begin{aligned}
err\_xi &:= \frac{1}{720}(-\cos(\xi)\, e^{\sin(\xi)} - 63\sin(\xi)\cos(\xi)\, e^{\sin(\xi)} \\
&+ 91\cos(\xi)^3\, e^{\sin(\xi)} - 210\sin(\xi)^2\cos(\xi)\, e^{\sin(\xi)} \\
&+ 245\sin(\xi)\cos(\xi)^3\, e^{\sin(\xi)} - 35\cos(\xi)^5\, e^{\sin(\xi)} \\
&- 105\sin(\xi)^3\cos(\xi)\, e^{\sin(\xi)} + 105\sin(\xi)^2\cos(\xi)^3\, e^{\sin(\xi)} \\
&- 21\sin(\xi)\cos(\xi)^5\, e^{\sin(\xi)} + \cos(\xi)^7\, e^{\sin(\xi)})(x-\pi)^6
\end{aligned}
$$

The two partial derivatives are zero at a critical point.

```
> sol := solve( {err_x=0, err_xi=0}, {x, xi} );
```

$$sol := \{\xi = \xi,\ x = \pi\}$$

The error is zero at this critical point.

```
> eval( err, sol );
```

$$0$$

Collect a set of critical values. The largest critical value then bounds the maximal error.

```
> critical := { % };
```

$$critical := \{0\}$$

The partial derivative err_xi is zero at a critical point on either of the two boundaries at $x = 2$ and $x = 4$.

```
> sol := { solve( err_xi=0, xi ) };
```

$$\begin{aligned}&sol := \{\arctan(\mathrm{RootOf}(\%1,\ index = 2),\\ &\mathrm{RootOf}(\_Z^2 + \mathrm{RootOf}(\%1,\ index = 2)^2 - 1)), \arctan(\\ &\mathrm{RootOf}(\%1,\ index = 5),\\ &\mathrm{RootOf}(\_Z^2 + \mathrm{RootOf}(\%1,\ index = 5)^2 - 1)), \arctan(\\ &\mathrm{RootOf}(\%1,\ index = 6),\\ &\mathrm{RootOf}(\_Z^2 + \mathrm{RootOf}(\%1,\ index = 6)^2 - 1)), \arctan(\\ &\mathrm{RootOf}(\%1,\ index = 1),\\ &\mathrm{RootOf}(\_Z^2 + \mathrm{RootOf}(\%1,\ index = 1)^2 - 1)), \arctan(\\ &\mathrm{RootOf}(\%1,\ index = 4),\\ &\mathrm{RootOf}(\_Z^2 + \mathrm{RootOf}(\%1,\ index = 4)^2 - 1)), \arctan(\\ &\mathrm{RootOf}(\%1,\ index = 3),\\ &\mathrm{RootOf}(\_Z^2 + \mathrm{RootOf}(\%1,\ index = 3)^2 - 1)), \frac{1}{2}\pi\}\\ &\%1 := -56 - 161\,\_Z + 129\,\_Z^2 + 308\,\_Z^3 + 137\,\_Z^4\\ &+ 21\,\_Z^5 + \_Z^6\end{aligned}$$

```
> evalf(sol);
```

$$\{-1.570796327 + 0.8535664710\,I,\ 1.570796327,\ -1.570796327 + 1.767486929\,I,\ -1.570796327 + 3.083849212\,I,\ -1.570796327 + 2.473801030\,I,\ 0.6948635283,\ -0.3257026605\}$$

Check the solution set by plotting the function.

```
> plot( eval(err_xi, x=2), xi=2..4 );
```

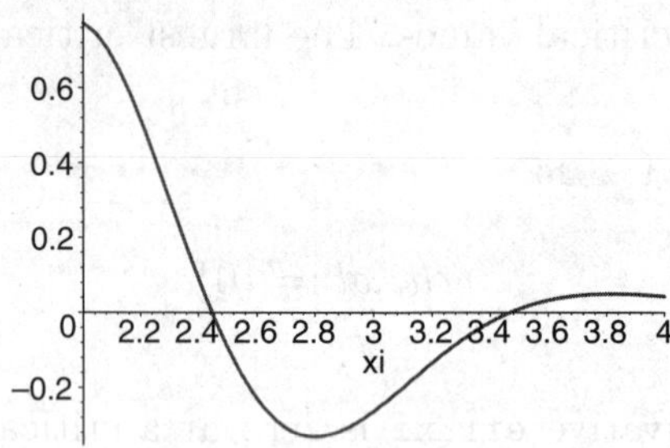

Two solutions to `err_xi=0` seem to exist between 2 and 4 where `solve` found none: $\pi/2$ is less than 2. Thus, you must use numerical methods. If $x = 2$, then ξ must be in the interval from 2 to a.

```
> sol := fsolve( eval(err_xi, x=2), xi, 2..a );
```

$$sol := 2.446729125$$

At that point the error is

```
> eval( err, {x=2, xi=sol});
```

$$0.07333000221\,(2 - \pi)^6$$

Add this value to the set of critical values.

```
> critical := critical union {%};
```

$$critical := \{0,\ 0.07333000221\,(2 - \pi)^6\}$$

If $x = 4$ then ξ must be between a and 4.

```
> sol := fsolve( eval(err_xi, x=4), xi, a..4 );
```

$$sol := 3.467295314$$

At that point, the error is

```
> eval( err, {x=4, xi=sol} );
```

$$-0.01542298119\,(4-\pi)^6$$

```
> critical := critical union {%};
```

$$critical :=$$
$$\{0,\ 0.07333000221\,(2-\pi)^6,\ -0.01542298119\,(4-\pi)^6\}$$

At the $\xi = a$ boundary, the error is

```
> B := eval( err, xi=a );
```

$$B := -\frac{1}{240}\,(x-\pi)^6$$

The derivative, $B1$, of B is zero at a critical point.

```
> B1 := diff( B, x );
```

$$B1 := -\frac{1}{40}\,(x-\pi)^5$$

```
> sol := { solve( B1=0, x ) };
```

$$sol := \{\pi\}$$

At the critical point the error is

```
> eval( B, x=sol[1] );
```

$$0$$

```
> critical := critical union { % };
```

$$critical :=$$
$$\{0,\ 0.07333000221\,(2-\pi)^6,\ -0.01542298119\,(4-\pi)^6\}$$

At the last boundary, $\xi = x$, the error is

```
> B := eval( err, xi=x );
```

$$B := \frac{1}{720}(-\sin(x)\,e^{\sin(x)} + 16\cos(x)^2\,e^{\sin(x)} - 15\sin(x)^2\,e^{\sin(x)} + 75\sin(x)\cos(x)^2\,e^{\sin(x)} - 20\cos(x)^4\,e^{\sin(x)} - 15\sin(x)^3\,e^{\sin(x)} + 45\sin(x)^2\cos(x)^2\,e^{\sin(x)} - 15\sin(x)\cos(x)^4\,e^{\sin(x)} + \cos(x)^6\,e^{\sin(x)})(x-\pi)^6$$

Again, find where the derivative is zero.

```
> B1 := diff( B, x );
```

$$B1 := \frac{1}{720}(-\cos(x)\,e^{\sin(x)} - 63\sin(x)\cos(x)\,e^{\sin(x)} + 91\cos(x)^3\,e^{\sin(x)} - 210\sin(x)^2\cos(x)\,e^{\sin(x)} + 245\sin(x)\cos(x)^3\,e^{\sin(x)} - 35\cos(x)^5\,e^{\sin(x)} - 105\sin(x)^3\cos(x)\,e^{\sin(x)} + 105\sin(x)^2\cos(x)^3\,e^{\sin(x)} - 21\sin(x)\cos(x)^5\,e^{\sin(x)} + \cos(x)^7\,e^{\sin(x)})(x-\pi)^6 + \frac{1}{120}(-\sin(x)\,e^{\sin(x)} + 16\cos(x)^2\,e^{\sin(x)} - 15\sin(x)^2\,e^{\sin(x)} + 75\sin(x)\cos(x)^2\,e^{\sin(x)} - 20\cos(x)^4\,e^{\sin(x)} - 15\sin(x)^3\,e^{\sin(x)} + 45\sin(x)^2\cos(x)^2\,e^{\sin(x)} - 15\sin(x)\cos(x)^4\,e^{\sin(x)} + \cos(x)^6\,e^{\sin(x)})(x-\pi)^5$$

```
> sol := { solve( B1=0, x ) };
```

$$sol := \{\pi\}$$

Check the solution by plotting.

```
> plot( B1, x=2..4 );
```

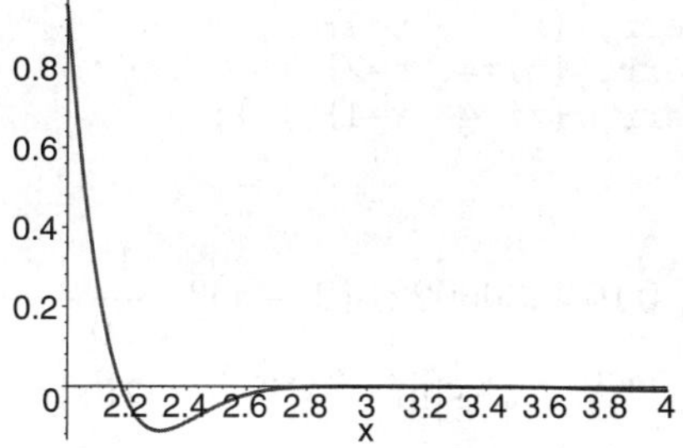

The plot of $B1$ indicates that a solution between 2.1 and 2.3 exists. The `solve` command cannot find that solution. Use numerical methods again.

```
> fsolve( B1=0, x, 2.1..2.3 );
```

$$2.180293062$$

Add the numerical solution to the set of symbolic solutions.

```
> sol := sol union { % };
```

$$sol := \{2.180293062,\ \pi\}$$

The following is the set of extremal errors at the $\xi = x$ boundary.

```
> { seq( B, x=sol ) };
```

$$\{0,\ 0.04005698601\,(2.180293062 - \pi)^6\}$$

Enlarge the set of large errors.

```
> critical := critical union %;
```

$$critical := \{0,\ 0.07333000221\,(2 - \pi)^6,$$
$$-0.01542298119\,(4 - \pi)^6,$$
$$0.04005698601\,(2.180293062 - \pi)^6\}$$

Add the error at the four corners to the set of critical values.

```
> critical := critical union
>     { eval( err, {xi=2, x=2} ),
>       eval( err, {xi=2, x=4} ),
>       eval( err, {xi=4, x=2} ),
>       eval( err, {xi=4, x=4} ) };
```

$$
\begin{aligned}
&\mathit{critical} := \{0,\ 0.07333000221\,(2-\pi)^6,\ \frac{1}{720}(-\sin(4)\,e^{\sin(4)}\\
&+16\cos(4)^2\,e^{\sin(4)} - 15\sin(4)^2\,e^{\sin(4)} + 75\sin(4)\cos(4)^2\,e^{\sin(4)}\\
&-20\cos(4)^4\,e^{\sin(4)} - 15\sin(4)^3\,e^{\sin(4)}\\
&+45\sin(4)^2\cos(4)^2\,e^{\sin(4)} - 15\sin(4)\cos(4)^4\,e^{\sin(4)}\\
&+\cos(4)^6\,e^{\sin(4)})(2-\pi)^6,\ \frac{1}{720}(-\sin(2)\,e^{\sin(2)}\\
&+16\cos(2)^2\,e^{\sin(2)} - 15\sin(2)^2\,e^{\sin(2)} + 75\sin(2)\cos(2)^2\,e^{\sin(2)}\\
&-20\cos(2)^4\,e^{\sin(2)} - 15\sin(2)^3\,e^{\sin(2)}\\
&+45\sin(2)^2\cos(2)^2\,e^{\sin(2)} - 15\sin(2)\cos(2)^4\,e^{\sin(2)}\\
&+\cos(2)^6\,e^{\sin(2)})(4-\pi)^6,\ -0.01542298119\,(4-\pi)^6,\\
&0.04005698601\,(2.180293062-\pi)^6,\ \frac{1}{720}(-\sin(4)\,e^{\sin(4)}\\
&+16\cos(4)^2\,e^{\sin(4)} - 15\sin(4)^2\,e^{\sin(4)} + 75\sin(4)\cos(4)^2\,e^{\sin(4)}\\
&-20\cos(4)^4\,e^{\sin(4)} - 15\sin(4)^3\,e^{\sin(4)}\\
&+45\sin(4)^2\cos(4)^2\,e^{\sin(4)} - 15\sin(4)\cos(4)^4\,e^{\sin(4)}\\
&+\cos(4)^6\,e^{\sin(4)})(4-\pi)^6,\ \frac{1}{720}(-\sin(2)\,e^{\sin(2)}\\
&+16\cos(2)^2\,e^{\sin(2)} - 15\sin(2)^2\,e^{\sin(2)} + 75\sin(2)\cos(2)^2\,e^{\sin(2)}\\
&-20\cos(2)^4\,e^{\sin(2)} - 15\sin(2)^3\,e^{\sin(2)}\\
&+45\sin(2)^2\cos(2)^2\,e^{\sin(2)} - 15\sin(2)\cos(2)^4\,e^{\sin(2)}\\
&+\cos(2)^6\,e^{\sin(2)})(2-\pi)^6\}
\end{aligned}
$$

Find the maximum of the absolute values of the elements of `critical`. First, map the `abs` command onto the elements of `critical`.

```
> map( abs, critical );
```

$$\{0, 0.07333000221\,(2-\pi)^6, -\frac{1}{720}(-\sin(4)\,e^{\sin(4)}$$
$$+16\cos(4)^2\,e^{\sin(4)} - 15\sin(4)^2\,e^{\sin(4)} + 75\sin(4)\cos(4)^2\,e^{\sin(4)}$$
$$-20\cos(4)^4\,e^{\sin(4)} - 15\sin(4)^3\,e^{\sin(4)}$$
$$+45\sin(4)^2\cos(4)^2\,e^{\sin(4)} - 15\sin(4)\cos(4)^4\,e^{\sin(4)}$$
$$+\cos(4)^6\,e^{\sin(4)})(2-\pi)^6, -\frac{1}{720}(-\sin(2)\,e^{\sin(2)}$$
$$+16\cos(2)^2\,e^{\sin(2)} - 15\sin(2)^2\,e^{\sin(2)} + 75\sin(2)\cos(2)^2\,e^{\sin(2)}$$
$$-20\cos(2)^4\,e^{\sin(2)} - 15\sin(2)^3\,e^{\sin(2)}$$
$$+45\sin(2)^2\cos(2)^2\,e^{\sin(2)} - 15\sin(2)\cos(2)^4\,e^{\sin(2)}$$
$$+\cos(2)^6\,e^{\sin(2)})(4-\pi)^6, 0.01542298119\,(4-\pi)^6, -\frac{1}{720}($$
$$-\sin(2)\,e^{\sin(2)} + 16\cos(2)^2\,e^{\sin(2)} - 15\sin(2)^2\,e^{\sin(2)}$$
$$+75\sin(2)\cos(2)^2\,e^{\sin(2)} - 20\cos(2)^4\,e^{\sin(2)} - 15\sin(2)^3\,e^{\sin(2)}$$
$$+45\sin(2)^2\cos(2)^2\,e^{\sin(2)} - 15\sin(2)\cos(2)^4\,e^{\sin(2)}$$
$$+\cos(2)^6\,e^{\sin(2)})(2-\pi)^6, -\frac{1}{720}(-\sin(4)\,e^{\sin(4)}$$
$$+16\cos(4)^2\,e^{\sin(4)} - 15\sin(4)^2\,e^{\sin(4)} + 75\sin(4)\cos(4)^2\,e^{\sin(4)}$$
$$-20\cos(4)^4\,e^{\sin(4)} - 15\sin(4)^3\,e^{\sin(4)}$$
$$+45\sin(4)^2\cos(4)^2\,e^{\sin(4)} - 15\sin(4)\cos(4)^4\,e^{\sin(4)}$$
$$+\cos(4)^6\,e^{\sin(4)})(4-\pi)^6,$$
$$0.04005698601\,(2.180293062-\pi)^6\}$$

Find the maximal element. The `max` command expects a sequence of numbers, so you must use the `op` command to convert the set of values into a sequence.

```
> max_error := max( op(%) );
```

$$max\_error := 0.07333000221\,(2-\pi)^6$$

Approximately, this number is

```
> evalf( max_error );
```

$$0.1623112756$$

You can now plot f, its Taylor approximation, and a pair of curves indicating the error band.

```
> plot( [ f(x), poly, f(x)+max_error, f(x)-max_error ],
>        x=2..4,
>        color=[ red, blue, brown, brown ] );
```

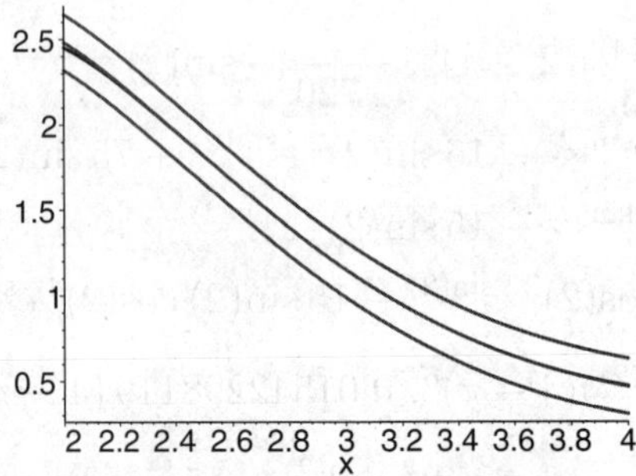

The plot shows that the actual error stays well inside the error estimate.

The Integral

The integral of a function can be considered as a measure of the area between the x-axis and the graph of the function. The definition of the Riemann integral relies on this graphical interpretation of the integral.

```
> f := x -> 1/2 + sin(x);
```

$$f := x \to \frac{1}{2} + \sin(x)$$

For example, the `ApproximateInt` command with `method = left`, `partition = 6`, and `output = plot` specified, from the `Student[Calculus1]` package draws the graph of f along with 6 boxes. The height of each box is the value of f evaluated at the left-hand side of the box.

```
> with(Student[Calculus1]):
```

```
> ApproximateInt( f(x), x=0..10, method=left, partition=6,
>                output=plot);
```

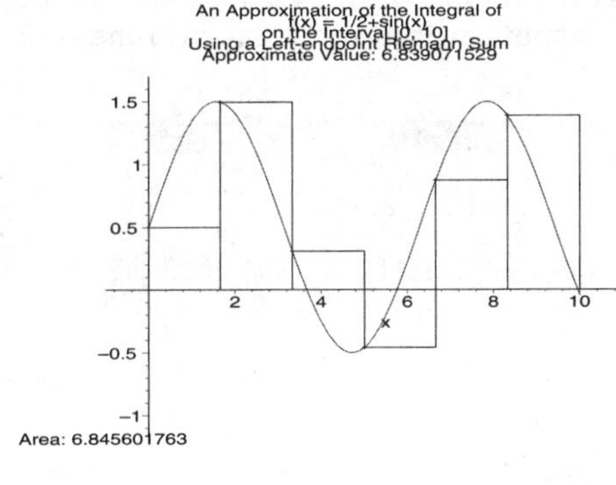

Change `output = plot` to `output = sum` to calculate the area of the boxes.

```
> ApproximateInt( f(x), x=0..10, method=left, partition=6,
>              output=sum);
```

$$\frac{5}{3}\left(\sum_{i=0}^{5}\left(\frac{1}{2}+\sin\left(\frac{5}{3}i\right)\right)\right)$$

Approximately, this number is

```
> evalf( % );
```

$$6.845601766$$

The approximation of the area improves as you increase the number of boxes. Increase the number of boxes to 12 and calculate the value of `ApproximateInt` for each of these boxes.

```
> seq( evalf(ApproximateInt( f(x), x=0..10, method=left,
>         partition=n^2)), n=3..14);
```

6.948089404, 6.948819108, 6.923289158, 6.902789477,
6.888196449, 6.877830055, 6.870316621, 6.864739771,
6.860504866, 6.857222009, 6.854630209, 6.852550664

Use the option `output = animation` to create an animation for the left Riemann sum.

```
> ApproximateInt( f(x), x=0..4*Pi, method=left, partition=6,
>               output=animation, iterations=7);
```

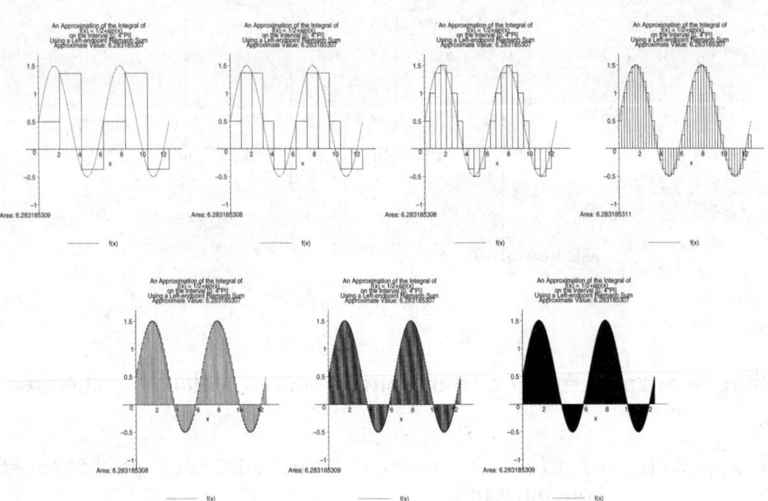

In the limit, as the number of boxes tends to infinity, you obtain the definite integral.

```
> Int( f(x), x=0..10 );
```

$$\int_{0}^{10} \frac{1}{2} + \sin(x)\, dx$$

The value of the integral is

```
> value( % );
```

$$-\cos(10) + 6$$

and in floating-point numbers, this value is approximately

```
> evalf( % );
```

$$6.839071529$$

The indefinite integral of f is

```
> Int( f(x), x );
```

$$\int \frac{1}{2} + \sin(x)\,dx$$

```
> value( % );
```

$$\frac{1}{2}\,x - \cos(x)$$

Define the function F to be the antiderivative.

```
> F := unapply( %, x );
```

$$F := x \to \frac{1}{2}\,x - \cos(x)$$

Choose the constant of integration so that $F(0) = 0$.

```
> F(x) - F(0);
```

$$\frac{1}{2}\,x - \cos(x) + 1$$

```
> F := unapply( %, x );
```

$$F := x \to \frac{1}{2}\,x - \cos(x) + 1$$

If you plot F and the left-boxes together, F increases faster when the corresponding box is larger, that is, when f is bigger.

```
> with(plots):
> display( [ plot( F(x), x=0..10, color=blue, legend="F(x)" ),
>            ApproximateInt( f(x), x=0..10, partition=14,
>            method=left, output=plot) ] );
```

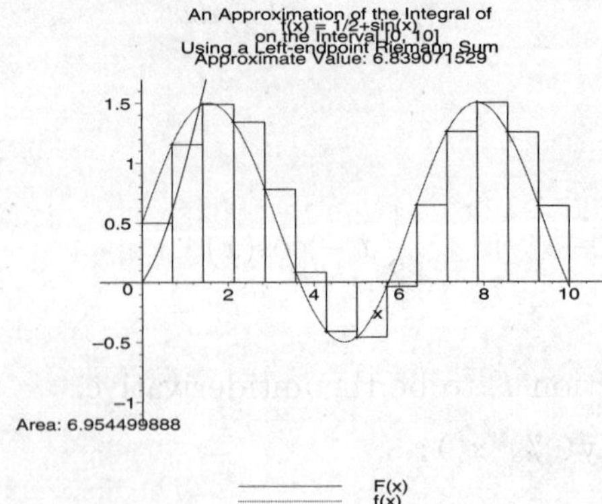

By specifying `method = right` or `method = midpoint` when using the `ApproximateInt` command, you can draw and sum boxes evaluated at the right-hand side or at the midpoint of the box.

Mixed Partial Derivatives

This section describes the `D` operator for derivatives and gives an example of a function whose mixed partial derivatives are different.

Consider the following function.

```
> f := (x,y) -> x * y * (x^2-y^2) / (x^2+y^2);
```

$$f := (x, y) \to \frac{x\,y\,(x^2 - y^2)}{x^2 + y^2}$$

The function f is not defined at $(0, 0)$.

```
> f(0,0);
Error, (in f) numeric exception: division by zero
```

At $(x, y) = (r\cos(\theta), r\sin(\theta))$ the function value is

```
> f( r*cos(theta), r*sin(theta) );
```

$$\frac{r^2\cos(\theta)\sin(\theta)\,(r^2\cos(\theta)^2 - r^2\sin(\theta)^2)}{r^2\cos(\theta)^2 + r^2\sin(\theta)^2}$$

As r tends to zero so does the function value.

```
> Limit( %, r=0 );
```

$$\lim_{r \to 0} \frac{r^2 \cos(\theta) \sin(\theta) \, (r^2 \cos(\theta)^2 - r^2 \sin(\theta)^2)}{r^2 \cos(\theta)^2 + r^2 \sin(\theta)^2}$$

```
> value( % );
```

$$0$$

Thus, you can extend f as a continuous function by defining it to be zero at $(0, 0)$.

```
> f(0,0) := 0;
```

$$\mathrm{f}(0,\, 0) := 0$$

The above assignment places an entry in f's *remember* table.

Note: A remember table is a hash table in which the arguments to a procedure call are stored as the table index, and the result of the procedure call is stored as the table value. For more information, refer to the `?remember` help page and the *Maple Advanced Programming Guide.*

Here is the graph of f.

```
> plot3d( f, -3..3, -3..3 );
```

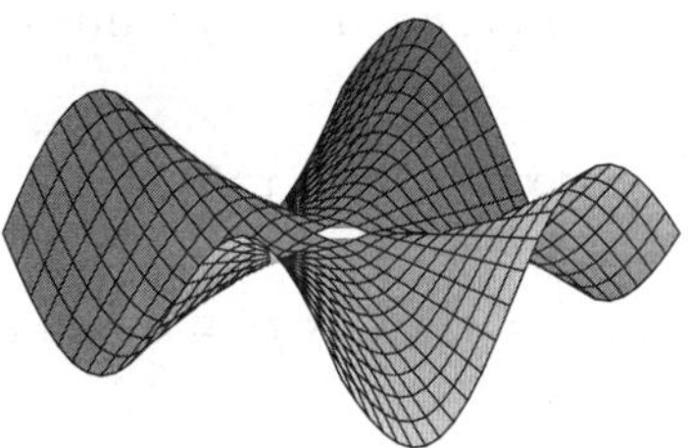

The partial derivative of f with respect to its first parameter, x, is

```
> fx := D[1](f);
```

$$fx := (x,\, y) \to \frac{y\,(x^2 - y^2)}{x^2 + y^2} + 2\,\frac{x^2\,y}{x^2 + y^2} - 2\,\frac{x^2\,y\,(x^2 - y^2)}{(x^2 + y^2)^2}$$

This formula does not hold at $(0, 0)$.

```
> fx(0,0);
Error, (in fx) numeric exception: division by zero
```

Therefore, you must use the limit definition of the derivative.

```
> fx(0,0) := limit( ( f(h,0) - f(0,0) )/h, h=0 );
```

$$\text{fx}(0, 0) := 0$$

At $(x, y) = (r\cos(\theta), r\sin(\theta))$ the value of **fx** is

```
> fx( r*cos(theta), r*sin(theta) );
```

$$\frac{r\sin(\theta)\,(r^2\cos(\theta)^2 - r^2\sin(\theta)^2)}{r^2\cos(\theta)^2 + r^2\sin(\theta)^2} + 2\,\frac{r^3\cos(\theta)^2\sin(\theta)}{r^2\cos(\theta)^2 + r^2\sin(\theta)^2}$$
$$-2\,\frac{r^3\cos(\theta)^2\sin(\theta)\,(r^2\cos(\theta)^2 - r^2\sin(\theta)^2)}{(r^2\cos(\theta)^2 + r^2\sin(\theta)^2)^2}$$

```
> combine( % );
```

$$\frac{3}{4}\,r\sin(3\,\theta) - \frac{1}{4}\,r\sin(5\,\theta)$$

As the distance r from (x, y) to $(0, 0)$ tends to zero, so does $|fx(x, y) - fx(0, 0)|$.

```
> Limit( abs( % - fx(0,0) ), r=0 );
```

$$\lim_{r\to 0}\left|-\frac{3}{4}\,r\sin(3\,\theta) + \frac{1}{4}\,r\sin(5\,\theta)\right|$$

```
> value( % );
```

$$0$$

Hence, fx is continuous at $(0, 0)$.

By symmetry, the same arguments apply to the derivative of f with respect to its second parameter, y.

```
> fy := D[2](f);
```

$$fy := (x, y) \to \frac{x\,(x^2 - y^2)}{x^2 + y^2} - 2\,\frac{x\,y^2}{x^2 + y^2} - 2\,\frac{x\,y^2\,(x^2 - y^2)}{(x^2 + y^2)^2}$$

```
> fy(0,0) := limit( ( f(0,k) - f(0,0) )/k, k=0 );
```

$$\text{fy}(0, 0) := 0$$

Here is a mixed second derivative of f.

```
> fxy := D[1,2](f);
```

$$fxy := (x, y) \to \frac{x^2 - y^2}{x^2 + y^2} + 2\,\frac{x^2}{x^2 + y^2} - 2\,\frac{x^2\,(x^2 - y^2)}{(x^2 + y^2)^2} - 2\,\frac{y^2}{x^2 + y^2} - 2\,\frac{y^2\,(x^2 - y^2)}{(x^2 + y^2)^2} + 8\,\frac{x^2\,y^2\,(x^2 - y^2)}{(x^2 + y^2)^3}$$

Again, the formula does not hold at $(0, 0)$.

```
> fxy(0,0);
Error, (in fxy) numeric exception: division by zero
```

The limit definition is

```
> Limit( ( fx(0,k) - fx(0,0) )/k, k=0 );
```

$$\lim_{k \to 0} -1$$

```
> fxy(0,0) := value( % );
```

$$\text{fxy}(0, 0) := -1$$

The other mixed second derivative is

```
> fyx := D[2,1](f);
```

$$fyx := (x, y) \to \frac{x^2 - y^2}{x^2 + y^2} + 2\,\frac{x^2}{x^2 + y^2} - 2\,\frac{x^2\,(x^2 - y^2)}{(x^2 + y^2)^2} - 2\,\frac{y^2}{x^2 + y^2} - 2\,\frac{y^2\,(x^2 - y^2)}{(x^2 + y^2)^2} + 8\,\frac{x^2\,y^2\,(x^2 - y^2)}{(x^2 + y^2)^3}$$

At $(0, 0)$, you must use the limit definition.

```
> Limit( ( fy(h, 0) - fy(0,0) )/h, h=0 );
```

$$\lim_{h \to 0} 1$$

```
> fyx(0,0) := value( % );
```

$$\mathrm{fyx}(0, 0) := 1$$

Note that the two mixed partial derivatives are different at $(0, 0)$.

```
> fxy(0,0) <> fyx(0,0);
```

$$-1 \neq 1$$

The mixed partial derivatives are equal only if they are continuous. As you can see in the plot of `fxy`, it is *not* continuous at $(0, 0)$.

```
> plot3d( fxy, -3..3, -3..3 );
```

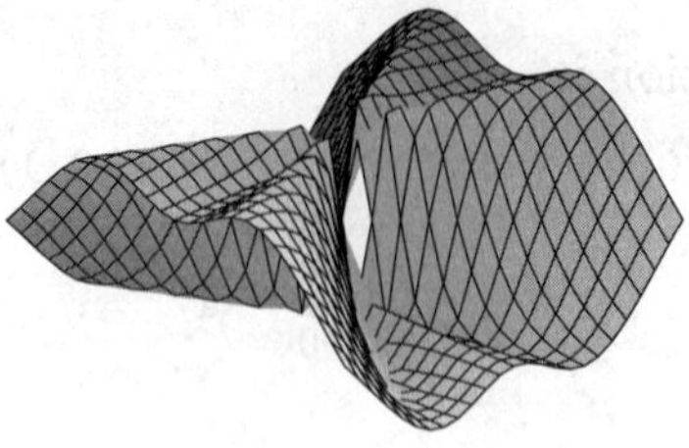

Maple can help you with many problems from introductory calculus. For more information, refer to the `?Student[Calculus1]` help page.

7.2 Ordinary Differential Equations

Maple provides you with tools for solving, manipulating, and plotting ordinary differential equations and systems of differential equations.

The dsolve Command

The most commonly used command for investigating the behavior of ordinary differential equations (ODEs) in Maple is **dsolve**. You can use this general-purpose command to obtain both closed form and numerical solutions to a wide variety of ODEs. This is the basic syntax of **dsolve**.

```
dsolve(eqns, vars)
```

- *eqns* is a set of differential equations and initial values
- *vars* is a set of variables with respect to which **dsolve** solves

The following example is a differential equation and an initial condition.

```
> eq := diff(v(t),t)+2*t = 0;
```

$$eq := (\frac{d}{dt}\,\mathrm{v}(t)) + 2\,t = 0$$

```
> ini := v(1) = 5;
```

$$ini := \mathrm{v}(1) = 5$$

Use **dsolve** to obtain the solution.

```
> dsolve( {eq, ini}, {v(t)} );
```

$$\mathrm{v}(t) = -t^2 + 6$$

If you omit some or all of the initial conditions, then **dsolve** returns a solution containing arbitrary constants of the form *_Cnumber*.

```
> eq := diff(y(x),x$2) - y(x) = 1;
```

$$eq := (\frac{d^2}{dx^2}\,\mathrm{y}(x)) - \mathrm{y}(x) = 1$$

```
> dsolve( {eq}, {y(x)} );
```

$$\{\mathrm{y}(x) = e^x\,\_C2 + e^{(-x)}\,\_C1 - 1\}$$

To specify initial conditions for the derivative of a function, use the following notation.

```
D(fcn)(var_value) = value
(D@@n)(fcn)(var_value) = value
```

- `D` notation represents the derivative
- `D@@n` notation represents the nth derivative

Here is a differential equation and some initial conditions involving the derivative.

```
> de1 := diff(y(t),t$2) + 5*diff(y(t),t) + 6*y(t) = 0;
```

$$de1 := (\frac{d^2}{dt^2}\,\mathrm{y}(t)) + 5\,(\frac{d}{dt}\,\mathrm{y}(t)) + 6\,\mathrm{y}(t) = 0$$

```
> ini := y(0)=0, D(y)(0)=1;
```

$$ini := \mathrm{y}(0) = 0,\ \mathrm{D}(y)(0) = 1$$

Again, use `dsolve` to find the solution.

```
> dsolve( {de1, ini}, {y(t)} );
```

$$\mathrm{y}(t) = -e^{(-3\,t)} + e^{(-2\,t)}$$

Additionally, `dsolve` may return a solution in parametric form, `[x=f(_T), y(x)=g(_T)]`, where `_T` is the parameter.

The `explicit` Option Maple may return the solution to a differential equation in implicit form.

```
> de2 := diff(y(x),x$2) = (ln(y(x))+1)*diff(y(x),x);
```

$$de2 := \frac{d^2}{dx^2}\,\mathrm{y}(x) = (\ln(\mathrm{y}(x)) + 1)\,(\frac{d}{dx}\,\mathrm{y}(x))$$

```
> dsolve( {de2}, {y(x)} );
```

$$\{y(x) = \_C1\}, \left\{\int^{y(x)} \frac{1}{\_a \ln(\_a) + \_C1} \, d\_a - x - \_C2 = 0\right\}$$

Use the **explicit** option to search for an explicit solution for the first result.

```
> dsolve( {de2}, {y(x)}, explicit );
```

$$\{y(x) = \_C1\},$$
$$\left\{y(x) = \mathrm{RootOf}\left(-\int^{\_Z} \frac{1}{\_f \ln(\_f) + \_C1} \, d\_f + x + \_C2\right)\right\}$$

However, in some cases, Maple may not be able to find an explicit solution. There is also an **implicit** option to force answers to be returned in implicit form.

The method=laplace Option Applying Laplace transform methods to differential equations often reduces the complexity of the problem. The transform maps the differential equations into algebraic equations, which are much easier to solve. The difficulty is in the transformation of the equations to the new domain, and especially the transformation of the solutions back.

The Laplace transform method can handle linear ODEs of arbitrary order, and some cases of linear ODEs with non-constant coefficients, provided that Maple can find the transforms. This method can also solve systems of coupled equations.

Consider the following problem in classical dynamics. Two weights with masses m and αm, respectively, rest on a frictionless plane joined by a spring with spring constant k. What are the trajectories of each weight if the first weight is subject to a unit step force $u(t)$ at time $t = 1$? First, set up the differential equations that govern the system. Newton's Second Law governs the motion of the first weight, and hence, the mass m times the acceleration must equal the sum of the forces that you apply to the first weight, including the external force $u(t)$.

```
> eqn1 :=
>   alpha*m*diff(x[1](t),t$2) = k*(x[2](t) - x[1](t)) + u(t);
```

$$eqn1 := \alpha\, m\, (\frac{d^2}{dt^2} x_1(t)) = k\,(x_2(t) - x_1(t)) + \mathrm{u}(t)$$

Similarly for the second weight.

```
> eqn2 := m*diff(x[2](t),t$2) = k*(x[1](t) - x[2](t));
```

$$eqn2 := m\,(\frac{d^2}{dt^2}\,x_2(t)) = k\,(x_1(t) - x_2(t))$$

Apply a unit step force to the first weight at $t = 1$.

```
> u := t -> Heaviside(t-1);
```

$$u := t \to \mathrm{Heaviside}(t-1)$$

At time $t = 0$, both masses are at rest at their respective locations.

```
> ini := x[1](0) = 2, D(x[1])(0) = 0,
>        x[2](0) = 0, D(x[2])(0) = 0 ;
```

$$ini := x_1(0) = 2,\, \mathrm{D}(x_1)(0) = 0,\, x_2(0) = 0,\, \mathrm{D}(x_2)(0) = 0$$

Solve the problem using Laplace transform methods.

```
> dsolve( {eqn1, eqn2, ini}, {x[1](t), x[2](t)},
>     method=laplace );
```

$$\Bigg\{x_2(t) = \frac{1}{2}(-2\,\alpha\,m + t^2\,k + t^2\,k\,\alpha - 2\,t\,k - 2\,t\,k\,\alpha + k + \alpha\,k$$

$$+ 2\,\alpha\cosh(\frac{\sqrt{\%1}\,(t-1)}{\alpha\,m})\,m)\mathrm{Heaviside}(t-1)\Big/(k$$

$$(1+\alpha)^2\,m) - 2\,\frac{\alpha\,(-1+\cosh(\frac{\sqrt{\%1}\,t}{\alpha\,m}))}{1+\alpha},\, x_1(t) = \frac{1}{2}(2\,m$$

$$- 2\cosh(\frac{\sqrt{\%1}\,(t-1)}{\alpha\,m})\,m + t^2\,k + t^2\,k\,\alpha - 2\,t\,k - 2\,t\,k\,\alpha$$

$$+ k + \alpha\,k)\mathrm{Heaviside}(t-1)\Big/(k\,m\,(1+\alpha)^2) + ($$

$$e^{(-\frac{\sqrt{\%1}\,t}{\alpha\,m})} + e^{(-\frac{\sqrt{\%1}\,t}{\alpha\,m})}\,\alpha + e^{(\frac{\sqrt{\%1}\,t}{\alpha\,m})} + e^{(\frac{\sqrt{\%1}\,t}{\alpha\,m})}\,\alpha + 2\,\alpha$$

$$- 2\,\alpha\cosh(\frac{\sqrt{\%1}\,t}{\alpha\,m}))/(1+\alpha)\Bigg\}$$

$$\%1 := -\alpha\,m\,k\,(1+\alpha)$$

Evaluate the result at values for the constants.

```
> ans := eval( %, {alpha=1/10, m=1, k=1} );
```

$$ans := \{x_2(t) = \frac{50}{121}$$
$$(\frac{9}{10} + \frac{11}{10}t^2 - \frac{11}{5}t + \frac{1}{5}\cosh(\frac{1}{10}\sqrt{-11}\sqrt{100}(t-1)))$$
$$\mathrm{Heaviside}(t-1) + \frac{2}{11} - \frac{2}{11}\cosh(\frac{1}{10}\sqrt{-11}\sqrt{100}\,t), x_1(t)$$
$$= \frac{50}{121}$$
$$(\frac{31}{10} - 2\cosh(\frac{1}{10}\sqrt{-11}\sqrt{100}(t-1)) + \frac{11}{10}t^2 - \frac{11}{5}t)$$
$$\mathrm{Heaviside}(t-1) + e^{(-1/10\sqrt{-11}\sqrt{100}\,t)} + e^{(1/10\sqrt{-11}\sqrt{100}\,t)}$$
$$+ \frac{2}{11} - \frac{2}{11}\cosh(\frac{1}{10}\sqrt{-11}\sqrt{100}\,t)\}$$

You can turn the above solution into two functions, say $y_1(t)$ and $y_2(t)$, as follows. First evaluate the expression `x[1](t)` at the solution to select the $x_1(t)$ expression.

```
> eval( x[1](t), ans );
```

$$\frac{50}{121}(\frac{31}{10} - 2\cosh(\frac{1}{10}\sqrt{-11}\sqrt{100}(t-1)) + \frac{11}{10}t^2 - \frac{11}{5}t)$$
$$\mathrm{Heaviside}(t-1) + e^{(-1/10\sqrt{-11}\sqrt{100}\,t)} + e^{(1/10\sqrt{-11}\sqrt{100}\,t)}$$
$$+ \frac{2}{11} - \frac{2}{11}\cosh(\frac{1}{10}\sqrt{-11}\sqrt{100}\,t)$$

Then convert the expression to a function by using `unapply`.

```
> y[1] := unapply( %, t );
```

$$y_1 := t \to \frac{50}{121}$$
$$(\frac{31}{10} - 2\cosh(\frac{1}{10}\sqrt{-11}\sqrt{100}(t-1)) + \frac{11}{10}t^2 - \frac{11}{5}t)$$
$$\mathrm{Heaviside}(t-1) + e^{(-1/10\sqrt{-11}\sqrt{100}\,t)} + e^{(1/10\sqrt{-11}\sqrt{100}\,t)}$$
$$+ \frac{2}{11} - \frac{2}{11}\cosh(\frac{1}{10}\sqrt{-11}\sqrt{100}\,t)$$

You can also perform the two steps at once.

```
> y[2] := unapply( eval( x[2](t), ans ), t );
```

$$y_2 := t \to \frac{50}{121}$$
$$(\frac{9}{10} + \frac{11}{10}\,t^2 - \frac{11}{5}\,t + \frac{1}{5}\cosh(\frac{1}{10}\,\sqrt{-11}\,\sqrt{100}\,(t-1)))$$
$$\mathrm{Heaviside}(t-1) + \frac{2}{11} - \frac{2}{11}\cosh(\frac{1}{10}\,\sqrt{-11}\,\sqrt{100}\,t)$$

Plot the two functions.

```
> plot( [ y[1](t), y[2](t) ], t=-3..6 );
```

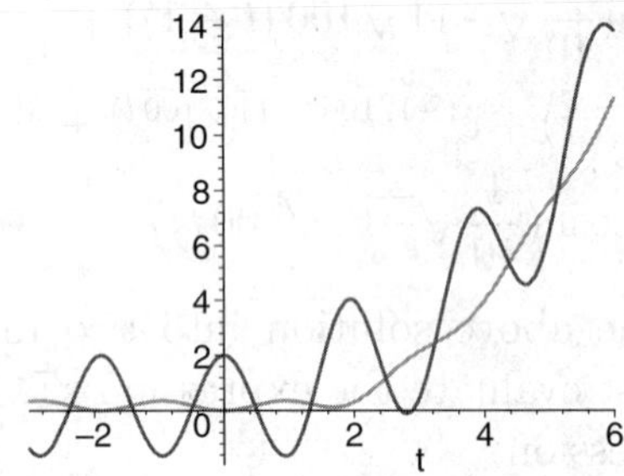

Instead of using `dsolve(..., method=laplace)`, you can use the Laplace transform method by hand. The `inttrans` package defines the Laplace transform and its inverse (and many other integral transforms).

```
> with(inttrans);
```

[*addtable*, *fourier*, *fouriercos*, *fouriersin*, *hankel*, *hilbert*, *invfourier*, *invhilbert*, *invlaplace*, *invmellin*, *laplace*, *mellin*, *savetable*]

The Laplace transforms of the two differential equations `eqn1` and `eqn2` are

```
> laplace( eqn1, t, s );
```

$$\alpha\, m\,(s^2\,\mathrm{laplace}(x_1(t),\,t,\,s) - \mathrm{D}(x_1)(0) - s\,x_1(0)) =$$
$$k\,(\mathrm{laplace}(x_2(t),\,t,\,s) - \mathrm{laplace}(x_1(t),\,t,\,s)) + \frac{e^{(-s)}}{s}$$

and

```
> laplace( eqn2, t, s );
```

$$m\,(s^2\,\mathrm{laplace}(x_2(t),\,t,\,s) - \mathrm{D}(x_2)(0) - s\,x_2(0)) =$$
$$k\,(\mathrm{laplace}(x_1(t),\,t,\,s) - \mathrm{laplace}(x_2(t),\,t,\,s))$$

Evaluate the set consisting of the two transforms at the initial conditions.

```
> eval( {%, %%}, {ini} );
```

$$\{\alpha\,m\,(s^2\,\mathrm{laplace}(x_1(t),\,t,\,s) - 2\,s) =$$
$$k\,(\mathrm{laplace}(x_2(t),\,t,\,s) - \mathrm{laplace}(x_1(t),\,t,\,s)) + \frac{e^{(-s)}}{s},$$
$$m\,s^2\,\mathrm{laplace}(x_2(t),\,t,\,s) =$$
$$k\,(\mathrm{laplace}(x_1(t),\,t,\,s) - \mathrm{laplace}(x_2(t),\,t,\,s))\}$$

You must solve this set of algebraic equations for the Laplace transforms of the two functions $x_1(t)$ and $x_2(t)$.

```
> sol := solve( %, { laplace(x[1](t),t,s),
>     laplace(x[2](t),t,s) } );
```

$$sol := \{\mathrm{laplace}(x_1(t),\,t,\,s) = \frac{(m\,s^2 + k)\,(2\,\alpha\,m\,s^2\,e^s + 1)}{e^s\,s^3\,m\,(k + \alpha\,m\,s^2 + \alpha\,k)},$$
$$\mathrm{laplace}(x_2(t),\,t,\,s) = \frac{k\,(2\,\alpha\,m\,s^2\,e^s + 1)}{e^s\,s^3\,m\,(k + \alpha\,m\,s^2 + \alpha\,k)}\}$$

Maple has solved the algebraic problem. You must take the inverse Laplace transform to get the functions $x_1(t)$ and $x_2(t)$.

```
> invlaplace( %, s, t );
```

$$\Big\{x_2(t) = k\Bigg(\frac{1}{2}(-2\,\alpha\,m + t^2\,k + t^2\,k\,\alpha - 2\,t\,k - 2\,t\,k\,\alpha + k$$

$$+\,\alpha\,k + 2\,\alpha\cosh(\frac{\sqrt{\%1}\,(t-1)}{\alpha\,m})\,m)\mathrm{Heaviside}(t-1)\Big/$$

$$(k^2\,(1+\alpha)^2) - 2\,\frac{\alpha\,m\,(-1+\cosh(\frac{\sqrt{\%1}\,t}{\alpha\,m}))}{k\,(1+\alpha)}\Bigg)/m, x_1(t) =$$

$$e^{(-\frac{\sqrt{\%1}\,t}{\alpha\,m})} + e^{(\frac{\sqrt{\%1}\,t}{\alpha\,m})} - 2\,\frac{\alpha\cosh(\frac{\sqrt{\%1}\,t}{\alpha\,m})}{1+\alpha}$$

$$-\,\frac{\mathrm{Heaviside}(t-1)\cosh(\frac{\sqrt{\%1}\,(t-1)}{\alpha\,m})}{k\,(1+\alpha)^2} + ($$

$$\frac{1}{2}\,k\,\mathrm{Heaviside}(t-1)\,(1+\alpha)\,t^2$$

$$-\,k\,\mathrm{Heaviside}(t-1)\,(1+\alpha)\,t + \mathrm{Heaviside}(t-1)\,m$$

$$+\,\frac{1}{2}\,\mathrm{Heaviside}(t-1)\,k + \frac{1}{2}\,\mathrm{Heaviside}(t-1)\,\alpha\,k$$

$$+\,2\,\alpha\,m\,k + 2\,\alpha^2\,m\,k)\Big/(m\,k\,(1+\alpha)^2)\Big\}$$

$$\%1 := -\alpha\,m\,k\,(1+\alpha)$$

Evaluate at values for the constants.

```
> eval( %, {alpha=1/10, m=1, k=1} );
```

$$\{x_2(t) = \frac{50}{121}$$
$$(\frac{9}{10} + \frac{11}{10}t^2 - \frac{11}{5}t + \frac{1}{5}\cosh(\frac{1}{10}\sqrt{-11}\sqrt{100}(t-1)))$$
$$\mathrm{Heaviside}(t-1) + \frac{2}{11} - \frac{2}{11}\cosh(\frac{1}{10}\sqrt{-11}\sqrt{100}\,t), x_1(t)$$
$$= e^{(-1/10\sqrt{-11}\sqrt{100}\,t)} + e^{(1/10\sqrt{-11}\sqrt{100}\,t)}$$
$$-\frac{2}{11}\cosh(\frac{1}{10}\sqrt{-11}\sqrt{100}\,t)$$
$$-\frac{100}{121}\mathrm{Heaviside}(t-1)\cosh(\frac{1}{10}\sqrt{-11}\sqrt{100}(t-1))$$
$$+\frac{5}{11}\mathrm{Heaviside}(t-1)\,t^2 - \frac{10}{11}\mathrm{Heaviside}(t-1)\,t$$
$$+\frac{155}{121}\mathrm{Heaviside}(t-1) + \frac{2}{11}\}$$

As expected, you get the same solution as before.

The `type=series` Option The series method for solving differential equations finds an approximate symbolic solution to the equations in the following manner. Maple finds a series approximation to the equations. It then solves the series approximation symbolically, using exact methods. This technique is useful when Maple standard algorithms fail, but you still want a symbolic solution rather than a purely numeric solution. The series method can often help with nonlinear and high-order ODEs.

When using the series method, Maple assumes that a solution of the form

$$x^c\left(\sum_{i=0}^{\infty} a_i x^i\right)$$

exists, where c is a rational number.

Consider the following differential equation.

```
> eq := 2*x*diff(y(x),x,x) + diff(y(x),x) + y(x) = 0;
```

$$eq := 2\,x\,(\frac{d^2}{dx^2}\,\mathrm{y}(x)) + (\frac{d}{dx}\,\mathrm{y}(x)) + \mathrm{y}(x) = 0$$

Solve the equation.

```
> dsolve( {eq}, {y(x)}, type=series );
```

$$y(x) = \_C1\,\sqrt{x}(1 - \frac{1}{3}x + \frac{1}{30}x^2 - \frac{1}{630}x^3 + \frac{1}{22680}x^4 - \frac{1}{1247400}x^5 + O(x^6)) + \_C2\,(1 - x + \frac{1}{6}x^2 - \frac{1}{90}x^3 + \frac{1}{2520}x^4 - \frac{1}{113400}x^5 + O(x^6))$$

Use **rhs** to select the solution, then convert it to a polynomial.

```
> rhs(%);
```

$$\_C1\,\sqrt{x}(1 - \frac{1}{3}x + \frac{1}{30}x^2 - \frac{1}{630}x^3 + \frac{1}{22680}x^4 - \frac{1}{1247400}x^5 + O(x^6)) + \_C2\,(1 - x + \frac{1}{6}x^2 - \frac{1}{90}x^3 + \frac{1}{2520}x^4 - \frac{1}{113400}x^5 + O(x^6))$$

```
> poly := convert(%, polynom);
```

$$poly := \_C1\,\sqrt{x}\,(1 - \frac{1}{3}x + \frac{1}{30}x^2 - \frac{1}{630}x^3 + \frac{1}{22680}x^4 - \frac{1}{1247400}x^5) + \_C2\,(1 - x + \frac{1}{6}x^2 - \frac{1}{90}x^3 + \frac{1}{2520}x^4 - \frac{1}{113400}x^5)$$

Plot the solution for different values of the arbitrary constants _C1 and _C2.

```
> [ seq( _C1=i, i=0..5 ) ];
```

$$[\_C1 = 0, \_C1 = 1, \_C1 = 2, \_C1 = 3, \_C1 = 4, \_C1 = 5]$$

```
> map(subs, %, _C2=1, poly);
```

$$[1 - x + \frac{1}{6}x^2 - \frac{1}{90}x^3 + \frac{1}{2520}x^4 - \frac{1}{113400}x^5,$$
$$\%1 + 1 - x + \frac{1}{6}x^2 - \frac{1}{90}x^3 + \frac{1}{2520}x^4 - \frac{1}{113400}x^5,$$
$$2\,\%1 + 1 - x + \frac{1}{6}x^2 - \frac{1}{90}x^3 + \frac{1}{2520}x^4 - \frac{1}{113400}x^5,$$
$$3\,\%1 + 1 - x + \frac{1}{6}x^2 - \frac{1}{90}x^3 + \frac{1}{2520}x^4 - \frac{1}{113400}x^5,$$
$$4\,\%1 + 1 - x + \frac{1}{6}x^2 - \frac{1}{90}x^3 + \frac{1}{2520}x^4 - \frac{1}{113400}x^5,$$
$$5\,\%1 + 1 - x + \frac{1}{6}x^2 - \frac{1}{90}x^3 + \frac{1}{2520}x^4 - \frac{1}{113400}x^5]$$
$$\%1 :=$$
$$\sqrt{x}\,(1 - \frac{1}{3}x + \frac{1}{30}x^2 - \frac{1}{630}x^3 + \frac{1}{22680}x^4 - \frac{1}{1247400}x^5)$$

```
> plot( %, x=1..10 );
```

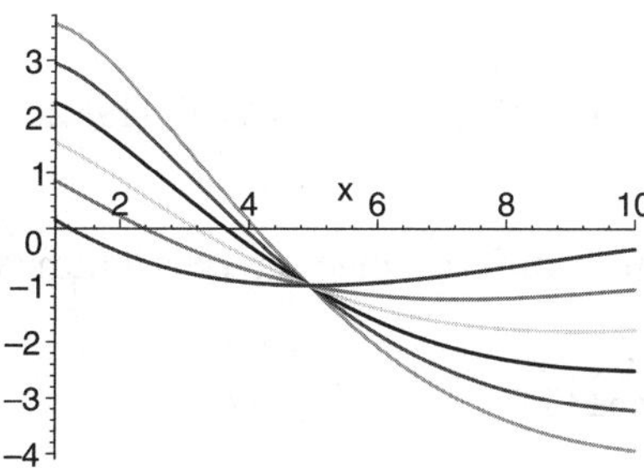

The `type=numeric` Option Although the series methods for solving ODEs are well understood and adequate for finding accurate approximations of the dependent variable, they do exhibit some limitations. To obtain a result, the resultant series must converge. Moreover, in the process of finding the solution, Maple must calculate many derivatives, which can be expensive in terms of time and memory. For these and other reasons, alternative numerical solvers have been developed.

Here is a differential equation and an initial condition.

```
> eq := x(t) * diff(x(t), t) = t^2;
```

$$eq := \mathrm{x}(t)\,(\frac{d}{dt}\,\mathrm{x}(t)) = t^2$$

```
> ini := x(1) = 2;
```

$$ini := x(1) = 2$$

The output from the dsolve command with the numeric option is a procedure that returns a list of equations.

```
> sol := dsolve( {eq, ini}, {x(t)}, type=numeric );
```

$$sol := \textbf{proc}(x\_rkf45)\ \ldots\ \textbf{end proc}$$

The solution satisfies the initial condition.

```
> sol(1);
```

$$[t = 1., x(t) = 2.]$$

```
> sol(0);
```

$$[t = 0., x(t) = 1.82574790049820024]$$

Use the eval command to select a particular value from the list of equations.

```
> eval( x(t), sol(1) );
```

$$2.$$

You can also create an ordered pair.

```
> eval( [t, x(t)], sol(0) );
```

$$[0., 1.82574790049820024]$$

The plots package contains a command, odeplot, for plotting the result of dsolve(..., type=numeric).

```
> with(plots):
```

```
> odeplot( sol, [t, x(t)], -1..2 );
```

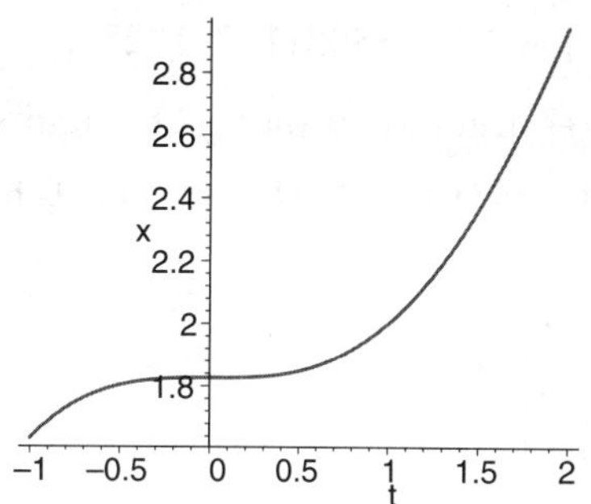

For the syntax of `odeplot`, refer to the `?plots,odeplot` help page. Here is a system of two ODEs.

```
> eq1 := diff(x(t),t) = y(t);
```

$$eq1 := \frac{d}{dt}\,\mathrm{x}(t) = \mathrm{y}(t)$$

```
> eq2 := diff(y(t),t) = x(t)+y(t);
```

$$eq2 := \frac{d}{dt}\,\mathrm{y}(t) = \mathrm{x}(t) + \mathrm{y}(t)$$

```
> ini :=  x(0)=2, y(0)=1;
```

$$ini := \mathrm{x}(0) = 2,\ \mathrm{y}(0) = 1$$

In this case, the solution-procedure yields a list of three equations.

```
> sol1 := dsolve( {eq1, eq2, ini}, {x(t),y(t)},
>    type=numeric );
```

$$sol1 := \mathbf{proc}(x\_rkf45)\ \ldots\ \mathbf{end\ proc}$$

```
> sol1(0);
```

$$[t = 0.,\ \mathrm{x}(t) = 2.,\ \mathrm{y}(t) = 1.]$$

```
> sol1(1);
```

$$[t = 1., \mathrm{x}(t) = 5.58216755967155986,$$
$$\mathrm{y}(t) = 7.82688931187210280]$$

Use the `odeplot` command to plot `y(t)` against `x(t)`,

```
> odeplot( sol1, [x(t), y(t)], -3..1, labels=["x","y"] );
```

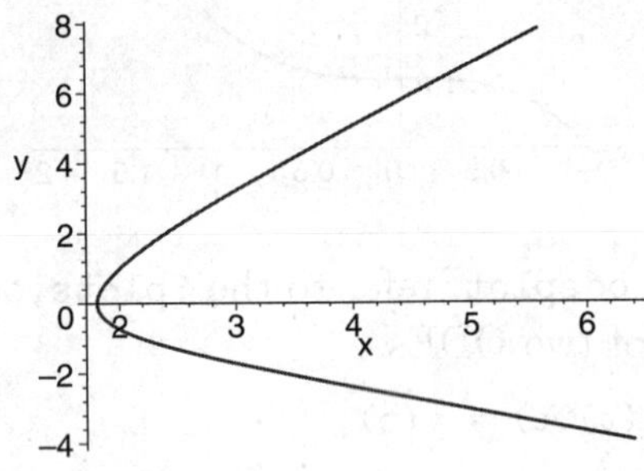

`x(t)` and `y(t)` against `t`,

```
> odeplot( sol1, [t, x(t), y(t)], -3..1,
>     labels=["t","x","y"], axes=boxed );
```

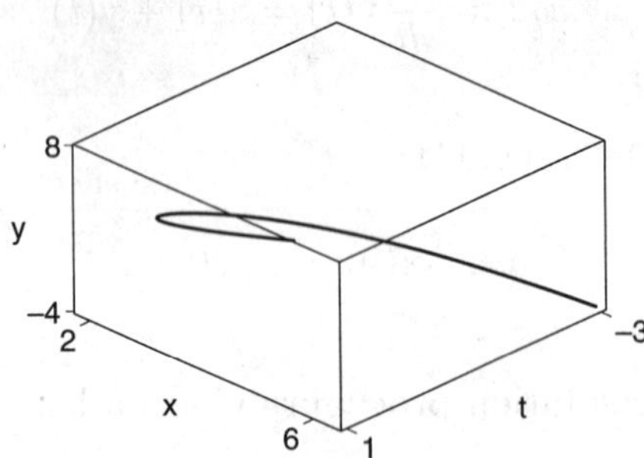

or any other combination.

Important: Use caution when using numeric methods because errors can accumulate in floating-point calculations. Universal rules for preventing this effect do not exist; no software package can anticipate all conditions. The solution is to use the `startinit` option to make `dsolve` (or rather the procedure which `dsolve` returns) begin at the initial value for every calculation at a point $(x, y(x))$.

You can specify which algorithm `dsolve(..., type=numeric)` uses when solving your differential equation. Refer to the `?dsolve,numeric` help page.

Example: Taylor Series

In its general form, a series method solution to an ODE requires the forming of a Taylor series about $t = 0$ for some function $f(t)$. Thus, you must be able to obtain and manipulate the higher order derivatives of your function, $f'(t)$, $f''(t)$, $f'''(t)$, and so on.

Once you have obtained the derivatives, substitute them into the Taylor series representation of $f(t)$.

```
> taylor(f(t), t);
```

$$\mathrm{f}(0) + \mathrm{D}(f)(0)\,t + \frac{1}{2}\,(\mathrm{D}^{(2)})(f)(0)\,t^2 + \frac{1}{6}\,(\mathrm{D}^{(3)})(f)(0)\,t^3 + \frac{1}{24}\,(\mathrm{D}^{(4)})(f)(0)\,t^4 + \frac{1}{120}\,(\mathrm{D}^{(5)})(f)(0)\,t^5 + \mathrm{O}(t^6)$$

As an example, consider Newton's Law of Cooling:

$$\frac{d\theta}{dt} = -\frac{1}{10}(\theta - 20), \qquad \theta(0) = 100.$$

Using the `D` operator, enter the above equation into Maple.

```
> eq := D(theta) = -1/10*(theta-20);
```

$$eq := \mathrm{D}(\theta) = -\frac{1}{10}\,\theta + 2$$

```
> ini := theta(0)=100;
```

$$ini := \theta(0) = 100$$

First obtain the required number of higher derivatives. Determine this number from the order of your Taylor series. If you use the default value of `Order` that Maple provides,

```
> Order;
```

$$6$$

then you must generate derivatives up to order

```
> dev_order := Order - 1;
```

$$dev\_order := 5$$

Use `seq` to generate a sequence of the higher order derivatives of `theta(t)`.

```
> S := seq( (D@@(dev_order-n))(eq), n=1..dev_order );
```

$$S := (\mathrm{D}^{(5)})(\theta) = -\frac{1}{10}(\mathrm{D}^{(4)})(\theta),\ (\mathrm{D}^{(4)})(\theta) = -\frac{1}{10}(\mathrm{D}^{(3)})(\theta),$$
$$(\mathrm{D}^{(3)})(\theta) = -\frac{1}{10}(\mathrm{D}^{(2)})(\theta),\ (\mathrm{D}^{(2)})(\theta) = -\frac{1}{10}\mathrm{D}(\theta),$$
$$\mathrm{D}(\theta) = -\frac{1}{10}\theta + 2$$

The fifth derivative is a function of the fourth derivative, the fourth a function of the third and so on. Therefore, if you make substitutions according to `S`, you can express all the derivatives as functions of `theta`. For example, the third element of `S` is the following.

```
> S[3];
```

$$(\mathrm{D}^{(3)})(\theta) = -\frac{1}{10}(\mathrm{D}^{(2)})(\theta)$$

Substituting according to `S` on the right-hand side, yields

```
> lhs(%) = subs( S, rhs(%) );
```

$$(\mathrm{D}^{(3)})(\theta) = -\frac{1}{1000}\theta + \frac{1}{50}$$

To make this substitution on all the derivatives at once, use the `map` command.

```
> L := map( z -> lhs(z) = eval(rhs(z), {S}), [S] );
```

$$L := [(\mathrm{D}^{(5)})(\theta) = \frac{1}{100}(\mathrm{D}^{(3)})(\theta),\ (\mathrm{D}^{(4)})(\theta) = \frac{1}{100}(\mathrm{D}^{(2)})(\theta),$$
$$(\mathrm{D}^{(3)})(\theta) = \frac{1}{100}\mathrm{D}(\theta),\ (\mathrm{D}^{(2)})(\theta) = \frac{1}{100}\theta - \frac{1}{5},$$
$$\mathrm{D}(\theta) = -\frac{1}{10}\theta + 2]$$

You must evaluate the derivatives at $t = 0$.

```
> L(0);
```

$$[(\mathrm{D}^{(5)})(\theta)(0) = \frac{1}{100}(\mathrm{D}^{(3)})(\theta)(0),$$
$$(\mathrm{D}^{(4)})(\theta)(0) = \frac{1}{100}(\mathrm{D}^{(2)})(\theta)(0),$$
$$(\mathrm{D}^{(3)})(\theta)(0) = \frac{1}{100}\mathrm{D}(\theta)(0),\ (\mathrm{D}^{(2)})(\theta)(0) = \frac{1}{100}\theta(0) - \frac{1}{5},$$
$$\mathrm{D}(\theta)(0) = -\frac{1}{10}\theta(0) + 2]$$

Generate the Taylor series.

```
> T := taylor(theta(t), t);
```

$$T := \theta(0) + \mathrm{D}(\theta)(0)\,t + \frac{1}{2}(\mathrm{D}^{(2)})(\theta)(0)\,t^2 + \frac{1}{6}(\mathrm{D}^{(3)})(\theta)(0)$$
$$t^3 + \frac{1}{24}(\mathrm{D}^{(4)})(\theta)(0)\,t^4 + \frac{1}{120}(\mathrm{D}^{(5)})(\theta)(0)\,t^5 + \mathrm{O}(t^6)$$

Substitute the derivatives into the series.

```
> subs( op(L(0)), T );
```

$$\theta(0) + (-\frac{1}{10}\theta(0) + 2)\,t + (\frac{1}{200}\theta(0) - \frac{1}{10})\,t^2 +$$
$$(-\frac{1}{6000}\theta(0) + \frac{1}{300})\,t^3 + (\frac{1}{240000}\theta(0) - \frac{1}{12000})\,t^4 +$$
$$(-\frac{1}{12000000}\theta(0) + \frac{1}{600000})\,t^5 + \mathrm{O}(t^6)$$

Evaluate the series at the initial condition and convert it to a polynomial.

```
> eval( %, ini );
```

$$100 - 8\,t + \frac{2}{5}t^2 - \frac{1}{75}t^3 + \frac{1}{3000}t^4 - \frac{1}{150000}t^5 + \mathrm{O}(t^6)$$

```
> p := convert(%, polynom);
```

$$p := 100 - 8\,t + \frac{2}{5}\,t^2 - \frac{1}{75}\,t^3 + \frac{1}{3000}\,t^4 - \frac{1}{150000}\,t^5$$

You can now plot the response.

```
> plot(p, t=0..30);
```

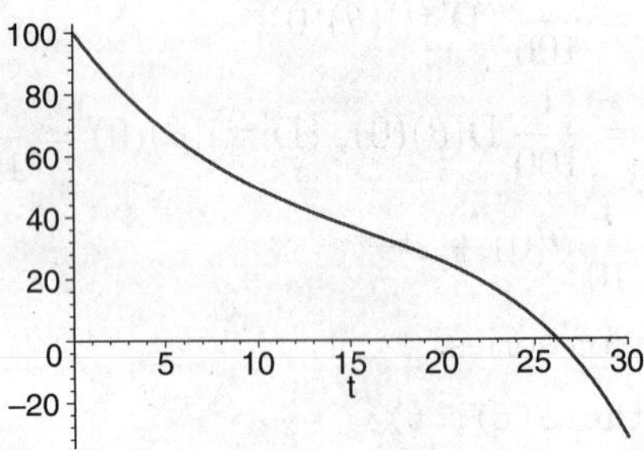

This particular example has the following analytic solution.

```
> dsolve( {eq(t), ini}, {theta(t)} );
```

$$\theta(t) = 20 + 80\,e^{(-1/10\,t)}$$

```
> q := rhs(%);
```

$$q := 20 + 80\,e^{(-1/10\,t)}$$

Thus, you can compare the series solution with the actual solution.

```
> plot( [p, q], t=0..30 );
```

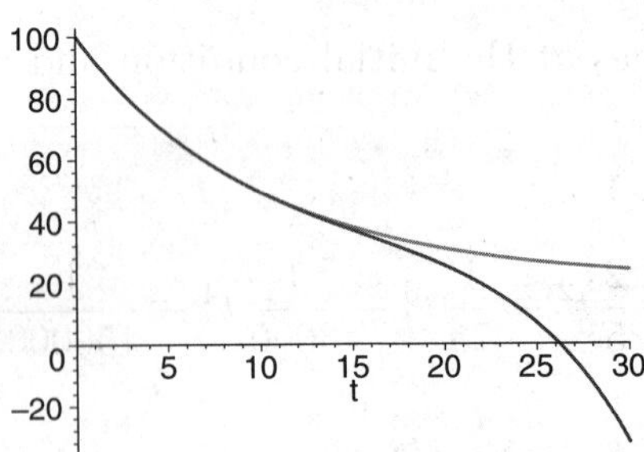

Instead of finding the Taylor series by hand, you can use the **series** option of the **dsolve** command.

```
> dsolve( {eq(t), ini}, {theta(t)}, 'series' );
```

$$\theta(t) =$$
$$100 - 8\,t + \frac{2}{5}\,t^2 - \frac{1}{75}\,t^3 + \frac{1}{3000}\,t^4 - \frac{1}{150000}\,t^5 + \mathrm{O}(t^6)$$

When You Cannot Find a Closed Form Solution

In some instances, you cannot express the solution to a linear ODE in closed form. In such cases, `dsolve` may return solutions containing the data structure `DESol`. `DESol` is a place holder representing the solution of a differential equation without explicitly computing it. Thus, `DESol` is similar to `RootOf`, which represents the roots of an expression. This allows you to manipulate the resulting expression symbolically prior to attempting another approach.

```
> de := (x^7+x^3-3)*diff(y(x),x,x) + x^4*diff(y(x),x)
>         + (23*x-17)*y(x);
```

$$de :=$$
$$(x^7 + x^3 - 3)\,(\tfrac{d^2}{dx^2}\,\mathrm{y}(x)) + x^4\,(\tfrac{d}{dx}\,\mathrm{y}(x)) + (23\,x - 17)\,\mathrm{y}(x)$$

The `dsolve` command cannot find a closed form solution to `de`.

```
> dsolve( de, y(x) );
```

$$\mathrm{y}(x) = \mathrm{DESol}\Bigg($$
$$\left\{(\tfrac{d^2}{dx^2}\,\_\mathrm{Y}(x)) + \frac{x^4\,(\frac{d}{dx}\,\_\mathrm{Y}(x))}{x^7 + x^3 - 3} + \frac{(23\,x - 17)\,\_\mathrm{Y}(x)}{x^7 + x^3 - 3}\right\},$$
$$\{\_\mathrm{Y}(x)\}\Bigg)$$

You can now try another method on the `DESol` itself. For example, find a series approximation.

```
> series(rhs(%), x);
```

$$\_Y(0) + D(\_Y)(0)\, x - \frac{17}{6}\, \_Y(0)\, x^2 +$$
$$(-\frac{17}{18}\, D(\_Y)(0) + \frac{23}{18}\, \_Y(0))\, x^3 +$$
$$(\frac{289}{216}\, \_Y(0) + \frac{23}{36}\, D(\_Y)(0))\, x^4 +$$
$$(\frac{289}{1080}\, D(\_Y)(0) - \frac{833}{540}\, \_Y(0))\, x^5 + O(x^6)$$

The `diff` and `int` commands can also operate on `DESol`.

Plotting Ordinary Differential Equations

You cannot solve many differential equations analytically. In such cases, plotting the differential equation is advantageous.

```
> ode1 :=
> diff(y(t), t$2) + sin(t)^2*diff(y(t),t) + y(t) = cos(t)^2;
```

$$ode1 := (\frac{d^2}{dt^2}\, y(t)) + \sin(t)^2\, (\frac{d}{dt}\, y(t)) + y(t) = \cos(t)^2$$

```
> ic1 := y(0) = 1, D(y)(0) = 0;
```

$$ic1 := y(0) = 1,\, D(y)(0) = 0$$

First, attempt to solve this ODE analytically by using `dsolve`.

```
> dsolve({ode1, ic1}, {y(t)} );
```

The `dsolve` command returned nothing, indicating that it could not find a solution. Try Laplace methods.

```
> dsolve( {ode1, ic1}, {y(t)}, method=laplace );
```

Again, `dsolve` did not find a solution. Since `dsolve` was not successful, try the `DEplot` command found in the `DEtools` package.

```
> with(DEtools):
```

`DEplot` is a general ODE plotter which you can use with the following syntax.

```
DEplot( ode, dep-var, range, [ini-conds] )
```

- *ode* is the differential equation to plot
- *dep-var* is the dependent variable
- *range* is the range of the independent variable
- *ini-conds* is a list of initial conditions

The following is a plot of the function satisfying both the differential equation `ode1` and the initial conditions `ic1` above.

```
> DEplot( ode1, y(t), 0..20, [ [ ic1 ] ] );
```

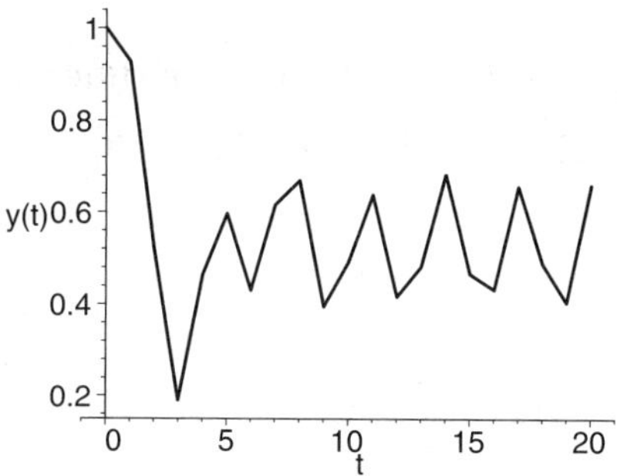

You can refine the plot by specifying a smaller `stepsize`.

```
> DEplot( ode1, y(t), 0..20, [ [ ic1 ] ], stepsize=0.2 );
```

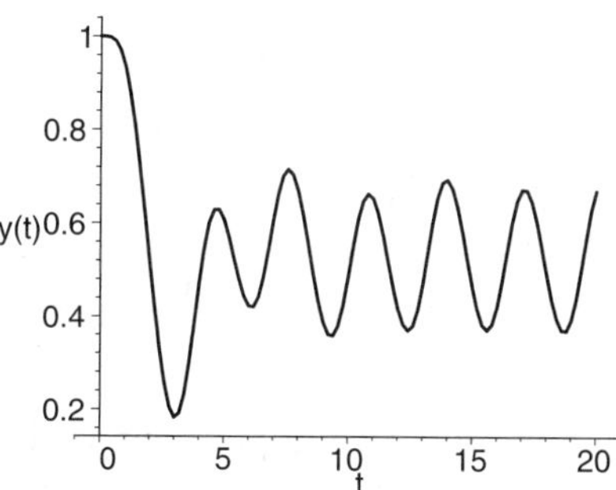

If you specify more than one list of initial conditions, `DEplot` plots a solution for each.

```
> ic2 := y(0)=0, D(y)(0)=1;
```

$$ic2 := y(0) = 0, D(y)(0) = 1$$

```
> DEplot( ode1, y(t), 0..20, [ [ic1], [ic2] ], stepsize=0.2 );
```

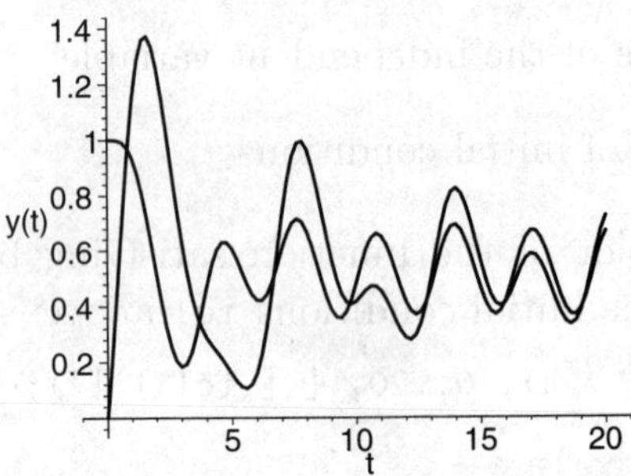

DEplot can also plot solutions to a set of differential equations.

```
> eq1 := diff(y(t),t) + y(t) + x(t) = 0;
```

$$eq1 := (\frac{d}{dt}\,y(t)) + y(t) + x(t) = 0$$

```
> eq2 := y(t) = diff(x(t), t);
```

$$eq2 := y(t) = \frac{d}{dt}\,x(t)$$

```
> ini1 := x(0)=0, y(0)=5;
```

$$ini1 := x(0) = 0, y(0) = 5$$

```
> ini2 := x(0)=0, y(0)=-5;
```

$$ini2 := x(0) = 0, y(0) = -5$$

The system {eq1, eq2} has two dependent variables, x(t) and y(t), so you must include a list of dependent variables.

```
> DEplot( {eq1, eq2}, [x(t), y(t)], -5..5,
> [ [ini1], [ini2] ] );
```

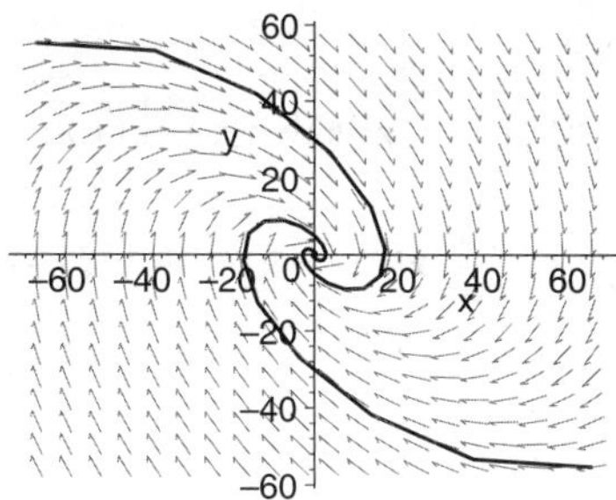

Note: `DEplot` also generates a direction field, as above, whenever it is meaningful to do so. For more details on how to plot ODEs, refer to the `?DEtools,DEplot` help page.

`DEplot3d` is the three-dimensional version of `DEplot`. The basic syntax of `DEplot3d` is similar to that of `DEplot`. For details, refer to the `?DEtools,DEplot3d` help page. The following is a three-dimensional plot of the system plotted in two dimensions above.

```
> DEplot3d( {eq1, eq2}, [x(t), y(t)], -5..5,
> [ [ini1], [ini2] ] );
```

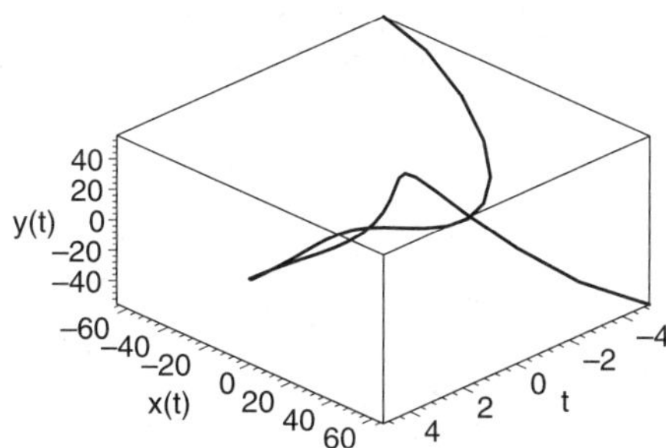

The following is an example of a plot of a system of three differential equations.

```
> eq1 := diff(x(t),t) = y(t)+z(t);
```

$$eq1 := \frac{d}{dt}\, \mathrm{x}(t) = \mathrm{y}(t) + \mathrm{z}(t)$$

```
> eq2 := diff(y(t),t) = -x(t)-y(t);
```

$$eq2 := \frac{d}{dt}\,\mathrm{y}(t) = -\mathrm{y}(t) - \mathrm{x}(t)$$

```
> eq3 := diff(z(t),t) = x(t)+y(t)-z(t);
```

$$eq3 := \frac{d}{dt}\,\mathrm{z}(t) = \mathrm{x}(t) + \mathrm{y}(t) - \mathrm{z}(t)$$

These are two lists of initial conditions.

```
> ini1 := [x(0)=1, y(0)=0, z(0)=2];
```

$$ini1 := [\mathrm{x}(0) = 1,\ \mathrm{y}(0) = 0,\ \mathrm{z}(0) = 2]$$

```
> ini2 := [x(0)=0, y(0)=2, z(0)=-1];
```

$$ini2 := [\mathrm{x}(0) = 0,\ \mathrm{y}(0) = 2,\ \mathrm{z}(0) = -1]$$

The DEplot3d command plots two solutions to the system of differential equations {eq1, eq2, eq3}, one solution for each list of initial values.

```
> DEplot3d( {eq1, eq2, eq3}, [x(t), y(t), z(t)], t=0..10,
>     [ini1, ini2], stepsize=0.1, orientation=[-171, 58] );
```

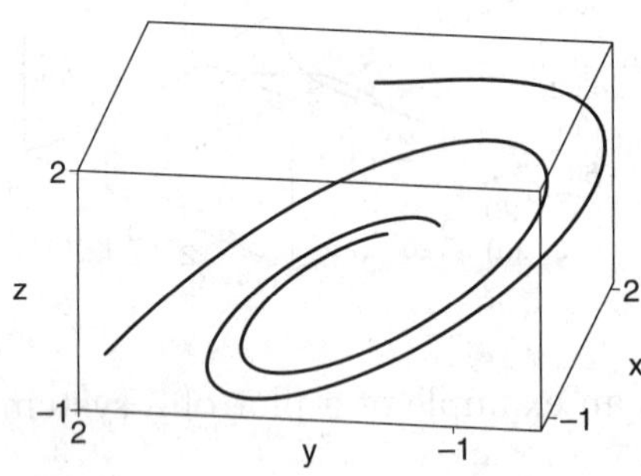

Discontinuous Forcing Functions

In many practical instances the forcing function to a system is discontinuous. Maple provides many ways to describe a system in terms of ODEs and include descriptions of discontinuous forcing functions.

The Heaviside Step Function Using the `Heaviside` function allows you to model delayed and piecewise-defined forcing functions. You can use `Heaviside` with `dsolve` to find both symbolic and numeric solutions.

```
> eq := diff(y(t),t) = -y(t)*Heaviside(t-1);
```

$$eq := \frac{d}{dt}\,\mathrm{y}(t) = -\mathrm{y}(t)\,\mathrm{Heaviside}(t-1)$$

```
> ini := y(0) = 3;
```

$$ini := \mathrm{y}(0) = 3$$

```
> dsolve({eq, ini}, {y(t)});
```

$$\mathrm{y}(t) = 3\,e^{((-t+1)\,\mathrm{Heaviside}(t-1))}$$

Convert the solution to a function that can be plotted.

```
> rhs( % );
```

$$3\,e^{((-t+1)\,\mathrm{Heaviside}(t-1))}$$

```
> f := unapply(%, t);
```

$$f := t \to 3\,e^{((-t+1)\,\mathrm{Heaviside}(t-1))}$$

```
> plot(f, 0..4);
```

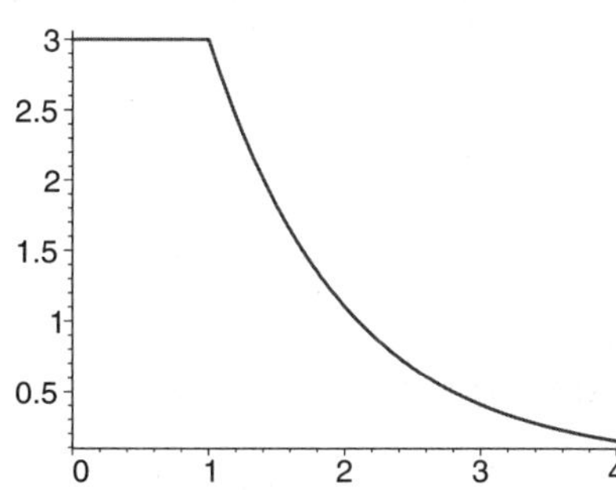

Solve the same equation numerically.

```
> sol1 := dsolve({eq, ini}, {y(t)}, type=numeric);
```

$$sol1 := \mathbf{proc}(x\_rkf45) \ldots \mathbf{end\ proc}$$

Use the odeplot command from the plots package to plot the solution.

```
> with(plots):
```

```
> odeplot( sol1, [t, y(t)], 0..4 );
```

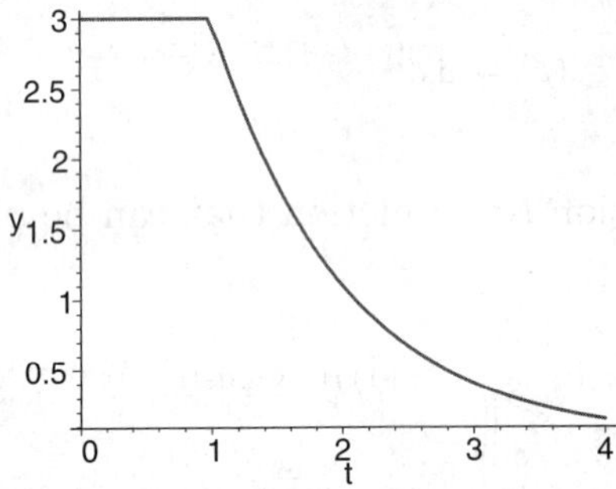

The Dirac Delta Function You can use the Dirac delta function in a manner similar to the Heaviside function above to produce impulsive forcing functions.

```
> eq := diff(y(t),t) = -y(t)*Dirac(t-1);
```

$$eq := \frac{d}{dt}\,\mathrm{y}(t) = -\mathrm{y}(t)\,\mathrm{Dirac}(t-1)$$

```
> ini := y(0) = 3;
```

$$ini := \mathrm{y}(0) = 3$$

```
> dsolve({eq, ini}, {y(t)});
```

$$\mathrm{y}(t) = 3\,e^{(-\mathrm{Heaviside}(t-1))}$$

Convert the solution to a function that can be plotted.

```
> f := unapply( rhs( % ), t );
```

$$f := t \to 3\,e^{(-\mathrm{Heaviside}(t-1))}$$

```
> plot( f, 0..4 );
```

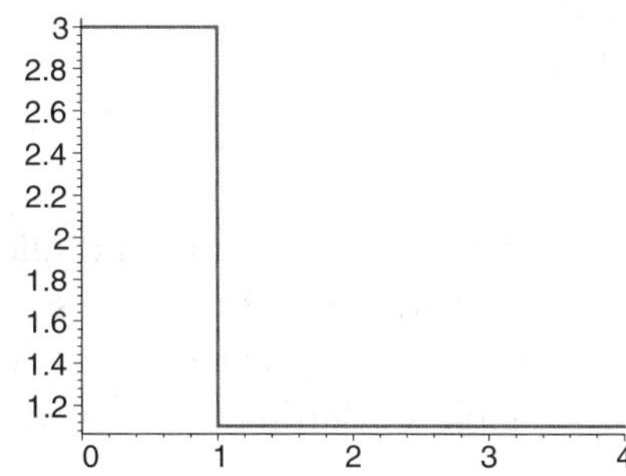

However, the numeric solution does not see the nonzero value of Dirac(0).

```
> sol2 := dsolve({eq, ini}, {y(t)}, type=numeric);
```

$$sol2 := \mathbf{proc}(x\_rkf45)\ \ldots\ \mathbf{end\ proc}$$

Use odeplot from plots to plot the numeric solution.

```
> with(plots, odeplot);
```

$$[odeplot]$$

```
> odeplot( sol2, [t,y(t)], 0..4 );
```

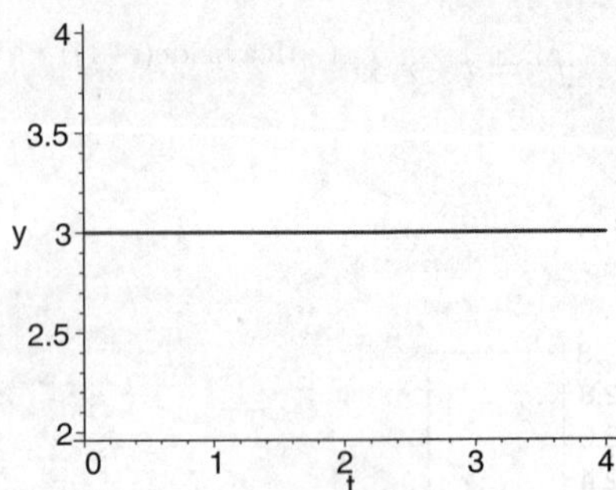

Piecewise Functions The `piecewise` command allows you to construct complicated forcing functions by approximating sections of it with analytic functions, and then taking the approximations together to represent the whole function. First, look at the behavior of `piecewise`.

```
> f:=  x -> piecewise(1<=x and x<2, 1, 0);
```

$$f := x \to \text{piecewise}(1 \le x \textbf{ and } x < 2,\ 1,\ 0)$$

```
> f(x);
```

$$\begin{cases} 1, & \text{if } , 1 - x \le 0 \text{ and } x - 2 < 0; \\ 0, & \text{otherwise.} \end{cases}$$

Note that the order of the conditionals is important. The first conditional that returns `true` causes the function to return a value.

```
> plot(f, 0..3);
```

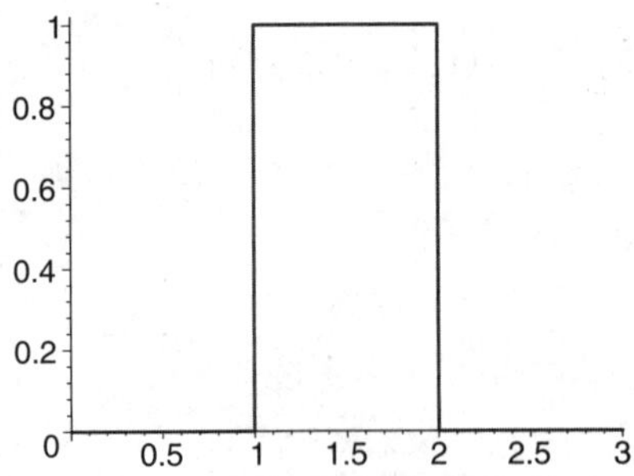

Thus, you can use this `piecewise` function as a forcing function.

```
> eq := diff(y(t),t) = 1-y(t)*f(t);
```

$$eq := \frac{d}{dt}\,\mathrm{y}(t) = 1 - \mathrm{y}(t)\left(\begin{cases} 1, & \text{if } 1 - t \le 0 \text{ and } t - 2 < 0; \\ 0, & \text{otherwise.} \end{cases}\right)$$

```
> ini := y(0)=3;
```

$$ini := \mathrm{y}(0) = 3$$

```
> sol3 := dsolve({eq, ini}, {y(t)}, type=numeric);
```

$$sol3 := \mathbf{proc}(x\_rkf45)\ \ldots\ \mathbf{end\ proc}$$

Use the `odeplot` command in the `plots` package to plot the result.

```
> with(plots, odeplot):
```

```
> odeplot( sol3, [t, y(t)], 0..4 );
```

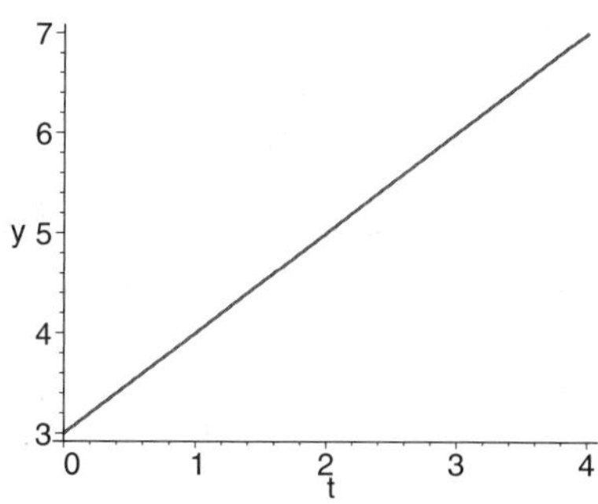

The `DEtools` package contains commands that can help you investigate, manipulate, plot, and solve differential equations. For details, refer to the `?DEtools` help page.

Interactive ODE Analyzer

The `dsolve[interactive](odesys,options)` command launches a graphical user interface for the investigation and solution of ODE and ODE systems.

If `odesys` is not given in the call to `dsolve[interactive]`, then `odesys` can be entered by using the interface; otherwise, the input equations are examined and used as a starting point for the application (these equations can be changed from within the graphical user interface).

For details about the command and interface, see `?dsolve,interactive` and `?worksheet,interactive,dsolveinterface`.

7.3 Partial Differential Equations

Partial differential equations (PDEs) are in general very difficult to solve. Maple provides a number of commands for solving, manipulating, and plotting PDEs. Some of these commands are in the standard library, but most of them reside in the `PDEtools` package.

The pdsolve Command

The `pdsolve` command can solve many partial differential equations. This is the basic syntax of the `pdsolve` command.

```
pdsolve( pde, var )
```

- *pde* is the partial differential equation
- *var* is the variable with respect to which `pdsolve` solves

The following is the one-dimensional wave equation.

```
> wave := diff(u(x,t), t,t) - c^2 * diff(u(x,t), x,x);
```

$$wave := (\frac{\partial^2}{\partial t^2}\,\mathrm{u}(x,\,t)) - c^2\,(\frac{\partial^2}{\partial x^2}\,\mathrm{u}(x,\,t))$$

To solve for `u(x,t)`, first load the `PDEtools` package.

```
> with(PDEtools):
> sol := pdsolve( wave, u(x,t) );
```

$$sol := \mathrm{u}(x,\,t) = \_\mathrm{F1}(c\,t + x) + \_\mathrm{F2}(c\,t - x)$$

Note the solution is in terms of two arbitrary functions, _F1 and _F2. To plot the solution you need a particular set of functions.

```
> f1 := xi -> exp(-xi^2);
```

$$f1 := \xi \to e^{(-\xi^2)}$$

```
> f2 := xi -> piecewise(-1/2<xi and xi<1/2, 1, 0);
```

$$f2 := \xi \to \text{piecewise}(\frac{-1}{2} < \xi \textbf{ and } \xi < \frac{1}{2}, 1, 0)$$

Substitute these functions into the solution.

```
> eval( sol, {_F1=f1, _F2=f2, c=1} );
```

$$\text{u}(x, t) = e^{(-(t+x)^2)} + \left(\begin{cases} 1 & -t+x < \frac{1}{2} \textbf{ and } t-x < \frac{1}{2} \\ 0 & \textit{otherwise} \end{cases}\right)$$

Use the **rhs** command to select the solution.

```
> rhs(%);
```

$$e^{(-(t+x)^2)} + \left(\begin{cases} 1 & -t+x < \frac{1}{2} \textbf{ and } t-x < \frac{1}{2} \\ 0 & \textit{otherwise} \end{cases}\right)$$

The **unapply** command converts the expression to a function.

```
> f := unapply(%, x,t);
```

$$f := (x, t) \to$$
$$e^{(-(t+x)^2)} + \text{piecewise}(-t+x < \frac{1}{2} \textbf{ and } t-x < \frac{1}{2}, 1, 0)$$

Plot the solution.

```
> plot3d( f, -8..8, 0..5, grid=[40,40] );
```

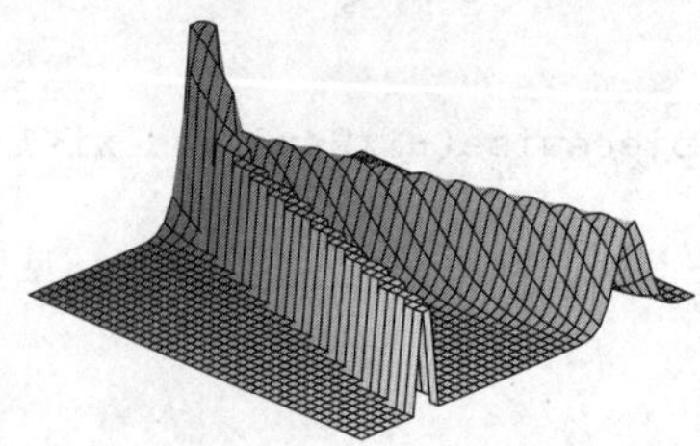

Changing the Dependent Variable in a PDE

The following is the one-dimensional heat equation.

```
> heat := diff(u(x,t),t) - k*diff(u(x,t), x,x) = 0;
```

$$heat := (\frac{\partial}{\partial t}\mathrm{u}(x,\,t)) - k\,(\frac{\partial^2}{\partial x^2}\mathrm{u}(x,\,t)) = 0$$

Try to find a solution of the form $X(x)T(t)$ to this equation. Use the aptly named HINT option of pdsolve to suggest a course of action.

```
> pdsolve( heat, u(x,t), HINT=X(x)*T(t));
```

$$(\mathrm{u}(x,\,t) = \mathrm{X}(x)\,\mathrm{T}(t))\ \&\mathrm{where}$$
$$[\{\tfrac{d}{dt}\,\mathrm{T}(t) = k\,\_c_1\,\mathrm{T}(t),\ \tfrac{d^2}{dx^2}\,\mathrm{X}(x) = \_c_1\,\mathrm{X}(x)\}]$$

The result here is correct, but difficult to read.

Alternatively, use product separation of variables with pdsolve (by specifying HINT='*') and then solve the resulting ODEs (by specifying the 'build' option).

```
> sol := pdsolve(heat, u(x,t), HINT='*', 'build');
```

$$sol := \mathrm{u}(x,\,t) = e^{(\sqrt{\_c_1}\,x)}\,\_C3\,e^{(k\,\_c_1\,t)}\,\_C1 + \frac{\_C3\,e^{(k\,\_c_1\,t)}\,\_C2}{e^{(\sqrt{\_c_1}\,x)}}$$

Evaluate the solution at specific values for the constants.

```
> S := eval( rhs(sol), {_C3=1, _C1=1, _C2=1, k=1, _c[1]=1} );
```

$$S := e^x\, e^t + \frac{e^t}{e^x}$$

You can plot the solution.

```
> plot3d( S, x=-5..5, t=0..5 );
```

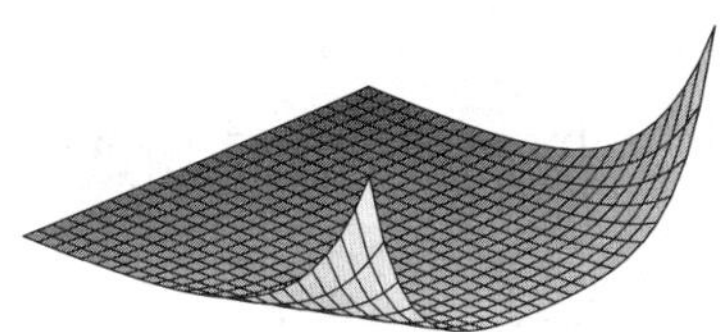

Check the solution by evaluation with the original equation.

```
> eval( heat, u(x,t)=rhs(sol) );
```

$$\%1\ \_C3\ k\ \_c_1\ e^{(k\ \_c_1\ t)}\ \_C1 + \frac{\_C3\ k\ \_c_1\ e^{(k\ \_c_1\ t)}\ \_C2}{\%1}$$
$$- k\,(\_c_1\ \%1\ \_C3\ e^{(k\ \_c_1\ t)}\ \_C1 + \frac{\_C3\ e^{(k\ \_c_1\ t)}\ \_C2\ \_c_1}{\%1}) = 0$$
$$\%1 := e^{(\sqrt{\_c_1}\, x)}$$

```
> simplify(%);
```

$$0 = 0$$

Plotting Partial Differential Equations

The solutions to many PDEs can be plotted with the PDEplot command in the PDEtools package.

```
> with(PDEtools):
```

You can use the PDEplot command with the following syntax.

```
PDEplot( pde, var, ini, s=range )
```

- *pde* is the PDE
- *var* is the dependent variable

- *ini* is a parametric curve in three-dimensional space with parameter s
- *range* is the range of s

Consider this partial differential equation.

```
> pde := diff(u(x,y), x) + cos(2*x) * diff(u(x,y), y) = -sin(y);
```

$$pde := (\frac{\partial}{\partial x} \mathrm{u}(x, y)) + \cos(2\,x)\,(\frac{\partial}{\partial y} \mathrm{u}(x, y)) = -\sin(y)$$

Use the curve given by $z = 1 + y^2$ as an initial condition, that is, $x = 0$, $y = s$, and $z = 1 + s^2$.

```
> ini := [0, s, 1+s^2];
```

$$ini := [0,\ s,\ 1 + s^2]$$

`PDEplot` draws the initial-condition curve and the solution surface.

```
> PDEplot( pde, u(x,y), ini, s=-2..2 );
```

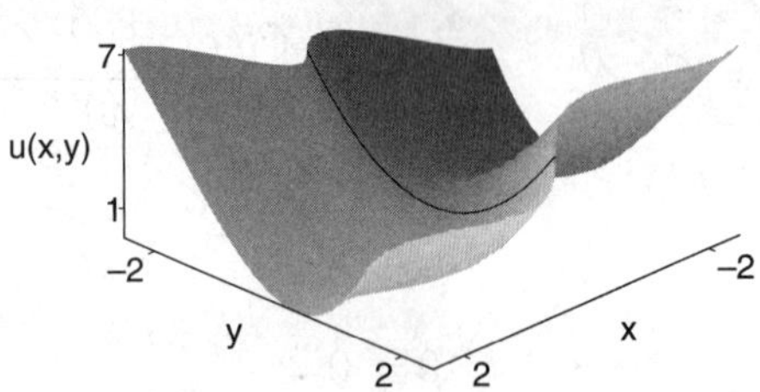

To draw the surface, Maple calculates these base characteristic curves. The initial-condition curve is easier to see here than in the previous plot.

```
> PDEplot( pde, u(x,y), ini, s=-2..2, basechar=only );
```

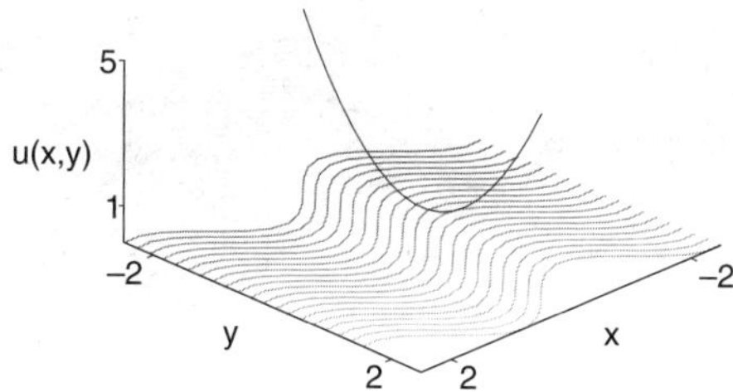

With the `basechar=true` option, `PDEplot` draws both the characteristic curves and the surface, as well as the initial-condition curve which is always present.

```
> PDEplot( pde, u(x,y), ini, s=-2..2, basechar=true );
```

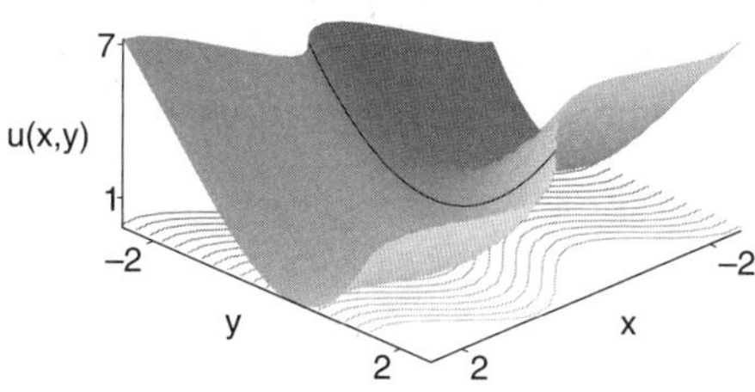

Many `plot3d` options are available. Refer to the `?plot3d,options` help page. The `initcolor` option sets the color of the initial value curve.

```
> PDEplot( pde, u(x,y), ini, s=-2..2,
>    basechar=true, initcolor=white,
>    style=patchcontour, contours=20,
>    orientation=[-43,45] );
```

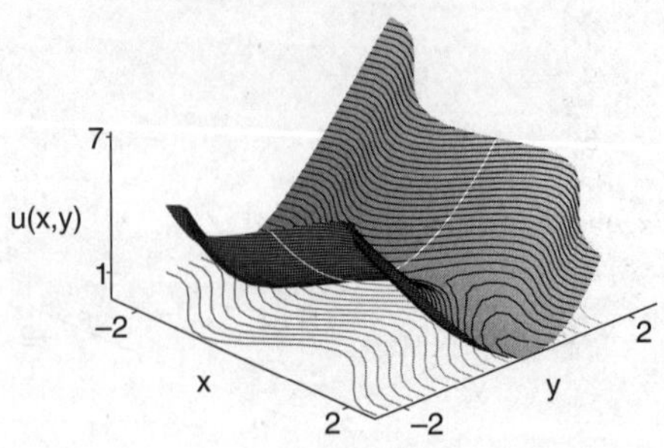

7.4 Conclusion

This chapter has demonstrated how Maple can be used to aid in the investigation and solution of problems using calculus. You have seen how Maple can visually represent concepts, such as the derivative and the Riemann integral; help analyze the error term in a Taylor approximation; and manipulate and solve ordinary and partial differential equations, numerically as well as symbolically.

8 Input and Output

Maple provides convenient ways to import and export raw numerical data and graphics. It presents individual algebraic and numeric results in formats suitable for use in FORTRAN, C, or the mathematical typesetting system LaTeX. You can export the entire worksheet as a file in any of the following formats: HTML or HTML with MathML, LaTeX, Maple Input, Maple Text, Maplet application, Plain Text, or Rich Text Format. You can cut and paste results, and export either single expressions or entire worksheets.

This chapter discusses the most common aspects of exporting and importing information to and from files. It introduces how Maple interacts with the file system on your computer, and how Maple can begin interacting with other software.

In This Chapter

- Reading Files
- Writing Data to a File
- Exporting Worksheets
- Printing Graphics

8.1 Reading Files

The two most common cases for reading files are to obtain data and to retrieve Maple commands stored in a text file.

- The first case is often concerned with data generated from an experiment. You can store numbers separated by whitespace and line breaks in a text file, then read them into Maple for study. You can accomplish these operations by using the Maple `ExportMatrix` and `ImportMatrix` commands.

- The second case concerns reading commands from a text file. Perhaps you have received a worksheet in text format, or you have written a Maple procedure by using a text editor and have stored it in a text file. You can cut and paste commands into Maple or you can use the `read` command.

The following section discusses the second case.

Reading Columns of Numbers from a File

If you generate data outside Maple, you must read it into Maple before you can manipulate it. Often such external data is in the form of columns of numbers in a text file. The file `data.txt` below is an example.

```
0 1 0
1 .5403023059 .8414709848
2 -.4161468365 .9092974268
3 -.9899924966 .1411200081
4 -.6536436209 -.7568024953
5 .2836621855 -.9589242747
6 .9601702867 -.2794154982
```

The `ImportMatrix` command reads columns of numbers. Use `ImportMatrix` as follows.

```
ImportMatrix( "filename", delimiter=string )
```

- *filename* is the name of the file to read
- *string* is the character that separates the entries in the file. The default value of *string* is a tab, represented by using `"\t"`. In `data.txt`, the entries are separated by spaces, so the value of *string* is `" "`

```
> L := ImportMatrix( "data.txt", delimiter="\t" );
```

$$L := \begin{bmatrix} 0 & 1 & 0 \\ 1 & 0.5403023059 & 0.8414709848 \\ 2 & -0.4161468365 & 0.9092974268 \\ 3 & -0.9899924966 & 0.1411200081 \\ 4 & -0.6536436209 & -0.7568024953 \\ 5 & 0.2836621855 & -0.9589242747 \\ 6 & 0.9601702867 & -0.2794154982 \end{bmatrix}$$

For example, you can plot the third column against the first. Use the `convert` command to select the first and the third entries in each column.

```
> convert( L[[1..-1],[1,3]], listlist );
```

$$[[0, 0], [1, 0.8414709848], [2, 0.9092974268], [3, 0.1411200081], [4, -0.7568024953], [5, -0.9589242747], [6, -0.2794154982]]$$

The `plot` command can plot lists directly.

```
> plot(%);
```

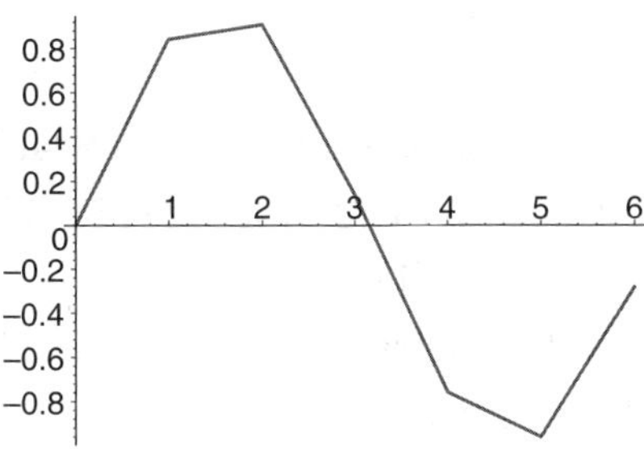

To select the second column of numbers, you can use the fact that `L[5,2]` is the second number in the fifth sublist.

```
> L[5,2];
```

$$-0.6536436209$$

You need the following data.

```
> L[ 1..-1, 2 ];
```

$$\begin{bmatrix} 1 \\ 0.5403023059 \\ -0.4161468365 \\ -0.9899924966 \\ -0.6536436209 \\ 0.2836621855 \\ 0.9601702867 \end{bmatrix}$$

Convert this data to a list, and then find the mean.

```
> convert(L[1..-1,2],list);
```

$$[1, 0.5403023059, -0.4161468365, -0.9899924966, -0.6536436209, 0.2836621855, 0.9601702867]$$

```
> stats[describe,mean](%) ;
```

$$0.1034788321$$

You can also perform calculations on your matrix L using the `LinearAlgebra` package.

```
> LinearAlgebra[Transpose](L) . L;
```

$$\begin{bmatrix} 91., & 1.30278930720000119, & -6.41489848119999984 \\ 1.30278930720000119, & 3.87483111270157598, & -0.109078174475632172 \\ -6.41489848119999984, & -0.109078174475632172, & 3.12516888746710864 \end{bmatrix}$$

For more information regarding options for use with `ImportMatrix`, refer to the `?ImportMatrix` help page.

Reading Commands from a File

Some Maple users find it convenient to write Maple programs in a text file with a text editor, and then import the file into Maple. You can paste the commands from the text file into your worksheet or you can use the `read` command.

When you read a file with the `read` command, Maple treats each line in the file as a command. Maple executes the commands and displays the results in your worksheet but it does *not*, by default, place the commands from the file in your worksheet. Use the `read` command with the following syntax.

```
read "filename";
```

For example, the file `ks.tst` contains the following Maple commands.

```
S := n -> sum( binomial(n, beta)
   * ( (2*beta)!/2^beta - beta!*beta ), beta=1..n );
S( 19 );
```

When you read the file, Maple displays the results but not the commands.

```
> read "ks.tst";
```

$$S := n \to \sum_{\beta=1}^{n} \mathrm{binomial}(n,\, \beta)\, (\frac{(2\,\beta)!}{2^{\beta}} - \beta!\, \beta)$$

$$1024937361666644598071114328769317982974$$

Inserting Commands If you set the `interface` variable `echo` to 2, Maple inserts the commands from the file into your worksheet.

```
> interface( echo=2 );
> read "ks.tst";

> S := n -> sum( binomial(n, beta)
>     * ( (2*beta)!/2^beta - beta!*beta ), beta=1..n );
```

$$S := n \to \sum_{\beta=1}^{n} \mathrm{binomial}(n,\, \beta)\, (\frac{(2\,\beta)!}{2^{\beta}} - \beta!\, \beta)$$

```
> S( 19 );
```

$$1024937361666644598071114328769317982974$$

The `read` command can also read files in Maple internal format. See **8.2 Writing Data to a File**.

8.2 Writing Data to a File

After using Maple to perform a calculation, you may want to save the result in a file. You can then process the result later, either with Maple or with another program.

Writing Columns of Numerical Data to a File

If the result of a Maple calculation is a long list or a large array of numbers, you can convert it to a Matrix and write the numbers to a file in a structured manner.

The `ExportMatrix` Command The `ExportMatrix` command writes columns of numerical data to a file, allowing you to import the numbers into another program. You can use the `ExportMatrix` command with the following syntax.

```
ExportMatrix( "filename", data )
```

- *filename* is the string containing the name of the file to which `ExportMatrix` writes the data
- *data* is a Matrix

Note: A list, vector, list of lists, or table-based matrix can be converted to a Matrix by using the `Matrix` constructor. For more information, refer to the `?Matrix` help page.

```
> L:=LinearAlgebra[RandomMatrix](5);
```

$$L := \begin{bmatrix} -66 & -65 & 20 & -90 & 30 \\ 55 & 5 & -7 & -21 & 62 \\ 68 & 66 & 16 & -56 & -79 \\ 26 & -36 & -34 & -8 & -71 \\ 13 & -41 & -62 & -50 & 28 \end{bmatrix}$$

```
> ExportMatrix("matrixdata.txt", L):
```

If the data is a Vector or any object that can be converted to type Vector, then `ExportVector` can be used. Lists and table-based vectors can be converted by using the `Vector` constructor. For more information, refer to the `?Vector` help page.

```
> L := [ 3, 3.1415, -65, 0 ];
```

$$L := [3, 3.1415, -65, 0]$$

```
> V := Vector(L);
```

$$V := \begin{bmatrix} 3 \\ 3.1415 \\ -65 \\ 0 \end{bmatrix}$$

```
> ExportVector( "vectordata.txt", V ):
```

You can extend these routines to write more complicated data, such as complex numbers or symbolic expressions. For more information, refer to the `?ExportMatrix` and `?ExportVector` help pages.

Saving Expressions in the Maple Internal Format

If you construct a complicated expression or procedure, you can save it for future use in Maple. If you save the expression or procedure in the Maple internal format, then Maple can retrieve it efficiently. Use the `save` command to write the expression to a filename ending with the characters ".m". Use the `save` command with the following syntax.

```
save nameseq, "filename.m";
```

- *nameseq* is a sequence of names; you can save only named objects. The `save` command saves the objects in ***filename*.m**
- `.m` indicates that `save` writes the file using the Maple internal format

Consider the following.

```
> qbinomial := (n,k) -> product(1-q^i, i=n-k+1..n) /
>                        product(1-q^i, i=1..k );
```

$$qbinomial := (n, k) \to \frac{\prod_{i=n-k+1}^{n} (1 - q^i)}{\prod_{i=1}^{k} (1 - q^i)}$$

```
> expr := qbinomial(10, 4);
```

$$expr := \frac{(1 - q^7)(1 - q^8)(1 - q^9)(1 - q^{10})}{(1 - q)(1 - q^2)(1 - q^3)(1 - q^4)}$$

```
> nexpr := normal( expr );
```

$$nexpr := (q^6 + q^5 + q^4 + q^3 + q^2 + q + 1)(q^4 + 1)(q^6 + q^3 + 1)$$
$$(q^8 + q^6 + q^4 + q^2 + 1)$$

You can save these expressions to the file `qbinom.m`.

```
> save qbinomial, expr, nexpr, "qbinom.m";
```

The `restart` command clears the three expressions from memory. Thus `expr` evaluates to its own name.

```
> restart:
> expr;
```

$$expr$$

Use the `read` command to retrieve the expressions that you saved in `qbinom.m`.

```
> read "qbinom.m";
```

Now `expr` has its value again.

```
> expr;
```

$$\frac{(1-q^7)(1-q^8)(1-q^9)(1-q^{10})}{(1-q)(1-q^2)(1-q^3)(1-q^4)}$$

For more information on the `read` command, see **8.1 Reading Files**.

Converting to LaTeX Format

TeX is a program for typesetting mathematics, and LaTeX is a macro package for TeX. The `latex` command converts Maple expressions to LaTeX format. You can perform conversion to LaTeX by using the `latex` command. Thus, you can use Maple to solve a problem, then convert the result to LaTeX code that can be included in a LaTeX document. Use the `latex` command in the following manner.

```
latex( expr, "filename" )
```

- *expr* can be any mathematical expression. Maple-specific expressions, such as procedures, are not translatable
- *filename* is optional, and specifies that Maple writes the translated output to the file you specified. If you do not specify a *filename*, Maple writes the output to the `default` output stream (your session)
- `latex` writes the LaTeX code corresponding to the Maple expression *expr* to the file *filename*. If *filename* exists, `latex` overwrites it. If you

omit *filename*, **latex** prints the LaTeX code on the screen. You can cut and paste from the output into your LaTeX document.

```
> latex( a/b );
```

```
{\frac {a}{b}}
```

```
> latex( Limit( int(f(x), x=-n..n), n=infinity ) );
```

```
\lim _{n\rightarrow \infty }\int _{-n}^{n}\!f
 \left( x \right) {dx}
```

The `latex` command:

- Produces code suitable for LaTeX math mode. However, it does not produce the command for entering and leaving math mode, and it does not attempt any line breaking or alignment.
- Can translate most types of mathematical expressions, including integrals, limits, sums, products, and matrices. You can expand the capabilities of `latex` by defining procedures with names of the form `'latex/`*`functionname`*`'`. Such a procedure formats calls to the function called *functionname*. You must produce the output of such formatting functions with the `printf` command.
- Uses the `writeto` command to redirect the output when you specify a *filename*.
- Does *not* generate the commands that LaTeX requires to put the typesetting system into mathematics mode (for example, $...$).

The following example shows the generation of LaTeX for an equation for an integral and its value.

Note: `Int`, the inert form of `int`, prevents the evaluation of the left-hand side of the equation that Maple is formatting.

```
> Int(1/(x^4+1),x) = int(1/(x^4+1),x);
```

$$\int \frac{1}{x^4+1}\,dx = \frac{1}{8}\sqrt{2}\ln(\frac{x^2+x\sqrt{2}+1}{x^2-x\sqrt{2}+1}) + \frac{1}{4}\sqrt{2}\arctan(x\sqrt{2}+1)$$
$$+\frac{1}{4}\sqrt{2}\arctan(x\sqrt{2}-1)$$

```
> latex(%);

\int \! \left( {x}^{4}+1 \right) ^{-1}{dx}=1/8
\,\sqrt {2}\ln  \left( {\frac {{x}^{2}+x\sqrt
{2}+1}{{x}^{2}-x\sqrt {2}+1}} \right) +1/4\,
\sqrt {2}\arctan \left( x\sqrt {2}+1 \right) +
1/4\,\sqrt {2}\arctan \left( x\sqrt {2}-1
 \right)
```

Section **8.3 Exporting Worksheets** describes how you can save an entire worksheet in LaTeX format.

8.3 Exporting Worksheets

You can save your worksheets by selecting **Save** or **Save As** from the **File** menu. By selecting **Export As** from the **File** menu, you can also export a worksheet in the following formats: HTML or HTML with MathML, LaTeX, Maple Input, Maplet application, Maple Text, Plain Text, and Rich Text Format. (Maple automatically appends an appropriate extension.) This allows you to process a worksheet outside Maple.

HTML and HTML with MathML

The `.html` file that Maple generates can be loaded into any HTML browser. MathML is the Internet standard, sanctioned by the World Wide Web Consortium (W3C), for the communication of structured mathematical formulae between applications. For more information about MathML, refer to the `?MathML` help page.

Translation of Maple Worksheets to HTML or HTML with MathML

- Animations are converted to animated GIFs.
- Embedded images and plots are converted to GIFs.
- HTML - Formatted mathematical output are converted to GIFs, with each line of mathematical notation corresponding to a separate GIF.
- HTML with MathML - Formatted mathematical output is encoded by using the MathML version 2.0 standard (default selection) or by using the MathML version 1.0 standard (optional selection).
- Hidden content is not exported.

- Hyperlinks to help pages are converted to plain text in HTML.
- Hyperlinks in worksheets are converted to links to HTML files. The links are renamed to be compatible with HTML. For example, a link in a Maple worksheet to a file named `example.mws` is converted to an html link to the file `example.html`.
- Page breaks that are entered manually in Maple are not exported to HTML.
- Sketch output is converted to GIF.
- Spreadsheets are converted to HTML tables.
- Worksheet styles are approximated by HTML style attributes on a text-object-by-text-object basis.

Maple worksheets that are exported to HTML translate into multiple documents when using frames. If the frames feature is not selected, only one page that contains the worksheet contents is created.

Exporting As HTML or HTML with MathML To export a Maple worksheet in HTML(HyperText Markup Language) format:

1. Open the worksheet to export.
2. From the **File** menu, select **Export As**. The **Export As** dialog opens.
3. Select **HTML** as a file type.
4. Specify a path and folder for the file.
5. Enter a filename.
6. Click **Export**. The **HTML Options** dialog opens.
7. In the **Image Subdirectory** field, enter the pathname for the directory where exported images are to be saved. Images in an HTML document cannot be saved in the HTML file. Each image is saved in its own GIF file. If the directory that you specified does not exist, it is created for you. All image directories are relative to the document. The default directory is `images`, and it is located under the same directory that was selected for the HTML document. For example, if the HTML document is saved in `/u/mydocs`, the default image directory will be `/u/mydocs/images`. An **Image Subdirectory** of "" causes the images to be saved in the same directory as the HTML file.

8. To export the worksheet as an HTML document with frames, select the **Use Frames** check box.

9. You can export mathematical expressions in various forms. Select **GIF** images, **MathML1.0**, **MathML2.0**, or **MathML2.0 with WebEQ**.

10. Click **OK**.

Example of Export to HTML Format The following is a Maple worksheet exported as HTML. Notice that other HTML documents (including a table of contents), which were created by the export process, are called within it.

```
<html>
<head>
<title>tut1.htm</title>
</head>
<basefont size=3>
<frameset cols="25%,*">
  <frame src="tut1TOC.htm" name="TableOfContents">
  <frame src="tut11.htm" name="Content">
<noframes>
Sorry, this document requires that your browser support
frames.
<a href="tut11.htm" target="Content">This link</a>
will take you to a non-frames presentation of the document.
</noframes>
</frameset>
</basefont>
</html>
```

The following is a portion of the `tut11.htm` file called in the above `tut1.htm` file.

```
<b><font color=#000000 size=5>Calculation</font></b>
</p>
<p align=left>
<font color=#000000>Look at the integral </font>
<img src="tut11.gif" width=120 height=60 alt="[Maple Math]"
align=middle>
<font color=#000000>. Notice that its integrand, </font>
<img src="tut12.gif" width=89 height=50 alt="[Maple Math]"
```

```
align=middle>
<font color=#000000>, depends on the parameter </font>
<img src="tut13.gif" width=13 height=32 alt="[Maple Math]"
align=middle>
<font color=#000000>.</font>
</p>
<p align=left>
<font color=#000000>Give the integral a name so that you
can refer to it later.</font>
</p>
<p align=left><a name="expr command">
<tt>&gt; </tt>
<b><font color=#FF0000>expr := Int(x^2 * sin(x-a),
x);</font></b>
</p>
<p align=center>
<img src="tut14.gif" width=169 height=49 alt="[Maple Math]">
</p>
<p align=left>
<font color=#000000>The value of the integral is </font>
<a href="tut4.html" target="_top">an anti-derivative</a>
<font color=#000000> of the integrand.</font>
</p>
```

LaTeX

The .tex file that Maple generates is ready for processing by LaTeX. All distributions of Maple include the necessary style files.

Translation of Maple Worksheets to LaTeX The following is a description of what happens when you export the worksheet.

- Displayed mathematics is translated into LaTeX 2e, using line-breaking algorithms to conform to the document width requested by the user.
- Hidden content is not exported.
- Images and sketches are not exported.
- Maple character styles are mapped directly onto LaTeX 2e macro calls.
- Maple paragraph styles are mapped onto LaTeX environments.
- Maple section headings are mapped onto LaTeX sections and subsections.

- Maple plots are rewritten in separate postscript files and links to those files are inserted in the LaTeX document.
- Maple spreadsheets are converted to LaTeX tables.

Exporting As LaTeX To export a Maple worksheet to LaTeX format:

1. Open the worksheet to export.
2. From the **File** menu, select **Export As**. The **Export As** dialog opens.
3. Select **LaTeX** as a file type.
4. Specify a path and folder for the file.
5. Enter a filename. Maple automatically appends a .tex extension.
6. Click **Export**.

Example of Export to LaTeX Format The following is a portion of a Maple worksheet exported as LaTeX.

```
\begin{verbatim}
%% Source Worksheet: tut1.mws
\documentclass{article}
\usepackage{maple2e}
\DefineParaStyle{Author}
\DefineParaStyle{Heading 1}
\DefineParaStyle{Maple Output}
\DefineParaStyle{Maple Plot}
\DefineParaStyle{Title}
\DefineCharStyle{2D Comment}
\DefineCharStyle{2D Math}
\DefineCharStyle{2D Output}
\DefineCharStyle{Hyperlink}
\begin{document}
\begin{maplegroup}
\begin{Title}
An Indefinite Integral
\end{Title}

\begin{Author}
by Author Name
\end{Author}
```

```
\end{maplegroup}
\section{Calculation}

Look at the integral
\mapleinline{inert}{2d}{Int(x^2*sin(x-a),x);}{%
$\int x^{2}\,\mathrm{sin}(x - a)\,dx$%
}. Notice that its integrand,
\mapleinline{inert}{2d}{x^2*sin(x-a);}{%
$x^{2}\,\mathrm{sin}(x - a)$%
}, depends on the parameter
\mapleinline{inert}{2d}{a;}{%
$a$%
}.
```

By default, the LaTeX style files are set for printing the `.tex` file using the `dvips` printer driver. You can change this behavior by specifying an option to the `\usepackage` LaTeX command in the preamble of your `.tex` file.

Section **8.4 Printing Graphics** describes how to save graphics directly. You can include such graphics files in your LaTeX document by using the `\mapleplot` LaTeX command.

Maple Input

Export a Maple worksheet as Maple Input so that it can be loaded into a command-line version of Maple.

Translation of Maple Worksheets to Maple Input The Maple **Export as Maple Input** facility translates a Maple worksheet into a `.mpl` file. The following describes what happens to various worksheet elements.

- Animations, embedded images and plots, hidden content, page breaks, sketches, spreadsheets, worksheet styles, page numbers, contents of collapsed sections, output, and standard math elements are all ignored.
- Hyperlinks are converted to plain text. The visible text of the link is present but information about the path is lost.
- Maple input, text, and standard math input regions are maintained.
- Text is preceded by the (`#`) character.

Important: When exporting a worksheet as Maple Input, your worksheet must contain explicit semicolons and not auto-inserted ones. The resulting exported **.mpl** file will not run in command-line Maple with auto-inserted semicolons.

Exporting As Maple Input Format To export a worksheet as Maple Input:

1. Open the worksheet to export.
2. From the **File** menu, select **Export As**. The **Export As** dialog opens.
3. Select **Maple Input** as a file type.
4. Specify a path and folder for the file.
5. Enter a filename.
6. Click **Export**.

Maplet Application

The Maple **Export As Maplet** facility translates a Maple worksheet into a `.maplet` file.

Translation of Maple Worksheets to Maplet Applications The following describes what happens to various worksheet elements.

- Animations, embedded images and plots, hidden content, page breaks, sketches, spreadsheets, worksheet styles, page numbers, contents of collapsed sections, output, and standard math elements are all ignored.
- Hyperlinks are converted to plain text. The visible text of the link is present but information about the path is lost.
- Maple input, text, and standard math input regions are maintained.
- Text is preceded by the (`#`) character.

Important: When exporting a worksheet as a Maplet application, your worksheet must contain explicit semicolons and not auto-inserted ones. The resulting exported **.maplet** file will not run in command-line Maple with auto-inserted semicolons.

Export As A Maplet Application To export a worksheet as a Maplet application:

1. Open the worksheet to export.
2. From the **File** menu, select **Export As**. The **Export As** dialog opens.
3. Select **Maplet** as a file type.
4. Specify a path and folder for the file.
5. Enter a filename.
6. Click **Export**.

The Maplet application can be displayed by using the `MapletViewer`.

Maple Text

Maple text is specially marked text that retains the worksheet's distinction between text, Maple input, and Maple output. Thus, you can export a worksheet as Maple text, send the text file by email, and the recipient can import the Maple text into a Maple session and regenerate most of the structure of your original worksheet.

Translation of Maple Worksheets to Maple Text When a Maple worksheet is translated into a Maple text file, the following describes what happens to various worksheet elements.

- Maple Input is preceded by a greater-than sign and a space (`> `).
- Text is preceded by a pound sign and a space (`# `).
- Page break objects inserted manually in Maple are not supported when exported as Maple Text.
- Hidden content is not exported.
- Graphics are not exported.
- Special symbols (and all output) are displayed in character-based typesetting.

Exporting As Maple Text To export a worksheet as Maple text:

1. Open the worksheet to export.
2. From the **File** menu, select **Export As**. The **Export As** dialog opens.
3. Select **Maple Text** as a file type.
4. Specify a path and folder for the file.
5. Enter a filename.
6. Click **Export**

Example of Export to Maple Text Format The following is a portion of a Maple worksheet exported as Maple text.

```
# An Indefinite Integral
# Calculation
# Look at the integral Int(x^2*sin(x-a),x);. Notice that its
# integrand, x^2*sin(x-a);, depends on the parameter a;.
# Give the integral a name so that you can refer to it later.
> expr := Int(x^2 * sin(x-a), x);

                             /
                            |    2
                  expr :=   |   x  sin(x - a) dx
                            |
                           /

# The value of the integral is an anti-derivative of the
# integrand.
> answer := value( % );
```

Opening A Worksheet in Maple Text Format To open a worksheet in Maple text format (as in the previous example):

1. From the **File** menu, select **Open**. The **Open** dialog appears.
2. Select **Text** as file type.
3. Double-click the desired file. The **Text Format Choice** dialog opens.
4. Select **Maple Text**.
5. Click **OK**.

Plain Text

Export a Maple worksheet as plain text so that you can open the text file in another application.

Translation of Maple Worksheets to Plain Text When a Maple worksheet is translated to Plain Text, the following describes what happens to various worksheet elements.

- Maple Input is preceded by a greater-than sign and a space (>).
- Text is preceded by nothing.
- Page break objects insert manually in Maple are not supported when export as plain text.
- Hidden content is not exported.
- Graphics are not exported.
- Special symbols like integral signs and exponents are dislayed in character-based typesetting.

Exporting As Plain Text To export a worksheet as plain text:

1. Open the worksheet to export.
2. From the **File** menu, select **Export As**. The **Export As** dialog opens.
3. Select **Plain Text** as a file type.
4. Specify a path and folder for the file.
5. Enter a filename. Maple automatically appends a .txt extension.
6. Click **Export**.

Example of Export to Plain Text Format The following is a portion of a Maple worksheet exported in plain text format.

```
An Indefinite Integral
Calculation
Look at the integral Int(x^2*sin(x-a),x);. Notice that its
integrand, x^2*sin(x-a);, depends on the parameter a;.
Give the integral a name so that you can refer to it later.
> expr := Int(x^2 * sin(x-a), x);
```

```
                    /
                   |   2
        expr :=    |  x  sin(x - a) dx
                   |
                  /
```

```
The value of the integral is an anti-derivative of the
integrand.
> answer := value( % );
```

RTF

The `.rtf` file that Maple generates can be loaded into any word processor that supports RTF.

Translation of Maple Worksheets to Rich Text Format The following describes what happens to various worksheet elements.

- Graphical, that is, non-textual items such as Plots, Standard Math, and Standard Math Input and Output, images, and Sketch output in the worksheet are converted to static images in the RTF file. Each line of math is converted to a separate image.
- Hidden content is not exported.
- Manual page breaks are translated to an RTF page break object.
- Page numbers are translated to RTF page numbers.
- Spreadsheet cells in the Maple worksheet are exported, along with the column and row headers, and converted to RTF tables.
- Standard Math and Standard Math Input are baseline aligned in Microsoft® Word.
- Worksheet styles are approximated by RTF styles.

Exporting As RTF Format To export a Maple worksheet in RTF (Rich Text Format):

1. Open the worksheet to export.
2. From the **File** menu, select **Export As**. The **Export As** dialog opens.
3. Select **Rich Text Format** as a file type.

4. Specify a path and folder for the file.

5. Enter a filename.

6. Click **Export**.

Example of Export to RTF Format The following is a portion of a Maple worksheet exported as RTF.

```
{\rtf1\ansi\ansicpg1252\deff0\deflang1033
{\fonttbl
{\f0 Times New Roman}
{\f1 Symbol}
{\f2 Courier New}
}
{\colortbl
\red205\green205\blue205;
\red255\green0\blue0;
\red0\green0\blue0;
\red0\green0\blue255;
}
{\stylesheet
{\s0 \widctlpar}
{\s1\qr footer_header}
{\*\cs12\f2\fs24\cf1\i0 \b \ul0 \additive Maple Input}
{\*\cs13\f0\fs24\cf2\i0 \b0 \ul0 \additive 2D Comment}
{\*\cs14\f0\fs24\cf1\i0 \b0 \ul0 \additive 2D Input}
{\*\cs15\f0\fs24\cf3\i0 \b0 \ul0 \additive 2D Output}
```

XML

Because Maple worksheets (.mw files) are saved in an XML-based format, you can display the structure of a Maple worksheet in XML applications.

Loading XML Files as Worksheets You can use the graphical user interface to open an existing `.xml` document as a worksheet to modify content or to change the file's appearance.

1. From the **File** menu, select **Open**. The **Open** dialog appears.

2. Select **Maple Worksheet as XML** to display all XML files.

3. From the **Files** list, select the XML file.

4. Click **OK**.

8.4 Printing Graphics

On most platforms, Maple by default displays graphics directly in the worksheet as *inline plots*. You can use the `plotsetup` command to change this behavior.

Note: Plots created with the default thickness of 0 are sometimes too faint for professionally published documents. It is recommended that you increase plot line thickness to 3 before submitting documents for professional printing. For information about this feature, see the `?plot[options]` help page.

Displaying Graphics in Separate Windows

To display graphics in separate windows on your screen, use the following command.

```
> plotsetup(window);
```

With your plot in a separate window, you can print it through the **File** menu as you would print any other worksheet.

The `plotsetup` command has the following general syntax.

```
plotsetup( DeviceType, plotoutput="filename",
           plotoption="options" )
```

- *DeviceType* is the graphics device that Maple must use
- *filename* is the name of the output file
- *options* is a string of options that the graphics driver recognizes

Sending Graphics in PostScript Format to a File

To send graphics in PostScript format to the file `myplot.ps`, use the following command.

```
> plotsetup( postscript, plotoutput="myplot.ps" );
```

Consequently, the plot that the following `plot` command generates does not appear on the screen but is sent to the file `myplot.ps`.

```
> plot( sin(x^2), x=-4..4 );
```

Graphics Suitable for HP LaserJet

Maple can also generate graphics in a form suited to an HP LaserJet printer. Maple sends the graph that the following `plot3d` command generates to the file `myplot.hp`.

```
> plotsetup( hpgl, plotoutput="myplot.hp",
>            plotoptions=laserjet );
> plot3d( tan(x*sin(y)), x=-Pi/3..Pi/3, y=-Pi..Pi);
```

To print more than one plot, you must change the `plotoutput` option between each plot. Otherwise, the new plot overwrites the previous one.

```
> plotsetup( plotoutput="myplot2.hp" );
> plot( exp@sin, 0..10 );
```

When you are finished exporting graphics, use the following command to once again display graphics in your worksheet.

```
> plotsetup( inline );
```

For a description of the plotting devices supported in Maple, refer to the `?plot,device` help page.

8.5 Conclusion

In this chapter, you have seen a number of Maple elementary input and output facilities: how to print graphics, how to save and retrieve individual Maple expressions, how to read and write numerical data, and how to export a Maple worksheet as a LaTeX or HTML document.

In addition, Maple has many low-level input and output commands, such as `fprintf`, `fscanf`, `writeline`, `readbytes`, `fopen`, and `fclose`. Refer to the corresponding help pages for details.

9 Maplet User Interface Customization System

By using the `Maplets` package, you can create windows, dialogs, and other visual interfaces that interact with a user to provide the power of Maple. Users can perform calculations, or plot functions without using the worksheet interface. This chapter is intended primarily for Maplet application users. Some information may be helpful to Maplet application authors.

In This Chapter

- Example Maplet
- Terminology
- How to Start the `Maplets` Package
- How to Invoke a Maplet Application from the Maple Worksheet
- How to Close a Maplet Application
- How to Work With Maplet Applications and the Maple Window
- How to Activate a Maplet Application Window
- How to Terminate and Restart a Maplet Application
- How to Use Graphical User Interface Shortcuts

9.1 Example Maplet Application

As a Maplet application author, you can create an interface that requests user input. For example, you can create an integration Maplet application with the following appearance and components.

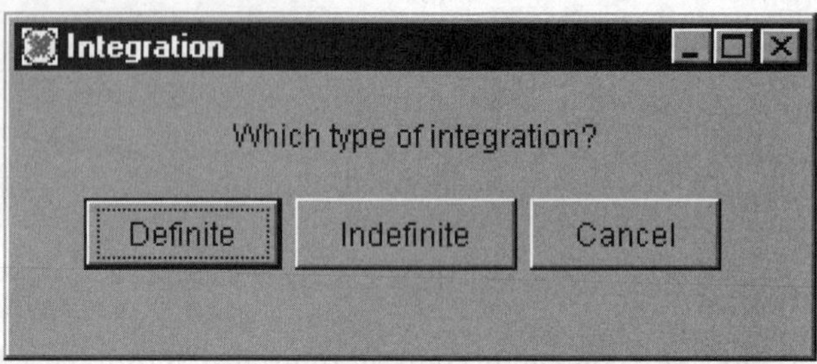

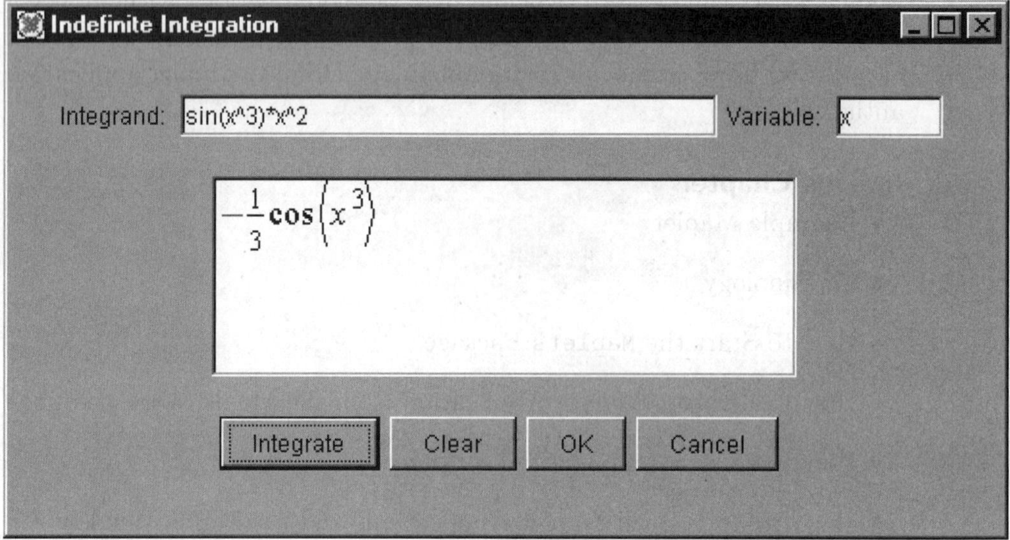

9.2 Terminology

Maplet Application A Maplet application is a collection of elements, including, but not limited to, windows, their associated layouts, dialogs, and actions. A Maplet application differs from windows and dialogs in that it contains windows and dialogs.

Maplet Application Author A programmer who uses Maple code to write a Maplet application.

Maplet Application User Someone who interacts with a Maplet application.

Layout Layout defines how elements within a Maplet application are displayed.

Window A window is a Maplet application element. A window should not be thought of as a Maplet application, but rather as one element within a Maplet application. A Maplet application can contain more than one window. Each window can contain many elements that control the layout and function of the window.

Dialog A dialog is a Maplet application element. Unlike a window, which can contain elements, for example, buttons or layout elements, a dialog element has a predefined structure. An author can specify options for a dialog, but cannot add elements.

9.3 How to Start the `Maplets` Package

If you receive a Maple worksheet with Maplet application code, you must first invoke the `Maplets` package. Press the ENTER key after these two possible execution groups:

```
> restart:
> with(Maplets[Elements]);
```

9.4 How to Invoke a Maplet Application from the Maple Worksheet

To start a maplet, press the ENTER key after the last colon (:), semicolon (;), or anywhere in an execution group to execute the Maplet application code. In the following example, the Maplet application is written as one execution group. You can press ENTER anywhere in the execution group to execute the code:

```
> mymaplet := Maplet ([
> ["Hello World", Button("OK", Shutdown())]
> ]):
> Maplets[Display](mymaplet);
```

In the following example, the Maplet application is written as two execution groups. The application must be defined before using the `Display` command.

```
> with(Maplets[Elements]):
> my2maplet := Maplet ([
> ["Hello World #2", Button("OK", Shutdown())]
> ]):
> Maplets[Display](my2maplet);
```

9.5 How to Close a Maplet Application

If the Maplet application contains a cancel button, click **Cancel**. Otherwise, click the appropriate Close icon for your platform. For example:

In UNIX:

1. Click the - icon in the upper left corner of the Maplet application window title bar. A drop-down list box appears.

   Note: The icon varies with window manager.

2. Select Close.

In Windows:

- Click the **X** icon in the upper right corner of the Maplet application window title bar. The Maplet application closes.

9.6 How to Work With Maplet Applications and the Maple Window (Modality)

When a Maplet application is running, the Maple worksheet is inaccessible. If you move the cursor across the worksheet, an icon (clock in UNIX (depending on your window manager), hourglass in Windows) appears, indicating that the worksheet is inaccessible. The Maplet application must be closed or allowed to complete an action before the Maple worksheet can be accessed.

9.7 How to Activate a Maplet Application Window

1. Click an input field in the Maplet application. The input field appears highlighted.

2. Enter the appropriate expression, numbers, or text as required.

9.8 How to Terminate and Restart a Maplet Application

With long computations, you may choose to stop the computation.

1. To terminate the current Maplet application process, click the **X** (or appropriate close icon for your platform) on the Maplet application title bar.

2. To restart the terminated application, run the Maplet application by using the `lastmaplet` tool.

```
> Maplets[Display](lastmaplet);
```

9.9 How to Use Graphical User Interface Shortcuts

Drop-down List Boxes

Some Maplet applications contain drop-down list boxes.

1. Enter the first character of any item in the list. The list automatically moves to an item that begins with the character entered.

2. Continue to enter the character until the desired selection is highlighted.

Note that this shortcut does not apply to editable drop-down lists created with the `ComboBox` element.

Space Bar and Tab Key

You can use the mouse to click a **Cancel** or **OK** button in a Maplet application. You can also use the TAB key and SPACE BAR.

1. Using the TAB key, position the cursor at the **Cancel** or **OK** button.

2. Press the SPACE BAR. The command is entered.

9.10 Conclusion

For more information on the Maplet User Interface Customization System, enter `?maplets` at the Maple prompt or refer to the *Maple Introductory Programming Guide.*

9.11 General Conclusion

This book aims to supply you with a good base of knowledge from which to further explore Maple. In this role, it focuses on the interactive use of Maple. Maple is a complete language and provides complete facilities for programming. The majority of Maple commands are coded in the Maple language, as this high-level, mathematically oriented language is superior to traditional computer languages for such tasks. The *Maple Introductory Programming Guide* introduces you to programming in Maple.

Index